Critical Compa~~ariso~~

Lead
this
of to
and
of cc
rangi
meth
ratio
the c
cour:

JOHN
Univ
Thou
(199

ROGI
Wash
Rebel

Critical Comparisons in Politics and Culture

edited by

John R. Bowen and Roger Petersen

PUBLISHED BY THE PRESS SYNDICATE OF THE UNIVERSITY OF CAMBRIDGE
The Pitt Building, Trumpington Street, Cambridge CB2 1RP, United Kingdom

CAMBRIDGE UNIVERSITY PRESS
The Edinburgh Building, Cambridge CB2 2RU, UK http://www.cup.cam.ac.uk
40 West 20th Street, New York 10011-4211, USA http://www.cup.org
10 Stamford Road, Oakleigh, Melbourne 3166, Australia

First published 1999

Printed in the United Kingdom at the University Press, Cambridge

Typeset in Plantin 10/12 pt   [CE]

A catalogue record for this book is available from the British Library

ISBN 0 521 65301 0 hardback
ISBN 0 521 65379 7 paperback

Contents

Figures

Contributors

FREDRIK BARTH is Professor of Anthropology at the University of Oslo, and Professor of Anthropology at Boston University.

JOHN R. BOWEN is Professor of Anthropology and Chair of the Committee on Social Thought and Analysis at Washington University in St. Louis.

BARBARA GEDDES is Professor and Chair of Political Science at the University of California, Los Angeles.

MIRIAM A. GOLDEN is Professor of Political Science at the University of California, Los Angeles.

ALLEN JOHNSON is Professor of Anthropology and Psychiatry at the University of California, Los Angeles.

DAVID D. LAITIN is the William R. Kenan Professor of Political Science and Director of the Center for the Study of Politics, History and Culture at the University of Chicago.

MARGARET LEVI is Professor of Political Science at the University of Washington, Seattle.

ROGER PETERSEN is Assistant Professor of Political Science at Washington University in St. Louis.

GREG URBAN is Professor of Anthropology at the University of Pennsylvania.

Acknowledgments

This volume grew out of two workshops and subsequent conversations among the authors over the course of several years. A conference on "Comparative Methods in Anthropology and Political Science," held at Washington University in St. Louis in 1994, began the project, and was followed by a second meeting in 1995. These sessions were funded by the Program in Social Thought and Analysis at Washington University, and by the Wenner-Gren Foundation; we thank the Foundation and the University for their support. We are grateful for the participation of Michael Burton, G. William Skinner, and Washington University colleagues at the workshops, and to comments on the introductory or concluding essays from Rogers Brubaker, Jack Knight, Adam Przeworski, and readers for Cambridge University Press. At the Press, Jessica Kuper provided encouraging and helpful comments.

Two of the chapters have appeared previously. The second part of Barbara Geddes' paper was published as "A Game Theoretic Model of Reform in Latin American Democracies," *American Political Science Review*, 85, 2 (1991), 371–92. David Laitin's chapter was published in substantially the same form as "National Revivals and Violence," *Archives Européennes de Sociologie*, 36 (1995), 3–43. Both articles are reprinted with permission from the editors. We thank Miriam Golden for providing the cover photograph.

1 Introduction: critical comparisons

John R. Bowen and Roger Petersen

Why compare?

The social sciences today are torn apart by a tension between two desires: to richly describe the world, showing its complexity and variability, and to robustly model the world, showing its relationships and regularities. We argue in this volume that engaging in comparisons of a few, well-understood cases reduces this tension. We offer, in effect, a case study of an encounter between two quite different disciplines, political science and anthropology. As students of society and culture, we found that we shared a stake in discovering processes and mechanisms underlying social phenomena, and that we found small-scale comparisons critical to that effort. And yet as participants in different disciplinary traditions, we continue to debate among ourselves about how best to compare, about how to interpret the patterns perceived, and about the ultimate goals of social research.

In a series of conferences and other exchanges, a collection of political scientists and anthropologists engaged in comparative study decided to put on the table what connected us and what divided us. Though a diverse lot – our objects of study run from ritual wailing to trade union disputes to agrarian transitions – we recognized in each other the dual commitment to understanding things both in their detail and in their general implications. We included no formal modelers or atheoretical monograph writers. All of us were engaged in comparative analysis of one sort or another, but some were also highly critical of much current comparative work.

We did, admittedly, approach our encounters with some fears – about disciplinary imperialisms, or about the Other's predilections for reductionism or mindless description. In truth, none of the worries have entirely been quashed, but they have been quelled, perhaps, as we have discovered that, yes, we do quite different things, and, indeed, that such is the point of the encounters. Here we wish to show and tell how these encounters ought to enrich comparative studies for social scientists generally as they have for us as a group.

In our discussions we noted a discordance between the richness of current comparative studies in our disciplines and the narrowness of how such work is described or prescribed in handbooks and review articles. Take two recent volumes (both discussed more fully below). King, Keohane, and Verba's *Designing Social Inquiry* (1994), a masterful prescriptive text in political science, delineates a set of requirements for valid "scientific inference" that effectively reads out of social science all comparative work designed to do anything other than test (or perhaps generate) causal hypotheses. By contrast, Holy's edited *Comparative Anthropology* (1987) argues that anthropological comparisons today are designed mainly to locate culturally specific meanings, and relegates to a "positivist" past all efforts to study social regularities. The gap between these two visions could be evidence that political scientists and anthropologists have absolutely nothing to say to one another – or it could be a sign that these summations are missing something of critical importance.

We began this project betting that the latter conclusion was the correct one, and we now think we were right. We prejudiced our experiment against finding agreement by bringing together, in the same room, political scientists whose work drew on rational choice theories with anthropologists whose work was highly concerned with the culturally specific. What we found we shared was a sense that the world's complexity demands some respect even as we try to understand or isolate processes and mechanisms.

This shared commitment to describing empirical richness and accounting for it has led us to critique and try to innovate beyond current ways of doing research in our own disciplines. For example, those of us who isolate a single set of motives or interests for modeling purposes (and only some of us do that) seek to retain in the analyses the specific processes and mechanisms characterizing each case. Sometimes doing so has required creating new ways of presenting material, as in the "analytical narrative" used by Margaret Levi and her colleagues. Conversely, our descriptions are shaped by efforts to understand processes and mechanisms – how and why things got to be the way they are. This effort, too, has required new ideas, as in the thesis advanced by Fredrik Barth and Greg Urban that variation both within and across cultural boundaries should be explained by reference to similar mechanisms. In both cases we are supplementing and critiquing standard images of what strategic models or cultural accounts can be.

It is, we argue, comparison that leads us to this critical use of our disciplinary tools – critical use, and not "application" of prefabricated tools (nor, for that matter, abandonment of social science). In this volume we show this more than tell it – we believe that exemplifying is more effective than prescribing – but we do also, here and in the other chapters, reflect explicitly on the value and limitations of particular kinds of comparisons. In design as well as in presentation, the volume is inductive, bottom-up, case-based, rather than deductive, prescriptive, law-giving. It offers the reader a set of examples to ponder, argue with, and perhaps draw from in planning comparative components for his or her own research.

Three concepts underlie these essays: comparisons, processes, and mechanisms. *Comparisons*, we argue, are at the heart of the matter for social science. We argue specifically for the value of controlled, or "small-n" comparisons of a few cases (or, as in David Laitin's chapter, a few sets of contrasting pairs). "Four plus or minus one" seems to capture what "a few" means in practice. Why comparisons, and why smallish ones, is detailed below, but the main message is that comparing several cases allows us to distinguish the important from the unimportant (or the relevant from the irrelevant, or the related from the contingent), and that limiting the number of cases allows us to deal more adequately with the complexity of social life.

We choose cases according to the questions we ask and the assumptions we make about this "complexity." When we study such "big" events as revolutions, trade union disputes, or enlistment in large standing armies (as in the projects by Margaret Levi and Miriam Golden), we may only have a few cases to start with, and the strengths and weaknesses of the analysis will depend to a great extent on the kind of information available about each (as Levi discusses).

We may decide to limit the scope of comparison to a region, or a type of society, to limit the differences between cases. This strategy of selecting closely related cases may be the result of different logics. We may, for example, be trying to control for shared features so as to isolate those elements that lead to a specific outcome, as in David Laitin's and Barbara Geddes' studies. Or we may be trying to study the variation and change in a cultural form across related societies, as in Greg Urban's and Fredrik Barth's studies. These pairs of studies start from very different questions – What are the general causal relations here? what are the specific processes of change here? – but they both depend on comparisons of closely related cases in order to find answers.[1] We may also decide to choose quite different cases so as to see if postulated relations hold up in very different contexts. David Laitin combines these two approaches; he uses the "most different case" strategy to see how well his hypothesis holds up once he has initially tested it from a "most similar case" approach.

We use comparisons not for their own sake, but because we find that they allow us to understand better *processes and mechanisms*, the how and why, narrative and explanation, of social phenomena. Mechanisms are specific patterns of action which explain individual acts and events; when linked they form a process. As developed in political theory (see Elster 1987), they are intended to apply over a wide range of settings, and they generally refer to psychological predispositions. For example, someone might continue to keep and repair an old automobile despite the likelihood of additional costly repairs because he or she figures that a lot has already been invested in the car. This mechanism, the "tyranny of sunk costs," may also keep spouses together who would otherwise separate because they cannot accept the fact that investments in the relationship have been in vain. This mechanism is both general, in that it can be applied to a wide variety of cases (cars and spouses), and specific, in that it can be used to explain why a particular event occurs.

A mechanism approach to explanation does not, however, seek a high degree of predictive power, nor does it aim at the creation of general laws. Sometimes spouses do break up, and other mechanisms ("the grass is greener," for instance) may be at work. "If p then *sometimes* q" is the closest to a prediction that can be made within this explanatory framework. The political scientists writing in this volume by and large adopt this approach, seeking a finer-grained account of several phenomena rather than a general law. This methodological choice, sometimes associated with rational choice theory (Johnson 1996), distinguishes them from other political scientists seeking predictive power through the use of a variable approach (see King, Keohane, and Verba 1994). It also brings them closer to the anthropologists in the collection (most of whom would otherwise see little affinity between their work and that stemming from rational choice) in their emphasis on understanding particular processes rather than generating highly simplified propositions about the general relationship among two or more variables. Indeed, in his concluding chapter, Bowen argues that in all the chapters the authors make their point most convincingly when they offer microhistorical accounts of processes, and often contrasts of processes across societies, rather than static comparisons of cases.

The political scientists included here are interested fundamentally in discovering mechanisms that lead people to undertake certain courses of action under certain conditions. Margaret Levi, for example, has as her main goal understanding the mechanisms that lead people to enlist (or not enlist) in armies. But she also constructs an analytical narrative of each country case, tracing specific macro-level pathways. Further, she tells another process story of building the model out of earlier work on taxation, looking for a very different domain against which to hone the model further, and then gradually building up knowledge of each case. (Levi thus chose her topic following a "most different case" strategy, and then compares cases of similar countries.)

For the anthropologists, both processes and mechanisms are desired objects of knowledge, but the better understanding of a particular process may be deemed more important than the uncovering of general mechanisms. Fredrik Barth's and Greg Urban's projects both involve redirecting comparative studies from the arrangement of predetermined cultural objects to the study of the processes by which forms are changed and transmitted. Ancillary to their studies, but mentioned by both as additional desiderata, is the uncovering of mechanisms that produce variation. Barth, in particular, seeks to link his fieldwork to studies of general cognitive mechanisms by which people forget and change information.

Although we find the two disciplines converging toward a renewed attention to controlled comparisons, each has its own quite distinct genealogy.

Anthropology

Anthropology exhibits continued nervousness about executing comparisons at all. When Robert Barnes (1987: 119) complains that "anthropology is permanently in crisis about the comparative method," it is the legacy of "the Comparative Method" that is at fault. This "Method" dates from the nineteenth century, and in particular from Lewis Morgan's (1871) philological studies and E. B. Tylor's (1889) cross-cultural comparisons, which he called the study of "adhesions." It is what Barth and Urban refer to as the museum approach to anthropology: isolating cultural traits and rearranging them according to such universalistic criteria as types of social structure or the relative complexity of tools.

The main traditions of American and British anthropology developed in large part as reactions to this acontextual isolation of traits. Boas and his cultural anthropology students in the United States emphasized the holistic properties of particular cultures; the founders of British social anthropology emphasized the interconnection of statuses and norms in particular societies. Yet both also engaged in comparisons of related societies or cultures. In the 1930s and 1940s Fred Eggan developed the term "controlled comparisons" to characterize studies of social variation and change in Native American societies of the southwest United States

(Eggan 1966). Regional comparisons were also used to generate and test ideas about processes, such as the rise of social stratification in the Pacific (Sahlins 1958), the development of witchcraft in Africa (Nadel 1952), or, returning to the US southwest, the development of personality through child-rearing practices (Whiting 1954). Sometimes regional comparisons were developed as contrasts, to show how different things could be along some axis within a region, as in Mead's (1935) contrasts of neighboring Melanesian societies.

Large-scale comparisons continued to be refined and expanded in the 1940s and 1950s, leading to today's "cross-cultural" method of universalistic comparisons based on a standard sample of cultures. This method typically focuses on the co-occurrence of social and cultural traits, sometimes using multiple regressions to explain the particular distribution of a feature such as "high women's status" or a certain residence rule (see Burton and White 1987).

By the 1970s and 1980s, comparative studies had been eclipsed by renewed emphases on interpretation and meaning. Large-scale cross-cultural analyses came in for particular criticism for their emphasis on traits over context, and their universalistic framework of bounded "cultures." First, critics argued, taking traits (such as "residence rules") as fixed features of cultures risks losing from the analysis many of the interesting features that good ethnography provides, including contextual determinacy (for example, residency choices depend on resources), and variation in local understandings (for example, genealogical ties to a co-resident can be reckoned in more than one way). As anthropologists turned more and more to the interpretation of local meanings, this criticism seemed increasingly telling.

Secondly, comparing across a universe of bounded, putatively independent "cultures" risks losing sight of the processes by which variation is created. The elements of a culture change over time and vary over space precisely because they have a dynamic interrelationship which can be causal and meaningful. Even in pursuit of the general hypotheses sought by practitioners of large-scale comparisons, regional variation can be a better source of data because of the control on certain variables (Mace and Pagel 1994). Although cross-cultural research has enjoyed a recent upsurge in interest, it is rarely even consulted by the majority of anthropologists; many consider it to have produced little of clear value, as recently noted by two of its major practitioners (Burton and White 1987).

Regional comparisons also have been neglected in the theoretical literature from the 1970s onward; Allen Johnson (1991) reviewed such studies and concludes that they have had little impact on the discipline as a whole. This neglect is probably due to the combined critiques of both cross-cultural comparisons and of ethnography itself. Work labeled "post-modern" has questioned the validity of all ethnographically produced knowledge (Clifford and Marcus 1987) and has further directed theoretical discussions away from comparisons. As the editor of a volume on comparative studies put it, "the line between comparativists and non-comparativists . . . is probably more sharply drawn than ever before" (Holy 1987: 9).

And yet comparative work thrives at the heart of the discipline, particularly at the level of collaborative efforts to understand better the nature of variation and processes within regions. Controlled, regional comparisons are more widely accepted in anthropology than are universalistic ones, because they preserve a relatively high degree of contextual specificity while moving beyond the boundaries of specific societies or cultures. Much of this kind of research has been intended mainly to point out regional variations on a theme, as in a collection of studies of eastern Indonesia social organization (Fox 1980) that points to the widespread symbolic importance of the house and of the "flow of life." Similar comparativist studies of culture areas can be found for Africa (Parkin 1980), South Asia (Yalman 1967), and lowland South America (Rivière 1984). More rarely do these anthropologists identify mechanisms generating variation within the area. Barnes (1980), for example, compares marriage payments across a number of eastern Indonesian societies not only to show variations on a theme but also to argue that a causal relationship holds between the degree of trade, the levels of bridewealth demanded, and the consequent difficulty of completing payments and converting an uxorilocal marriage to a virilocal one. Mandlebaum (1988) describes the widespread ideas and practices leading to the seclusion of women across south Asia, and then explains variation in these ideas and practices by reference to women's labor participation (see also Miller 1981).

Regional analyses have been perhaps most central to studies of New Guinea societies, where they also have achieved a noteworthy theoretical sharpness. An earlier emphasis on identifying subregions by the preponderance of particular diagnostic features (for example, competitive feasting, intensive sweet-potato cultivation) has yielded to more recent studies (for example Godelier and Strathern 1990; Knauft 1993) that emphasize the ways in which different questions (for example, the spread of social organizational forms, the development of stratification) will highlight different possible configurations of subregions. Thus an initial concern with mapping of cultural forms has been succeeded by a new focus on examining the processes that generate variation (Barth

1987; Hays 1993). This change in comparative strategies is often associated with the work of Fredrik Barth, and Barth's chapter for this volume focuses on ways to study generative social processes by comparing social forms within and across cultural boundaries. Because the same set of processes may develop variation within and across cultural boundaries, this approach takes cultural forms, and not bounded cultures, as the units of analysis.

For anthropology, the emphasis in this volume on process and mechanisms recalls much of the original purpose of undertaking controlled comparisons. Eggan's studies in the US southwest were a rebuke, albeit disguised, to the scientistic claims of his teacher A. R. Radcliffe-Brown that such societies had no history and that they therefore could only be understood in terms of the functional consequences of particular social forms. The comparison of neighboring societies, combined with what was known of early history, was intended precisely to reintroduce historical processes and mechanisms of change into social anthropology. What is different about today's work is in part the emphasis on comparisons of more highly interpreted realms of culture, such as the ritual wailing explored by Greg Urban and the Islamic rituals studied by John Bowen, and longitudinal analyses, as in Johnson's work. The goal of these and other analyses is understanding the processes by which cultural forms are learned, transmitted, and transformed.

Political science

Unlike anthropology, political science contains a subfield devoted to comparative studies. Arend Lijphart's much-cited 1971 article, "Comparative Politics and the Comparative Method," contains a view of the evolving role of small-scale comparisons within that subfield. Lijphart wrote (1971: 685): "If at all possible one should use the statistical (or perhaps even the experimental) method instead of the weaker comparative method." The strength of small-scale or "small-n" comparisons, Lijphart continued, lay in their ability to help create coherent hypotheses in a "first stage" of research. A statistical "second stage" would test these hypotheses "in as large a sample as possible."

Twenty-five years later, while some comparative research is conducted in the manner Lijphart recommended, much is not (see Collier 1991). In fact, the methodological coherence and division of labor envisioned by Lijphart has never developed. On the contrary, one might say that the sub-discipline of comparative politics has become either remarkably diverse or terribly fragmented, depending on one's perspective.[2]

Furthermore, as exemplified by the work and arguments of the political scientists below, small-scale comparisons are no longer a second choice to statistical approaches, nor are they simply used to generate hypotheses as a "stage" in the research process. They are used for both theory-building and theory testing, and they form a complete research program in their own right. In order to understand the continued prominence and even resurgence of these controlled comparisons in comparative politics, it is necessary to understand both the disillusionment with other research approaches, and the innovations in small-scale comparison.

During the 1950s, political science moved away from describing the legal-formal aspects of political systems towards a more behavioralist approach. Substantively the field was dominated by the issue of "development." The Social Science Resource Council Committee on Comparative Politics became the most influential institutional actor helping to create from the late 1950s to the early 1970s a large literature on development. Many of the works produced in this era put forth universalistic typologies and chronological models: developing nations could, and would (and should), follow the Western path toward democracy with the help of institutions and processes already witnessed in the United States.

By the late 1960s, however, faith in the universalistic processes that work toward outcomes of social justice was shaken by events throughout the world. Developing countries did not follow the expected paths, and Vietnam was a disaster. The last great grand synthesis of the field, Huntington's *Political Order in Changing Societies* (1968), reflected the original developmentalists' loss of optimism. The Social Science Resource Council Committee on Comparative Politics was disbanded. The backlash against the developmentalists produced a whole new set of general models. Dependency theory, corporatism, and bureaucratic-authoritarianism are the most well-known and direct responses to the perceived failures of the developmentalist approach.

However, these general models proved inadequate in explaining the complexity of modern politics: Asian newly industrialized countries (NICs) produce booming economies while other developing economies flounder; military regimes fade from Latin America while fundamentalist revolutionary regimes appear elsewhere; communist regimes fall but former communists win elections; mass ethnic killing in Rwanda and the former Yugoslavia occur simultaneously with peaceful change in South Africa and the Middle East; and so on. As complexity increased, two dominant approaches, model-building at the level of grand theory and large-scale statistical studies, went into relative decline.

The focus of the political comparativists in this volume is less on sweeping general models and more on explaining better-defined phenomena. Miriam Golden explains a set of labor actions in industrialized states; Barbara Geddes explains bureaucratic reform in Latin America; David Laitin isolates a set of conditions explaining nationalist violence; Margaret Levi's work explains variation in conscription policies and responses in several Western states. Following William Riker (1990), Golden describes her choice of topic and scope by asserting that "a narrow focus to attain a proper solution is a better research strategy than a broad focus that fails to generate conclusive results. By narrowing the focus of the phenomena under study, we reduce the trade-off between analytic rigor and empirical accuracy." An increasing number of comparativists have come to agree with this argument.

While large-scale studies are still prevalent in comparative politics, faith in cross-cultural and cross-national statistical study has diminished with increased awareness of problems associated with conceptual "stretching," unreliable measures, and improper specification of domain and units.[3] As Sartori (1970) has pointed out, the very concepts used to define independent and dependent variables often translate across societies only with the greatest difficulty. As more cases are included in a given study, the basic concepts are often "stretched" to incorporate them, sometimes to the point of meaninglessness. Furthermore, heightened appreciation of cultural difference has generated skepticism of statistical measures. For instance, does the gap between expected income and actual income really measure relative deprivation in both France and Indonesia? Does "income" have the same meaning and relevance in both societies? When does the social scientist know which cases belong in the sample if knowledge of cases is superficial (as in most large-scale studies)?

In addition to some of the more intractable methodological problems involved with large-scale statistical studies, some scholars are not satisfied with the very nature of the explanation that such work provides. Rather than simply identifying probabilistic relationships between sets of variables, many comparativists would rather work to identify the nature of causal linkages among parts of a process. The work of David Laitin (see chapter 2) comprises such an effort.

Many of today's political comparativists are skeptical of the abilities of general models and large-scale statistical work to capture the complexity of their subject matter; however, they remain committed to social science methods that allow for generality. Skepticism has not produced the desire to do purely descriptive and highly specific work. Margaret Levi speaks for many comparativists when she writes in chapter 8 that "an overemphasis on specificity . . . obscures the commonality among cases and places." It is at this point that small-scale controlled comparison comes into play. Through a focus on process and mechanism within the detailed study of the cases, much of the complexity of political life can be addressed while maintaining an ability to generalize. Through a focus on control, the benefits of social science logic (for example, covariation and falsifiability) are preserved.

Despite fragmentation in actual practice, there is a political science tradition of attempting to delineate one fundamental logic that underlies all comparative study, both quantitative and qualitative, and perhaps all of social science. In their influential 1970 work, Adam Przeworski and Henry Teune (1970: 86) conclude: "Although the phenomena under consideration vary from discipline to discipline, the logic of scientific inquiry is the same for all social sciences. As the theories explaining social events become general, the explanations of particular events will cut across presently accepted borders of particular disciplines." In another influential book published nearly two and a half decades later, Gary King, Robert Keohane, and Sidney Verba (1994: 4) write: "A major purpose of this book is to show that the differences between the quantitative and qualitative traditions are only stylistic and are methodologically and substantively unimportant. All good research can be understood – indeed, is best understood – to derive from the underlying logic of inference."[4] Charles Ragin's work on comparative method (1987) sees differences between variable-oriented and case-oriented methods but believes these differences are reconcilable. He proposes a synthetic approach employing Boolean algebra.

Our approach differs. While we applaud the search for common ground, we believe that the differences among the disciplines are more than a matter of style. Certainly, the prevailing goals vary among fields, if not the respective logics. Rather than trying to convince social science practitioners that there is one underlying logic, or developing a new synthesis, we believe that interdisciplinary progress might best be made by presenting choices and trade-offs made in the course of quite distinct research projects. We believe that knowing a wider range of possible ways of comparing will both help individual researchers in their own work and help build bridges across disciplines.

Although not its central concern, this volume thus indirectly addresses the notion of "one social science logic" that seems to preoccupy some political scientists. If both political scientists and anthropologists choose similar strategies when confronted with similar dilemmas of comparison, despite their different rhetorics and style, support for the idea of one pervasive logic is provided. On the other hand, if substantial and consistently different research choices are made, then the outlines of different logics of inquiry emerge. We will let the reader be the judge on this issue.

Validity and generality

Despite the convergence of these two fields on small-scale comparisons, real contrasts emerged from our discussions about what political scientists and anthropologists wish to emphasize. Both disciplines encourage their practitioners to develop ideas about how the world works that are faithful to those workings and that also have some degree of generality. But in our discussions the anthropologists tended to emphasize above all the validity of their knowledge, and the political scientists the value of constructing a model that can explain more than one case.

By "validity" we mean the degree to which the account of something picks up processes, ideas, or relationships that are indeed there in the world. Insisting on "validity" does not imply a correspondence theory of truth (that a true description maps one-to-one onto the world), but only that some descriptions are better than others, and that the kinds of things anthropologists do when in the field – checking with many people, listening in on discussions, and living through events – are particularly good ways to arrive at a good description. (We do not intend the statistical meaning of "validity.")

Greg Urban emphasizes that what appears to be a "simple" description of a cultural form already requires several levels of comparative activity, for members as well as observers of a society. Urban began his study of ritual wailing from his puzzlement that what seemed to be crying was performed in contexts of welcoming someone home. He then tried to understand the behavior he had seen by comparing different instances of it in the Amazonian society where he was living, looking for when it is performed and what meanings people seem to be imputing to it. He points out that this process of comparing within a culture is precisely what children in the society do when learning their culture. Now, Urban could have stopped there and simply reported how things worked in the one society. But his interest is mainly in the processes by which culture is transmitted within and across boundaries, so he began to look for similar phenomena elsewhere. The problem arose that in other, related societies what he might have taken to be a central component of the wailing, for example the "cry break" or creaky voice, were missing or difficult to hear, even though the forms were used in the same way. Urban concludes that we cannot begin with a singly defined phenomenon and then see if a society has it or not, because the form changes as it is transmitted. Instead, he urges that we take the processes of transmitting forms (and generating variation in them) as our object of study. The most valid knowledge of the cultural form even in one society, then, already takes into account the possible directions of its change.

Fredrik Barth joins Urban in attributing some of what they see as comparativist mistakes in anthropology to the close historical relationship of the discipline to the ethnographic museum, where things often were, and are, laid out according to function. This layout implies the prior assumption that the objects, despite their differing cultural contexts, are essentially the same. Such thinking, write Urban and Barth, has led some anthropologists to treat ideas and behavior similarly – as things that can be classified according to one-word rules, forms, or functions.

Barth questions the usefulness of comparing either cultures or "traits." He offers two arguments. First, that isolating cultural traits – a rule about whom one marries, or the general status of women – and subjecting them to cross-cultural statistical analysis omits their context-specific character and may systematically, not just randomly, distort the analysis. To take an example from another prominent anthropologist, Pierre Bourdieu (1972) argues that members of Kabyle society in Algeria say that a man ought to marry a cousin related to him through other males, and this may be coded as the preferred marriage for comparative analyses, but this trumpeted "rule" disguises the fact that many couples are brought together through female ties; men then reinterpret the marriage to highlight (often more distant) male ties.

Secondly, Barth argues that the most important mechanisms generating variation may operate across societal boundaries, and thus are not definitive of specific cultures or societies. It is artificial, he writes, to distinguish between the variation one finds across societies from that which one finds within a single place if both are generated by similar mechanisms.

One could suggest that part of his argument follows the logic of comparisons set out by John Stuart Mill. Thus, Barth writes that studying the diversity within the larger New Guinea area in which he worked helped him to focus on those features of Baktaman ritual that were "foundational," as he puts it, and those features that were due to "the flux of free variation." This moment of his analysis is a variant of Mill's analysis of differences: eliminating those elements which are not found in a number of closely related cases (Zelditch 1971). Barth also looked for covariation between elements of ritual and elements of context, within Baktaman society or across societies. But his goal is not to use such a method to explain variation, but rather to differentiate elements that vary from elements that do not, and then explain variation by studying the processes through which people learn, transmit, and alter knowledge.[5]

Barth and Urban highlight the importance of studying variation and processes of transmission within and across societies as a comparative study. Their chapters raise the following question about theory and objects of study: to what extent is their position (for variation, against comparing bounded units) a function of the kind of cultural objects they study? Ritual form may be inherently less amenable to correlational analyses than, say, local-level conflict. On the other hand, studying the transmission of discourses of ethnic identity and nationalism is hardly far-fetched, as Benedict Anderson's *Imagined Communities* (1983) exemplifies.

Barth's final point suggests one possible way of relating studies of variation to other forms of analysis. He cautions that *descriptions* of variation do not lead directly to *explanations* of variation. Explaining variation requires us to draw on hypotheses about why people act or think in certain ways in general: for example, what cognitive processes might have generated variation in ritual, or how differences in political structure might have produced variation in Balinese village form.

Miriam Golden's analysis of trade union disputes began, like Urban's study, with an anomaly. After years of studying trade unions in Italy, she puzzled over the fact that unions called strikes that were virtually unwinnable, in that the stated goal of the strike, preventing job loss, clearly could not be reached. Why this apparently irrational behavior? she wondered. She then compared decisions to call strikes in several industrialized countries, and found a second anomaly. Although union leaders say they strike to prevent downsizing, they do not seem to respond more forcefully when more jobs are at risk. She concluded that the real motivation behind strikes was protecting the union itself. The Italian strikes were realistically conceived; they failed because leaders overestimated employees' willingness to follow their strike call. Golden's argument is convincing precisely because she attends to the details of process in each of her cases: what leaders and followers knew, how they assessed their chances, what happened after the strike call.

Although both use comparative strategies to better understand basic processes and mechanisms, Urban and Golden follow very different logics of research. Urban's question is fundamentally about cultural processes, although he studies mechanisms of transmission and learning, whereas Golden's is fundamentally about mechanisms that shape decisions, although she studies processes of union formation. One can imagine a series of Urban-like questions asked of Golden: how did union leaders learn what ought to be fought for and what did not matter? in what ways did ideas and norms about strikes, leadership, wages, and so forth spread across these societies (through pamphlets and books, congresses and visits)? One can also imagine a series of Golden-like questions asked of Urban: what leads someone to initiate wailing? are there risks or costs if one fails to wail at the correct time or in the correct way? (These questions may be more interesting to Urban than the questions anthropologists usually expect to hear from other social scientists, such as: under what conditions would one expect to see wailing associated with welcome across cultures? In fact, that question is more likely to emerge from the large-n tradition of cross-cultural research in anthropology than from the political scientists included here.)

Golden explicitly rejects the idea that the best way to discover union leaders' beliefs, knowledge, and intentions is to ask the leaders directly. Because she believes that they will systematically distort their answers to such questions, she decided to build a model of their actions based on comparative data and inferences from a number of strike decisions, rather than from in-depth interviews. In our discussions some of us disagreed with this decision on grounds that, if systematic, differences between leaders' statements about their own actions and Golden's inferences could be quite interesting. We share the goal of discovering what union leaders know and intend to do; we differed, and continue to differ about how important actors' self-reports, rhetorics, and debates are to the analysis.

Generality is the second desiderata that guides our work. By "generality" we mean the capacity of an idea or hypothesis to account for a number of cases. (The political scientists tended to favor the term "robustness" to refer to the narrower concept of a model's capacity to explain a number of cases.) As Urban points out, even understanding the meaning of a single cultural form in one small-scale society requires a degree of generality, in that the hypothesis about what the form means must stand up over a number of its occurrences. Such hypotheses, whether about meaning, decisions, or social processes, imbue an account with some degree of generality, in that the account concerns more than a single event.

The nature of the material also shapes the meaning that "generality" has in these contributions. John Bowen analyzes variation in local forms of religious practice, when all practitioners develop local rituals with many of the same Islamic prescriptive texts in mind. Variation is within a controlled domain, and one would expect certain elements (such as the efficacy of sacrifice, or the importance of self-abnegation) to appear in many societies. Certain general associations might appear, although the analysis is mainly intended to explore a field of variation – as in the analyses by Urban and Barth (on New Guinea) of local ritual knowledge. But in the latter cases ritual knowledge is not encompassed by textual or other authority and thus can change from one case to the next, in the manner of "family resemblances," until endpoint cases share no features. The relatively controlled nature of the Islamic prescriptions makes possible a series of successive contrasts, within Gayo society, within the larger province, and finally between Indonesia and Morocco.

All of us find ourselves tacking back and forth between model building and the interpretation of data, but we differentially highlight particular moments in that movement. Some of us stress the way in which new observations lead to new theoretical understandings, as when Urban's cried welcome led to a new set of ideas about cultural processes, or Johnson's return visit to his Brazilian research site led him to revise his understanding of how political-economic changes reshape worker consciousness.

Like many projects, Johnson's research was begun from a combination of personal experience, theoretical training, and the lack of correspondence between the two. Having been trained to think of peasant consciousness as class consciousness, Johnson was surprised to find peasants thinking primarily in terms of patron-client networks during his fieldwork on Boa Ventura in Brazil. He developed a model of peasant behavior based on "client consciousness," as opposed to a view of "proletarian consciousness" dominant in the literature of the time. But he also wished to explain the conditions under which client consciousness would become proletarian consciousness. In order to accomplish this task, he returned to Boa Ventura twenty-two years after his original research. Class consciousness had not developed, he found, largely because of state welfare interventions. The comparison thus usefully points to limitations of models that take insufficient account of the various policies that states might pursue. Johnson then compares the Boa Ventura case with transitions from patron-client systems to more capitalistic ones elsewhere in Latin America, in countries where state intervention was less beneficial to peasants. He finds, as his revised model would predict, peasant revolt and the development of class consciousness. His model thus employs two stages of comparison: longitudinal, to develop a hypothesis about change (which can also be seen as experimental, a sub-genre of comparison), and controlled, regional comparisons, to check this hypothesis against other cases, noting especially cases where the major intervening variable (state welfare policy) was present or absent.

Others of us underscore the way in which an observed set of differences in the world could be explained by a new model of social action, as when Golden is able to explain the differential likelihood of strike calls by a model emphasizing union leaders' perceptions of the current threats to union strength, or when Laitin accounts for different degrees of violence.

In order to explain the use of violence in some cases of national revival but not others, David Laitin begins with a paired contrast, between Catalonia and Basque Country. He builds an explanatory model, whose critical mechanism is the tipping point where sufficiently many people participate in the movement to make the costs of participation drop. He then looks to explain why it is more difficult for nationalist leaders to recruit followers in some cases than others, finding answers in such factors as social networks and language histories. When these tipping points are more difficult to reach, leaders sometimes choose a violent course of action in order to raise the ante of sticking with the status quo and push more people toward commitment. Laitin then moves from the Catalonia/Basque Country contrast to one between Ukraine and Georgia, to enhance the plausibility of the account.

Laitin calls this kind of research emphases "dependent variable driven," in that observed differences in the world are the catalyst for a research project. Laitin agrees with Barth that comparisons need to be complemented by general hypotheses before one can claim to have explained differences.

Some of us place still more emphasis on the process of constructing and testing a model – but some of these model-driven projects also began with an intriguing puzzle. Barbara Geddes started with knowledge of Brazilian politics and society. She was struck by Brazil's relatively high growth rate and successful civil service reform. Her curiosity about Brazil's unusual path compared with those followed by other Latin American countries led her to ask a general question: under what conditions is civil service reform enacted in Latin America? Like Johnson, Geddes found a dominant paradigm, in her case that of collective action, insufficient to explain the case at hand. She then fashioned a model that reflected real Brazilian social-political life. Her model compares politicians' attitudes toward civil service reform by whether they are members of the dominant party or not, and works well for Brazil.

At this point Geddes had accounted for the Brazilian case, but because the model had been built to fit that case it did not yet test a general hypothesis. The pay-off matrix of the game did suggest that if a country had political parties of equal size, individual politicians, seeking greater electoral support, might support civil service reform. Geddes thus selected the four other Latin American countries with sufficiently long periods of democracy on which to try out this proposition. Her selection controlled to some degree for the Iberian political culture of the region and (because the four countries all were in a middle income range) for gross differences in economic development. A further set of contrasts was provided by changes in some of these countries from equal-size party situations to dominance by one party, a change that led to a scaling back of reform, as the model predicted.

Running through all these quite distinct research histories is the necessity of comparison to check an initial understanding against a broader field of data. This move toward comparison is not a specific method, but a necessary logical part of any research process that we can imagine. Comparisons, it should be remembered, are part of how we understand any social phenomenon, because we necessarily compare different utterances of what may or may not be the "same" expression, or different occurrences of what may or may not be the "same" ritual. They are part of how we account for any set of events, because we necessarily wish to specify which values of one or more variables lead to a certain occurrence and which do not.

In the end we see in our own work trade-offs between generality and validity, but agree that we must understand social life on the micro-level, in terms of how people come to know and act as they do. We disagree as to how best to do this. Some of us adopt a relatively thin view of intentions in modeling, others start with a thicker view. Some believe that actors' statements are necessary data; others disagree. But we see these decisions as strategic ones for purposes of obtaining particular kinds of results, and not as statements of ontological positions. Indeed, we would argue that creating analytical models not only is compatible with fieldwork or historical research but ultimately *requires* it for gathering sufficient information about strategies, decisions, and beliefs.

But we also emphasize that the fullest understanding of these events will incorporate the larger structure within which events and institutions are embedded. In our discussions, William Skinner (whose paper was not, in the end, included) pointed out that if you control for macro-region, apparently contradictory theories can often be resolved. Regarding the ongoing debates about peasant economic motivations, for example, debates often associated with the work of James Scott and Samuel Popkin, we might regularly find "maximizing peasants" in certain spaces of a macro-structure, and peasants focusing on minimizing risk and ensuring overall survival in other such spaces. David Laitin commented that macro-structural analysis, when fully elaborated, should be considered as fundamental in any attempt at a controlled comparison. If such data were available, suggested Laitin, and it showed that his cases differed on the macro-dimension – for example, Catalonia is a regional system with a city at its center, while Basque Country is not, with the expectation that the former would be more integrated – this factor would become the basis for new hypotheses and better controls for future comparisons.

"Critical comparisons," we believe, can best be made when, as we are engaged in our discipline-specific work of analyzing, modeling, comparing, we keep in the backs of our minds other possible strategies, other versions of social science. Our goal for this volume is to provide a set of cases that can be held in mind, some in the forefront, some in reserve, as reminders of other courses we might wish to take.

Notes

1   Although we concentrate on small-n comparisons, we recognize the value of other research designs, including both large-scale comparisons and, at the other end of the continuum, the use of a single case in "crucial case" designs. In the latter approach, the researcher analyzes one case judged to be the most likely case to fit the theory. Failure to fit then leads the researcher to abandon or modify the theory. We emphasize comparisons of multiple cases because we find them better able to generate new theory and shed light on already developed theories (see Eckstein 1975; Rogowski 1995).

2   For generally positive views, see Verba (1991) and Wiarda (1991). Both mention the "islands of theory" concept of comparative politics first suggested by Stanley Hoffman: "He [Hoffman] argued cogently and convincingly that, because the comparative politics field had lost its earlier unity, those active in the field should now accept this fact realistically rather than simply lamenting it or wishing it away. Rather, what we have now are various 'islands of theory' appropriate for the several, quasi-self-contained parts of the field – political culture studies, political socialization studies, political party studies, interest group studies, political economy studies, voting behavior studies, public policy studies, government performance and effectiveness studies, and the like" (Wiarda 1991: 245). See Almond (1990) for a collection of essays on the divisions within comparative politics and political science on the whole.

3   We do not wish to be overly negative about cross-national statistical models in political science. These models continue to produce fine statistical work, particularly on party and electoral systems, and may be most appropriate for understanding such issues as the relationship between GNP and the stability of democracy, where multiple mechanisms are in play.

4   Five critical reviews of this work are found in "The Qualitative-Quantitative Disputation: Gary King, Robert O. Keohane, and Sidney Verba's Designing Social Inquiry: Scientific Inference in Qualitative Research," *American Political Science Review*, 89: 454–481.

5   Stanley Lieberson (1991) argues that, taken alone, the Mill method cannot provide adequate accounts of why anything happened, in part because variables that will be dismissed as causal (because, say, present in two contrasted cases) may none the less play a causal role, and in part because the interaction of variables is not captured.

2　National revivals and violence

David D. Laitin

Nationalist movements seeking to make commensurate the boundaries of state and nation have in many cases employed or induced violence. Algeria, Basque Country (in Spain), Nazi Germany, Northern Ireland, Serbia, Somalia and Vietnam are gruesome examples. Yet the aims of comparable movements, similar in goals and apparently similar in context, have been resolved by relatively peaceful means. Quebec, Andhra Pradesh, Flanders, Italy and Catalonia are shining exemplars. This paper will employ the tools of game theory and the comparative method in political science (Lijphart 1971; Skocpol and Somers 1980; Collier 1991) to address the question: why are some nationalist movements peaceful in strategy and outcome while others create carnage? The answer is not to be found in the great forces of history, having to do with capitalism, state formation and inequality. Rather, the conditions that lead to violence require a microfoundation based upon social organization in rural and small-town life, tipping phenomena in political recruitment, and spiraling effects of fortuitous events.

Predominant approaches to the study of nationalism and violence have relied upon the identification of broad social processes that help to place nationalism in deep historical context (Kohn 1944). These approaches have pointed to the fact that nationalism is a modern social formation that emerged in the wake of industrial capitalism and concomitant modernization (Gellner 1983; Hobsbawm 1990). Capitalism in seventeenth-century Europe unleashed productive energies in a number of core zones, and these zones drew migrants from relatively depressed localities. This process, called "social mobilization" (Deutsch 1954), unhooked people from loyalties to tribe, village, and region. Before capitalism, each locality had a distinct dialect and culture. But with modernization, the cultures of the people who inhabited the core capitalist zones began to dominate, and set common standards across wide regions.

States in the pre-capitalist period were multinational, and boundaries were set by dynastic marriages, wars, and geographic convenience. The cultures of the populations inside those boundaries were of little relevance to leaders or subjects. But capitalism, the Enlightenment, and the Protestant Reformation all brought notions of individual citizenship to the consciousness of the newly powerful social classes (Bendix 1978). Kings were pressured to justify their domination by acting in the interest of their "people." Symbols that pointed to the common culture of the people, associated with the cultures of core economic zones, became powerful tools of legitimation, in large part because they connected the modern (a powerful state) with the neo-traditional (symbols of a national language, ancestry, and territory). In this way "nations" were "invented" (Hobsbawm 1990: 10) or "imagined" (Anderson 1983).

English, French and Spanish kings all sought to emphasize a common "national" culture to help bring coherence and efficiency to state rule. The full power of nationalist ideas, brilliantly demonstrated by Napoleon's ability to conscript soldiers who were committed to the "national" cause, led rulers elsewhere in the world to replicate French success by emphasizing national symbols to legitimate state domination (Posen 1993a). Groups of people who shared a common culture but lacked a state were similarly impressed, and sought states for their nations. The enormous success of the early nationalist projects and the universally available symbolic material (a mythic history, a common language, an attachment to a territory) made for easy replication of the project all over the world. This is what Anderson (1983) means when he writes of the "modular" quality of nationalism. Due to this quality and to the deeply felt needs of people for a sense of community in the anomic modern world, nationalist ideologies have remained powerful throughout the twentieth century (Smith 1979).

These broad outlines of nationalism have been astutely drawn in macrosociology. But the tale of violence is a more difficult one to tell. Historical sociologists are well aware that nationalism grew in England in a relatively benign fashion, but in Germany it was associated with hatred of minorities, genocide and imperialist war. Many attempts have been made to stipulate the connections between types of nationalism and likelihood of violence, for example by distinguishing the examples of states creating nations (France, England) from nations creating states (Italy, Germany). Other typologies (for example, Gellner 1983) identified additional patterns of nationalist development, but in none of these works is there a clear empirical or theoretical line drawn between nationalism on the one hand, and violent outcomes on the other.

The most compelling work differentiating types of nationalism (Hayes 1931; Haas 1993) does indeed point to special conditions that turn nationalism into an "integral" or exclusionary form, and one prone to violence. Integral nationalism is attributed to a number of factors, generally summed up by the term "modernization breakdowns". Under conditions of capitalist development, if a cultural minority becomes extremely rich as compared with the majority group, leaders of the majority group can use the symbols of nationalism to punish or to extort from the successful group, and this has a violent element to it. Or if a national state finds itself economically weak compared with a neighboring state, its leaders could use symbols of nationalism to mobilize the population toward extraordinary efforts at "catch-up". This may ultimately lead to military action in which the backward state seeks to seize valuable resources through war or imperialism; alternatively it could lead to the persecution of minorities within the state's boundaries who are held responsible for the failure to develop. Nationalist violence (in the form of internal "ethnic wars") in the postcolonial states of Africa and Asia is often attributed to the fact that these colonial peoples suffered the uprooting that went with capitalism but few of the economic benefits. This was the ultimate breakdown in modernization.

In general, macrosocial theorists argue that capitalism induces vast social change and a powerful ideology of legitimation (that is, nationalism). Those who are losers in the processes of change will employ the powerful ideology in a violent way to confront the winners. Psychological theories are often employed here (Gurr 1970; Davies 1969) to elucidate the reasons why people who are "relatively deprived" or who face "status inferiority" can be induced to act violently.

The comparative method

The comparative method employed in this chapter helps to undermine the cogency of formulations that find the taproots of nationalist violence in capitalism, modernization breakdowns, postcolonialism, poverty, relative deprivation or status inferiority. It does so by systematically seeking variation in outcomes (the dependent variable) when the putative cause (the independent variable) is present in all cases. If colonialism is associated with violence in Algeria but peace in Tunisia, the comparative method instructs us to look elsewhere for causes of Algerian violence. Looking at only one case (for example, Algeria) may lead an historian or anthropologist to draw links between the colonial experience and the violent war for national liberation. The comparative method suggests that those links are tenuous.

Or consider the cases of Catalonia and Basque Country when national revival movements reemerged in both of these Spanish regions in the 1960s. The variation on the dependent variable – high levels of

violence in the Basque movement; low levels of violence in Catalonia –
is sharp. Yet the macrosociological conditions can be controlled for: the
international context, the experience of the civil war and Franco's
authoritarian rule, and relative economic prosperity in comparison with
the rest of Spain are for both regions the same. We can therefore
discount these variables as explanatory of Basque violence or Catalan
peace. The Basque/Catalan comparison serves as this chapter's first step
in employing the comparative method.

The next step requires an identification of crucial differences between
the cases, as plausible explanations for their different outcomes. These
differences need to be formulated as variables, and therefore some
degree of abstraction is necessary. The reason for this is that the goal of
the comparative method is not simply to explain the set of cases under
consideration, but to identify general social and political processes. The
putative cause must therefore be formulated so that other scholars will
be able to determine whether that factor was present in other cases.

I then move to game theory to complement the comparative method. I
do so because the identification of plausible connections between independent and dependent variables only suggests association, but not
cause. The empirical relationships become powerful if they are part of a
deductively driven "story", one which provides a rationale as to how and
why the situation on the independent variable leads to specified outcomes
on the dependent variable. This story should suggest mechanisms that
drive the variations in the predicted directions. The stronger the theory
(its assumptions are reasonable; the number of independent variables is
few; its applications to other cases are wide; its account of the cases at
hand is plausible), the more confident one is that the empirical association has causal properties. Game theory is surely not the only approach
to the telling of a deductively driven story, but it is a compelling one.

The comparative method, like Citibank, never sleeps. It requires us to
refine our stories in light of new cases that are themselves carefully
controlled. In this chapter I apply the lessons from the Spanish cases
and game theory to the rise of nationalist movements in the former
Soviet Union. I therefore construct another controlled comparison,
between Ukraine and Georgia. In Ukraine, the establishment of national
sovereignty in the period 1989–94 has been peaceful. In Georgia, facing
similar constraints and opportunities, there has been intra-national and
inter-national violence continuing through the late 1990s. Can the
variables identified in the Spanish cases and illuminated by theory apply
to post-Soviet nationalism? To the extent that they can, the theory is
said to be "robust."

This chapter will demonstrate that the variables identified in the

Spanish cases do indeed help illuminate differences in the post-Soviet cases. This is not to say that the two pairs are similar. The end of Franquist rule is quite distinct from the collapse of Soviet rule. Nor is this to say that the nature of violence in Basque Country is parallel to that in Georgia. Rather, I wish to take methodological advantage of the considerable differences in the sets of pairs by claiming that if a similar set of mechanisms operates in a wide range of cases, then the theory behind these mechanisms must be robust indeed. To the extent to which the paired comparisons yield similar patterns of association that are deductively plausible, we can say that a satisfactory theory of nationalism and violence is emerging.

This chapter seeks to bridge the divide, identified in John Bowen and Roger Petersen's introduction to this volume, between validity and robustness (or generality). Valuing validity and therefore examining only four cases, I have tried to capture the social reality within each of the national revivals on its own terms. Valuing generality as well, I have tried to push compelling explanations into new arenas, wanting to learn the extent to which explanations for violence in the context of national revivals can serve beyond a single case. Rather than emphasizing one goal at the expense of the other, I have sought in this chapter to engage in a systematic back-and-forth movement between the reality of the cases and the implications of those realities for general propositions about national revivals and violence. Let us now move on to the cases and the theory, to see the extent to which the comparative method can perform as promised.

The search for theory: Catalonia and Basque Country

Catalonia and Basque Country are two regions of Spain whose linguistically distinct cultures have survived in popular memory and practice despite centuries of rationalization strategies by the leaders of the Spanish state.[1] Both regions were early to industrialize compared with the political center in Castile. Nineteenth-century regional revivals in both regions are related to their industrial advance, although in Catalonia the vanguard nationalists were the bourgeoisie seeking autonomy from mercantilist Spain, while in Basque Country the vanguard were the rural notables fearing the consequences of the high Basque bourgeoisie becoming Spaniards (Shafir 1995). Both regions, due to industrial vibrancy throughout the twentieth century, became magnets for migrants from rural Spain, and these migrants were considered to be "foreigners." The immigrant communities posed a demographic threat to the indigenous populations, making the regional nationalists fear the loss of their distinctive cultures. This threat became very real, for after the civil war (1936–39) General Francisco Franco imposed coercive rationalization policies in Basque Country and Catalonia, and suppressed all manifestations of regional distinctiveness. Under these conditions, migrants had no need or opportunity to assimilate into the regional culture, and the non-coopted autochthonous populations, of virtually all political persuasions, associated dictatorship with Castilian hegemony. It became an article of faith amongst the democratic opposition to Franco that regional autonomy was a prerequisite for Spanish democracy.

Anti-Franco nationalist movements consolidated in Catalonia and Basque Country in the 1960s. Their programs were similar, as radicals in both regions called for "independence" from Spain. Both sought the creation of newly constituted political units from a set of separate provinces. In fact, the radicals wanted more, and that was to unify the largest conceivable territory under the regional flag: Basque nationalists sought to incorporate Navarre, which is the historical center of medieval Basque power, but its residents today mostly see themselves as Navarrese, and very few have empathy for Basque nationalist aspirations; Catalan nationalists sought to include Valencia and the Balearic Islands, two provinces of what they call "the Catalan countries", and places from which many of Catalonia's leading language revivalists come, but whose peoples mostly see themselves as having separate languages and cultures from Catalonia. Once Basque and Catalan nationalism became mobilized, many activists were arrested by Franquist police. In response, both movements made amnesty a leading element of their political platforms. In the period of democratic transition, the leading regional parties, the PNV (Basque Nationalist Party) in Basque Country and the CDC (Democratic Convergence of Catalonia) in Catalonia, were both led by bourgeois moderates who had support among autochthonous professionals and managers as well as a strong rural base. The leaders of both parties were quite willing to give up the goal of independence in order to achieve the transfer of most state functions to the regional level. These leaders had economic and social ties to "Spain" and were ambivalent about their own nationalism. Both movements, then, earned the scorn of more radical elements in their own region who would not have compromised on the goal of independence.

Despite these similarities in historical experience, the nationalist revival movement in Catalonia has been relatively peaceful, with terrorist groups effectively marginalized by the Catalans themselves, while the nationalist revival movement in Basque Country has been bloody.

The Basque terrorist organization, ETA (Euskadi and Freedom), had up till 1990 been responsible for about 780 deaths, an endless string of kidnappings, and bombings of power stations, tourist centers, and state property. Targets for murder have been Spanish military and police forces as well as Basques themselves who cooperated with the Spanish state or joined all-Spanish parties, or who refused to pay a "revolutionary tax." In one bloody attack, ETA terrorists murdered a Basque politician who was associated with the all-Spain UCD (Central Democratic Union) party. They dragged his dead body to the UCD party headquarters in Vitoria and left it in front of the building. Several Basque socialists, members of the Spanish Socialist Workers' Party (PSOE), were also murdered by ETA terrorists. No wonder their terrorism made ordinary Basques fear to make any public statement in favor of accommodation with Spain (Elorriaga 1983).

The Catalans have not been immune to nationalist violence. In the 1960s, radical separatist organizations formed, and a small breakaway group of the Partit Socialista d'Alliberament Nacional (Socialist Party of National Liberation) even advocated military insurrection. In the late 1960s the Front d'Alliberament Catalá (Catalan Liberation Front) engaged in violent, but not murderous, acts (Díez 1995: 370–71; Reinares 1990: 355). The organization Terre Lliure (Free Land) formed later still, and recruited among young Catalans who were appalled by the willingness of CDC officials to compromise away the cherished goal of full independence. Violence as a tactic was always debated in radical Catalanist circles, and never completely rejected (*Esprai* 1988; *Catalunya* 1988). In 1981 Terre Lliure activists engaged in kidnappings and bombings which were reminiscent of ETA's tactics. But these activities were quickly contained from within the Catalan nationalist movement, and terrorism did not become normalized.

With such similarities in regional history and nationalist goals, why should one nationalist movement be marked by terrorism, and the other by political negotiation? This question has indeed captured the imagination of the leading social scientists who study Spain, but they have not been able to provide a coherent answer. Carr and Fusi (1979: 159) emphasize that there is "no simple explanation" and Gunther *et al.* (1986: 313) warn that the answer is "complex." The reason for the complex (and often convoluted) explanations is this "paradox" (Payne 1975: 250): Catalonia has been an historical thorn in the side of the Spanish state while Basque nationalism was only a local irritant; this should have us "predicting" (Carr, in Shafir 1995: 87) Catalan terrorism and Basque negotiation! Certainly a study of early twentieth-century working-class movements (such as in Romero 1968) would suggest the hypothesis that it is the Catalans who have an elective affinity for violence. Despite the confusions in the literature, it is instructive to examine the efforts by historical sociologists, political scientists, and anthropologists to explain Basque terrorism and Catalan negotiation, because my micro viewpoint will build upon their insights.

Historical sociology of Catalonia and Basque Country

Historical sociologists (Linz 1973; Díez 1995; Shafir 1995) differentiate between nineteenth-century Basque and Catalan nationalism by focusing on the social classes that played vanguard political roles. Basque nationalism was the program of the rural notables who lost status in the face of rapid industrial development in the steel producing cities. The leading industrialists required capital investment from a wide network, and Basque bankers set up branches throughout Spain to raise capital. The industrial and financial bourgeoisie saw Basque nationalism as provincial and backward; they had a cosmopolitan outlook, and saw themselves as Spaniards. In opposition to them, Basque nationalists in the nineteenth century linked themselves with neo-traditional Carlism. In the twentieth century, with the high bourgeoisie closely linked with Franco, a nationalist alliance formed between the left-wing nationalist forces in the cities with the traditional nationalists in the rural areas. Deep divisions within Basque society, and the odd marriage of the anticlerical left and the lower clergy, it is argued, brought a moralistic fervor to modern Basque nationalism.

In Catalonia, the industrial and financial bourgeoisies never lost control over the nationalist movement, even if many of them were ambivalent about a full nationalist program. In the late nineteenth century, Catalan industrialists unsuccessfully lobbied for legislation in Madrid that would facilitate the development of joint stock companies and set up trade barriers to limit textile imports from England. These failures plus the loss in the 1898 "Spanish-American" war of Cuba and the Philippines, where Catalan industrialists had near-monopoly rights, impelled the Catalan bourgeoisie to lead a cross-class alliance in support of Catalan regional autonomy. The hegemonic bloc that formed in Catalonia was able to bargain successfully with the Spanish state both in the 1930s and again in the late 1970s, and this reduced the space for an alliance of disaffected rural folk and urban radicals to challenge the bourgeoisie in the name of nationalism.

The patterns adduced through historical sociological inquiry are compelling images of the two nationalist movements; yet the links between the independent variable (the leading social groups in the nationalist movement) and the dependent variable (the level of violence in the strategic plan to fulfill their programs) are obscure. The explanations have a post-hoc quality: if Catalonia had the terrorism, it would be plausible to link the achievement of cross-class hegemony with the ability to organize a war of maneuver against the forces of the Spanish state; and then one could link the failure of hegemony in Basque nationalism with the need to make the best bargain possible short of going to war. The broad macrohistorical patterns can account for virtually any level of violence in the nationalist movements under study.

Survey research approaches to Catalan and Basque nationalism

Survey research, in collecting public opinion data throughout Spain, has sought to get a grasp on the differences between the levels of violence in the two nationalist movements by studying the structure of popular beliefs and opinions. Political outcomes, in this view, are the result of underlying values and feelings. The survey data, for example those compiled by Gunther *et al.* (1986), unfortunately, can support an argument going either way. Perhaps their greatest virtue, however, is in their power to discredit standard "political science" explanations, three of which will be outlined here.

1. *Racialist ideology*. It is often argued, based on a study of the nationalist writings of Sabino de Arana, that Basque nationalism is more "racist" and exclusionary than Catalan nationalism, and thus more intolerant. Catalan nationalism has often emphasized the mixed nature of the Catalan people, as the country is seen as a trading crossroads. Catalans promote themselves as more inclusive and open than other Spaniards. Survey data show that more Basques than Catalans define membership based on "willingness to defend the nation." While not racialist, this attitude reflects a rather intolerant view, counting as Basques only those willing to fight for a national cause (Shabad, personal communication). But other data show that Basques are more likely than Catalans to include as fellow nationals anyone who lives and works in their region, and they may thus be more tolerant about membership (Gunther *et al.* 1986: 318–30; see also Shafir, citing the surveys of Juan Linz (1995: 123–26)). On the basis of these data, it would be possible to find an elective affinity for both intolerance (violence) and pluralism (bargaining) in both regions.

2. *Cross-cutting cleavages*. Going back to the work of Simmel, social scientists have noted that where people are linked to different sets of others in different social arenas (for example, work, family, and church),

they are more likely to hold moderate political views and to seek democratic compromises. This is because your opponent on one issue might well become your ally on the next. The data in Gunther *et al.* (1986: 376–7) show that the Basques have higher levels of cross-cuttingness in their pattern of cleavages (class, religion, region and left-right) than do the Catalans. Because of the high *salience* and stark polarization of one of those cleavages – region – in Basque Country, Gunther *et al.* argue that it is the salience of the relevant cleavage rather than the degree of cross-cuttingness that explains the level of violence. Whether they are correct or not, their data deal a blow to standard cleavage theory.

3. *Symbolic power of cultural institutions.* A high percentage of Catalans, through the use of the Catalan language, are militantly regionalist. The percentage of Basques who are monolingual Spanish speakers is far higher. If the omnipresence of a cultural institution such as language facilitates collective action, we should expect Catalan nationalism to be far more militant than that of the Basques. To be sure, it could be argued, as a UCD official did (reported in Gunther *et al.* 1986: 331) that "There is a greater anguish in the [Basque] demands, because there are greater threats to the survival of their culture," but if the power of cultural symbols and their imminent disappearance can *both* predict militant political action, we are stuck with a theory that cannot be disconfirmed.

Still other survey data show that Basque identification with an exclusive autonomous community and their support of a revolutionary nationalist party are at much higher levels than the Catalans'. But when analyzed over time, Díez concludes that these attitudes are more the product of the events engendered by ETA than an explanation for ETA's activities (1995: 429–30).

Survey research has performed a service in helping us to eliminate well-regarded theories from consideration in the explanation for the differences in the Basque and Catalan strategic repertoires. But the concentration of research attention on attitudes and values as an explanation for violent action has been less fruitful. The attitudes themselves give ambiguous signals, and are more likely a response to events rather than an explanation of them.

Anthropological explanations for Basque and Catalan nationalism

Anthropologists have made important inroads in understanding the reproduction of Basque culture and the sources of the culture of violence that has marked Basque Country since the mid 1960s (Perez-Agote 1984; Ramírez 1991; Zulaika 1988). In an evocative treatise, Zulaika describes the setting in which young men find emotional appeal in joining a movement that asks them to murder people whom they have known all their lives but who have become informers for the Spanish police. If American boys in the 1950s invariably rooted for the "cowboys" in their genocidal forays against "Indians," young Basque boys saw in ETA an organization that would help realize them as men and citizens. To his horror, Zulaika himself felt pulled by those same forces to seek admission into ETA. While Zulaika spurns the task of providing a social "cause" for this appeal to join ETA in rural Basque Country, he provides a cultural context. For example, he analyzes the symbolic meanings of the words "yes" and "no" in the Basque language and in Basque literature and finds that they have sharp and uncrossable boundaries. This cultural feature inter alia sustains a politics in which unyielding opposition seems normal and moral. Basque culture, Zulaika points out, refused to yield to the attractions of modern urban "Spain"; it refused to compromise with the authoritarian Franco state; and in the 1960s ETA asked members of this culture to stand firm in its opposition to Spanish centralism.

However enlightening and subtle the analysis, the epistemological problem with Zulaika's story is that it cannot explain the centuries of assimilation by Basques into Spanish cultural and political life. Basques became multi-cultural, and said both "yes" and "no" to Castilian culture. Finding a deep cultural basis to explain ETA terrorism invariably runs into the problem of not being able to explain the more long lasting phenomenon: Basque participation in the construction and imagining of the Spanish nation.

There is yet another problem in a reliance on Zulaika's anthropological interpretations to explain Basque violence. The complementary exercise of probing into the symbolic bases of Catalan self-understandings does not lead to an unambiguous prediction of Catalan non-violence in the pursuit of autonomist goals. While Catalanist anthropologists (for example, DiGiacomo 1985) have emphasized the importance of the Catalan notion of *seny*, a feet-on-the-ground practical spirit that rewards calculation and compromise, it is important to point out that within the Catalan symbolic repertoire is the concept of *rauxa* ("impulsiveness") which anthropologists would have appealed to if Catalans had centered their politics in rebellious activities in the late Franco years (Laitin and Rodríguez 1992). Indeed, it has been pointed out (Freedman 1988) that Catalan legends have an important genre of heroic battles that their ancestors supposedly fought to the credit of the nation. Catalans have a cultural repertoire that can give support to cowardly accommodation or heroic rebellion. So do the Basques.

The microfoundations of nationalist violence

While previous research in Catalonia and Basque Country has not adequately explained the differential outcome in regard to violence, and while none of these theories has been put to a "robustness" test in other countries, many of the ideas are worth developing for wider testing. In this section I shall develop three propositions about violence in the course of regionally based nationalist movements, and in subsequent sections I will see how well those propositions hold up in the Catalonia–Basque Country comparison and, for a check on robustness, see how well they hold up in explaining the post-Soviet high levels of communal violence in Georgia and low levels in Ukraine. To the extent that propositions developed from one paired comparison hold up in a second paired comparison, a strong case can be made for their plausibility.

My focus on microfoundations is justified by the perplexity that macrotheorists have faced in regard to violence. If similar macrostructures are associated with divergent outcomes in regard to violence, perhaps the variables that explain the violence have to do with microsocial processes that translate broad social goals into everyday tactics. In order to develop a microtheory of nationalist violence, it is incumbent on the theorist to provide a plausible and compelling "story" as to why many individuals would themselves take the risks of armed combat to achieve uncertain results that will be shared equally by those who have engaged in the combat and those who have not. My microanalysis has identified three separate stories, which I shall now tell.

A necessary condition: dense rural social structure

Violent movements require recruits. Two conditions are necessary to find willing fighters. First, there must be a social stratum in which violence is part of a usual cultural repertoire. Studies in criminology have focused not on the middle classes (who will lead these movements, but find themselves initially unable to engage in violent activities themselves) but on lower-middle-class and working-class youths in urban ghettoes, small towns and rural societies (Mardin 1978; Waldmann 1985).

Second, such youths who are members of local social (as opposed to political or economic) groups make the best recruits for violent bands

(Petersen 1991, 1993). Consider three ideal-typical rural or small-town societies: one where there is a strong presence of a nationalist party in virtually every village; a second where the principal form of village solidarity is based upon irrigation societies and other work-sharing groups; the third where there is a strong presence of local social groups, from outing clubs to boy scouts. An initial proposition is that a necessary condition for nationalist guerrilla action against state authority is a rural society that is rich in social membership groups. Here is why.

In the first type, nationalist parties are easily penetrated by the leading centralist parties of the state, since the leaders of the nationalist parties find themselves in more regular negotiation with centralist than with local forces. An incentive for leaders of nationalist parties is to present to the localities hard-won compromises as packages that are the best available. Because war against the state, if it is to be led by nationalist party leaders, would require a coherent army, and because this army will have a low probability of beating an already established state army, the likelihood of leaders of nationalist parties supporting a violent war against the state is very low.

In the second type, with dense agricultural groups, the likelihood of guerrilla action (in localized combat, conventional armies are impossible to form) is low, in large part because any member of a rural work group who seeks to commit himself to a life of political/military action is necessarily shirking his economic duties. There will therefore be a strong incentive for leaders of rural work groups to deter such defections from work team duties. Furthermore, since work groups are publicly visible, any guerrilla action that is supported by such groups can be easily identified by state police, and the principle of collective guilt might well be followed. It is therefore imprudent for guerrilla action to take place based on rural work group solidarity.

Localized social groups, however, are the ideal nesting ground for guerrilla action. While economic groups have norms of fairness, social groups have norms of honor. If a leading individual of a scouting group commits himself to a nationalist guerrilla band, other members would be dishonored if they betrayed him, and in fact would feel social pressure to join in with that leader. Furthermore, since most local social groups have membership lists that are as private as those of masons, group members will not fear reprisal if they remain members of groups many of whose members are active in guerrilla or terrorist movements. The greater the number of such groups, the higher the likelihood that a critical mass of leaders will commit themselves to an underground terrorist campaign to fulfill their national dreams.

Explaining the incentives to violence: a tipping game phenomenon

The tipping game, first developed by Schelling (1978) to explain phenomena such as neighborhood stability, can be applied to the dynamics of recruitment to national causes. To illustrate the tipping mechanism, I shall first present a model showing the difficulties nationalist leaders face in seeking support for a switch of the language of public education from that of the center to that of the region (Laitin 1989). This model can be expanded so as to specify the point in the national project when leaders would have an incentive to use violent tactics.

Consider a region in a country in which over the centuries a significant percentage of people have begun to use the language of the political center as the language of education, work, and even everyday life at home. Many in the small towns and rural areas are bilingual but only a few are monolingual in the language of the region, a language which no longer has the institutional support (in schools, or in administration) to survive in the long term. There will inevitably be a corps of national historians, poets and philologists who keep the national language "alive"; they will have the seeds for any counter-hegemonic nationalist movement if and when leading sectors of the regional society cultivate such a movement.

The national revival will require, inter alia, that people who rely principally on the state language for getting information, watching television, and writing letters begin to equip themselves (and more importantly, their children) to operate in the regional language. This will be a costly investment especially if, for lack of a critical mass of speakers of the regional language, the movement fails. Each person in the region needs to calculate the costs and benefits of re-aligning him- or herself with the regional language, based on subjective assessments of the probability of others making a similar choice.

The calculation for making such an investment in the regional language is based on (i) the economic pay-offs for learning the regional language; (ii) the status gain or loss from the regional society for learning or not learning the regional language; and (iii) the changes in (i) and (ii) based upon the percentage of citizens in the region who have already invested in the regional language as the language of the future "nation."

Suppose that the average pay-offs for individuals to switch to the local language are considerably lower than the average pay-offs for individuals to continue relying principally on the language of the center. And suppose that the initial movers into the regional language (who will have higher individual pay-offs than the societal average) get great honor from the community for their bravery and good jobs as regional leaders

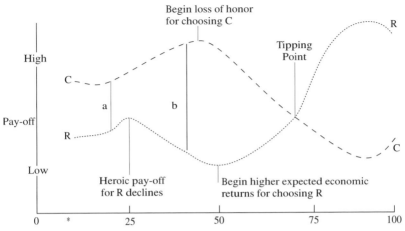

Percentage of people in the region who switch from the language of the center as their primary medium of instruction in their education to the regional language.

CC – pay-offs for people who receive instruction through the medium of the central language

RR – pay-offs for people who receive instruction through the medium of the regional language

* – status quo before beginning the nationalist movement

Figure 2.1. A tipping model game.

and teachers, but that these early successes only reward a small percentage of movers, and at about 25 percent, those who move to the regional language are no longer regarded as regional heroes. Suppose further that economic returns in the form of professional employment for learning the regional language only begin to kick in after more than half the people of the region are operating fully in this language. Suppose finally that negative sanctions (loss of local honor) for using the language of the center do not become strong (especially in the cities) until 45 percent of the population switches primary language allegiance. If these suppositions are formalized, the tipping game might look like Figure 2.1.

Two aspects of Figure 2.1 are noteworthy here. First, it is individually irrational for those with average or below-average pay-offs for switching to do so at the early stages of a national movement. Second, after initial successes into the regional language camp, the national movement will have a harder time (given the increasing divergence in average pay-offs) in recruiting people to make a personal investment in the future of the regional language (that is, $a < b$). This difference will be exacerbated by the fact that the early switchers were those with an above average pay-off for "R." This will make the potential pool of switchers at 40 percent R to have lower average support for R (all other things equal) than the potential population at 20 percent R. My hypothesis about violence follows from this second point. The hypothesis is that the wider the difference between a and b, the more likely that at "40 percent switch" the early movers (whom I call "language vigilantes") will see terrorism as a useful tactic in raising the costs for accepting the linguistic status quo. By terrorizing prominent regional actors who haven't switched, the vigilantes raise the status costs of not-switching. By terrorizing the police forces of the political center, the vigilantes seek to create greater regional solidarity and thereby raise the benefits for switching. Terrorism, then, is a viable tactic in the national revival tipping game for language vigilantes when the differences in pay-offs from identifying with the center and those for identifying with the region begin to increase in a direction unfavorable to the national cause.

Sustaining mechanisms: a random event, the value of stunning but small victories, the tyranny of sunk costs, and the culture of violence

The third set of mechanisms accounts for how violence is sustained. The basic proposition here is that violence gets going in only a small subset of cases for which the necessary conditions exist, and for which there are strong incentives to use it. Fortune chooses a small subset for a cycle of violence to get going. Once violence begins, it will be sustained by three factors: (i) if the regional population perceives the tactical victories but is blind to the strategic losses; (ii) if the costs of leaving the terrorist organization are high; and (iii) if a "culture" of violence becomes institutionalized.

Nationalist movements active in regions of established states invari-ably face police forces and state militias that are far more institutional-ized and have far greater access to firepower than do the challengers. Under such conditions, it would be irrational for anyone to join an army that is likely to be crushed. Suppose, however, that a small commando group stages a revolutionary event, such as an assassination of a leading politician from the center. In most cases, these efforts will fail; but when they succeed – I shall call this a "random" event that cannot be explained by social structural factors – these events have the power to galvanize support from potential recruits who now see the group as "successful." If the focus is on tactics, terrorist organizations can point to incredible strings of victories, and such pointing can have the effect of framing perceptions in the region that the balance of power is on their side.

A stunning random "victory," and the concomitant reevaluation of the chances for independence by people from the region, will lead to a new tyranny – the tyranny of sunk costs (Petersen 1991). After new recruits join an illegal military organization, and after they commit a criminal act, it is extremely difficult, psychologically and for security reasons, for them to change their minds and return to political quiescence (Fanon 1968). This tyranny of sunk costs acts to sustain a movement long after its original goals, or even its original characterization of the "center," are lost in the fog of commando actions and state reprisals.

This action-reprisal-action cycle that escalates between nationalist movement and state authority (or other enemies of the regional movement) creates what can be called a "culture of violence" (Shabad and Llera 1994) in which ordinary people become indifferent to violence and begin to see it as part of "ordinary" life. The cultural expectation of violence helps perpetuate it, as it joins the set of plausible actions that anyone in society might use to fulfill one's political agenda.

Retelling the stories of Basque and Catalan nationalist revival

The micro-mechanisms discussed in the previous section were developed with an eye on differentiating the Basque and Catalan regionalist movements. It will be no surprise that I find key differences in the two regions on each of these mechanisms. The real "test" will be to see the level of their robustness, once we move to another context, in the defunct Soviet Union. But even if there will be no surprises, it is worthwhile to lay out the key differences in the two regions of Spain.

Social structure

Virtually all anthropological accounts of Basque society point to the importance of low-membership village-based social groups. Each village has its own mountain-climbing clubs, called *mendigoitzale*, and the regular outings have always proven to be occasions for male bonding and political intrigue. Furthermore, it is characteristic of Basque society that young boys join into gangs, or *cuadrillas*, of about six to ten in a group. Pranks and petty vandalism make up the repertoire of these groups' activities. As members grow older, the groups transform into drinking societies. In the words of Gurrutxaga (quoted in Díez 1995: 449), "It seems that development in Guipuzcoa facilitates the diffusion of nationalism, because it is founded on small towns, where mechanisms of social control become more significant and where there is a very dense network of interpersonal relationships."

While the foundation of ETA membership was among middle-class and well-educated urban intellectuals, by the mid-1970s ETA's recruitment base went to the small and medium-sized cities, where recruits were among semi-qualified workers in small factories (Reinares 1990: 364). These became, as Mardin (1978) and Waldmann (1985) would have us predict, the commandos in ETA's terrorist program. In Clark's (1984) study of ETA, he finds that it was the climbing clubs and the *cuadrillas* that were the source of ETA recruitment. In his data base of eighty-one ETA militants, not one (and this is consistent with Petersen's theory) was from a farming village. The great majority came from small towns where young men commuted to work in small nearby factories. They were workers during the day, but embedded themselves in Basque culture at night. Unlike farmers, they were not members of local economic, but only social groups. The solidarity of these groups allowed for clandestine recruitment and a culture of group honor that made it nearly intolerable for group members to become police informers.

If Basque Country was strong in local social groups, it was weak on the level of local party organizations linked to Spanish-wide political institutions. The leaders of such parties, as Petersen's theory indicates, would have an interest in developing bargains with political power at the center. To be sure, the PNV had built a strong centralized (for the region) party with excellent local links. This could help explain why the PNV had been able by the late 1980s to cooperate with the Spanish state in marginalizing ETA from the Basque region (Maravall, personal communication). But ETA was able, until the 1990s, to immunize itself from this sort of bargaining. ETA's political wing, Herri Batasuna, entered parliamentary competition, but forbade the winners from occupying their seats. HB parliamentarians could not enrich their careers by trying to sell a peaceful compromise to their mass base (Reinares 1990: 378).

If the anthropological work on Basque Country emphasizes locally based social groups, Catalanist research emphasizes the importance of economic based groups (unions) and their links to national political parties. Díez (1995: 432) mentions that in the late Franco period, it was Catalonia that had far more political party activity than Basque Country, and points out that "While ETA faced little competition in becoming the symbolic center of Basque opposition to Franco, revolutionary nationalist groups in Catalonia ... faced strong competition from other more moderate political groups." Political parties are more likely to bargain than to fight; this helps explain the lower level of violent nationalism in Catalonia.

If Catalonia was strong in party development, it was weaker in the development of small-town autonomous social groups. Most important here is that Barcelona, Catalonia's capital, is about fifteen times more populous than Basque Country's largest city, and while Barcelona's youth participated in many clubs, these young men did not have continuous face-to-face interactions with their neighborhood cohort into their adult years. Barcelona life was too anonymous, with too many varied opportunities for youth, for the *cuadrilla*-type relationships to be sustained. Even small-town life in Catalonia was different from Basque Country. In one study of the rural Alto Panadés (Hansen 1977: 115), the author reported that prior to the mid-nineteenth century, the only voluntary groups were run by Catholic brothers. And when secular social organizations began to form, all the clubs were led by men who were "the *caciques* of one or another of the national parties. The prominence of the national party in part determined the prominence of the *cacique* on the local level ... The local *cacique* was far more than a vote deliverer for the national party and a patronage dispenser at the local level ... [He] was a man who took care of things for people." According to the logic of the group bases for terrorist organization, the Catalan type of rural group is too easily coopted through extra-local accommodations between leaders of the social groups and state-level authorities. Another anthropological study that focused upon the "culture of opposition" in Franquist Catalonia saw labor unions and the church as the major organizations in village life. Some emphasis was put on the scouting clubs (which were supported by the church) and mountain groups; so it would be fair to say that Catalan village life had some potential, albeit less than that in Basque Country, for triggering a violent opposition group (Johnston 1991: ch. 4).

The anthropological evidence suggests that the social conditions for a commando-like structure were more supportive in Basque Country than in Catalonia, but this doesn't necessarily mean that it would have been impossible in Catalonia (we don't know the thresholds), nor does it mean that violence was a logical outcome of the Basque social structure. We have seen only that a necessary condition has been more fully met in the Basque than in the Catalan case.

Tipping phenomena

The historical sociological approach identified a hegemonic Catalan and a divided Basque nationalist elite. Politically, this manifested itself clearly amid the collapse of the Second Republic. Unlike Basque Country, Catalonia had a successfully operating regional government in the Second Republic. Its president, Josep Tarradellas, spent the Franco years in exile in France. He became a symbol of Catalan aspirations, even though the younger generation of leaders, such as Jordi Pujol, felt that it was their turn to rule. Because of Tarradellas's legitimacy, however, radical Catalans could not easily renounce his leadership publicly, or undermine Tarradellas' negotiations with Adolfo Suérez, the prime minister of Spain who managed the transition. Meanwhile, in Basque Country the republican leadership broke up into separate groups amid the civil war. One faction went into exile while another remained to fight the war. The government in exile did not retain the same symbolic weight for Basques after 1975 as it did for Catalans. The intra-Basque political competition remains more salient than intra-Catalan. Shabad (1992: 39) writes that within Basque Country, the greatest hostility is between HB and the PNV (which was willing to compromise with Madrid), rather than between a united set of Basque nationalist parties against the ruling and non-regionalist PSOE.

What, however, are the mechanisms which translate elite division into violence and elite unity into negotiation? Here is where the tipping game might provide an answer, by examining more closely the recruitment dynamics within the autochthonous society, starting from a period of optimism in Basque Country when opposition to Franco began to be expressed in a nationalist frame. The radical nationalists in the early years won a small but significant percentage of the Basque population over to the *abertzale* (national liberation point of view) side. But the great majority, although sympathetic to the *abertzale* position, were unwilling to cut their ties with Spain. Leaders experienced the difficult problem of convincing fellow-Basques to change vastly their everyday behavior for uncertain gains. One way to change the calculations of those who remained Spaniards in their way of thinking and living was to raise the costs for doing so, at first by harassment and perhaps later by terror.

Although ETA was not directly involved in battles over cultural revitalization, one way to think about ETA's recruitment dilemma, at least in a metaphorical way, is to analyze the dilemmas facing those who sought to promote the Basque language as the principal language for Basque everyday life, education, and administration. Learning the Basque language for many urban Basques, and especially for those in Alava or Navarra, would be a great burden, with only uncertain rewards. For immigrants, learning a language that shared no roots with Indo-European languages would be especially burdensome. It would be hard for anyone rationally to assume that Basque would replace Castilian within one's lifetime.

Meanwhile the Catalan nationalists had an easier task. The Catalan language had been a language of science and written literature for centuries. From the cultural renaissance in the mid-nineteenth century to the Second Republic (1931–36), there was an outpouring of publications in Catalan. The language is of the Romance family, and unlike Euskera, can be learned easily by Castilian-speaking immigrants. Passive understanding takes months; active participation perhaps a few years. When the Catalan nationalists passed the Law of Linguistic Normalization (1983) in Catalonia, may people reasonably expected that if their children did not learn Catalan, their future (for example, in university admissions) would be imperiled.

Basque radicals faced a more difficult situation as they sought to "tip" their region in the direction of a Basque-centered culture. Their strongest supporters had a difficult time learning the Basque language. These radical leaders had a more daunting task than did the Catalans in altering subjective pay-offs. Early movers to Basque cultural styles were local heroes. When it became irrational for any more Basques similarly to adjust, radicals could raise the costs of maintaining the status quo by intimidating those who refused to shift. The sources of harassment and perhaps even terror can be found in a rational calculation by radicals that the movement would stagnate without adding the cost of fear to those who find comfort in the status quo.

ETA was not playing a language tipping game, but the logic may well be the same. My hypothesis is that the violence aimed at Spanish police authorities, and the kidnappings and "revolutionary taxation" of Basque industrialists were instrumental actions designed at reconfiguring the pay-off function of fellow Basques in their assessments of the value of maintaining a "Spanish" life style. *The difficulty of the tip, rather than the probability of it, provides an incentive for violent tactics.* This micro-explanation, linked to the macro-sociological situation of a divided Basque elite and a united Catalan elite, provides a coherent story of why violence in Basque country became a viable, even rational, nationalist strategy.

Sustaining mechanisms

ETA emerged in 1959 when a coalition of youth groups, frustrated with the passivity of the older generation in the PNV, merged ideas of ethnolinguistic nationality, anti-colonial guerrilla warfare, and marxism. The groups that formed were subject to schisms of every sort, and were only a marginal element in the underground anti-Franco movement in Basque Country. In 1965, members agreed on a theory of revolutionary change: to involve the state in an "action-repression-action spiral" that would serve nationalist purposes, as this spiral would draw ever larger numbers of Basques into the revolutionary camp. Nine years after its formation, with membership no larger than in the one hundreds, a pair of ETA members were stopped at a roadblock after a bank robbery. One was hauled from the car and shot; the other was imprisoned and tortured. True to its ideology, ETA targeted an especially fierce police commissioner, and murdered him. The results played into ETA's theoretical hand. Franco declared a "state of exception" over the entire country, engaging in just the kind of repressive actions ETA leaders had counted on, and ETA attracted new recruits. Extensive repression by Spanish police was effective, however, and by 1970 ETA membership declined from 600 to about 100. In December of that year, the infamous trial of ETA militants held at Burgos, when, amongst others, two Basque priests were charged, outraged public opinion internationally, and helped ETA recoup its forces. And three years later, in what was then perhaps the most stunning terrorist victory in modern European history, ETA commandos assassinated Luís Carrero Blanco, the Spanish prime minister and heir apparent to Franco. ETA membership quickly doubled. Finally, the execution in 1975 of two ETA prisoners yielded a general strike and turned the victims into martyrs (Reinares 1990: 366). Through these events, ETA became the frame for many small-town Basque youths who desperately wanted to be in the nationalist picture. ETA became as well so mythic in its identification with Basque values that it was able to expand its recruitment into rural society (Reinares, personal communication).

This vignette of ETA history (see Clark 1984, Payne 1975, and Zulaika 1988 for richer accounts) illustrates two points. First, identifying the social conditions that led to the emergence of ETA does not help to explain why violence, terror, murder and kidnapping became defining characteristics of the contemporary Basque nationalist revival. Groups like ETA form in many different kinds of societies, and are probably not different in outlook from the Catalan organization Terre Lliure. But a random event – like being caught in a roadblock – which was blown up into an affair of state catalyzed the group into a major representative force that delineated Basque aspirations. The assassination of Carrero Blanco, which succeeded because he followed the same route to church every morning for a period of years, was equally random and invigorating. Without this type of fortune for ETA, the PNV could well have become the hegemonic voice of Basque aspirations, and social scientists would be looking into Basque history and social structure to find the roots of peaceful nationalism.

Second, the early assassinations, the successful kidnapping of a Basque industrialist who had bullied unions, the collection of a "revolutionary tax" from a wide segment of nervous Basque businessmen, and the ease in stealing arms and ammunition from Spanish armories all gave ETA operatives (as well as potential recruits) a clear sense of endless tactical triumphs. The value of regular small victories was more powerful in ETA calculations than the degree of progress toward the ultimate goal. The cloud of tactical victories certainly overshadowed any calculations concerning the probability of a life of freedom in newly democratic Spain.

Once the Basque culture of violence had been established through the overvaluing of stunning tactical victories, anti-ETA Basque nationalists found themselves in a political bind. One high PNV operative responded in an interview that it was unrealistic to work towards ETA goals, but quickly added that "If I were to say today that I am Spanish, that I renounce Basque independence, I would be immediately kicked out of my party." A PNV senator, Joseba Eloségui, said in 1984 that "the fathers of ETA members belong to the PNV, and they propose that the *peneuvista* [member of PNV] father denounce his *etarra* [terrorist] son to the Guardia Civil ..." (Shabad and Llera 1994; the quotation is taken from a prepublication manuscript). ETA's élan prevented responsible Basque politicians from denouncing its use of violence.

ETA not only influenced the political agenda by policing *peneuvistas*, but was able to police defectors from within its ranks. To be sure, ETA policing of the Basque population was limited to only a few zones in the wider country, and it was relatively easy for commando members to return to normal civilian life (Clark 1984: 152). Furthermore, the Spanish Minister of the Interior in 1980 developed an amnesty program that eventually reintegrated 200 former terrorists into civil society. Yet those who considered amnesty found themselves subject to terrorist death threats (Reinares 1990: 389–93). Violence is sustained when those already implicated in terrorist acts fear reprisals if they defect from their organizational roles.

A cycle of violence never got under way in Catalonia, even though the generational tensions that led to ETA doubtlessly existed in Catalonia, and radical groups in Catalonia debated terrorism with a vocabulary similar to that of the ETA organizers. Terre Lliure (*Esprai* 1988) and the "Marxist social current" (Johnston 1991: 68) certainly had elements that were hard to distinguish from those of ETA.

Cultures of violence are not eternal, nor can they be ascribed to any national group. The Catalans, it is to be remembered, were the violent anarchists of the early twentieth century and the peaceful regionalists of the late twentieth century. The Basques were known for their centuries-long peaceful incorporation into the Castile-Léon crown. A combination of social organization and random events can enculturate a people anew into a lifestyle that turns terrorists into heroes, and in which ordinary citizens become callous. Cultures, once institutionalized, are resistant to change, but they are not eternal.

A critical test: Georgia and Ukraine

The collapse of the Soviet Union and the rise of the union Republics as new nation-states provides a nice robustness test. As with the Catalan/ Basque case, leaders in Georgia and Ukraine both had similar problems in regard to the establishment of a nationalist program. However, the results differed immensely. In Georgia, democratic elections did not lead to peaceful rule but rather to a violent intra-Georgian anti-government insurgency and a set of wars between Georgians and minority ethnic groups. In Ukraine, democratic elections were bitterly fought, but the winner was able to establish himself in authority without internecine war, and a subsequent election led to a peaceful transfer of presidential power. Furthermore, despite a host of cultural minorities in Ukraine, the first years of independence went by without inter-ethnic guerrilla warfare, even though on two occasions war clouds hovered over Crimea.

Virtually all the union republics in the Soviet Union were multiethnic in composition but had a single group (called in the Soviet Union the "titular" nationality) after which the republic was named and to which most central largesse went. In the context of the union, minority groups in union republics were assured protection from Moscow, and ambitious people from those groups could orient themselves to the status hierarchy of the union. Meanwhile, members of the "titular" nationality could orient their future either to the republic or to the union. After the collapse of the Soviet Union, ethnic minorities in the newly independent republics were subject to the will of the titulars, and this situation was an invitation to conflict.

In Georgia, with the rapid outmigration of Armenians, Jews and Russians since 1959, Georgians make up nearly 70 percent of the population, with Armenians at 9 percent and Russians at 7.4 percent (Suny 1988: 299). Most of the other minority populations live on the border with Turkey and in the mountainous regions of the Caucasus bordering on the Russian Federation. The Ossetians cross the border between Georgia and Russia. In the latter, North Ossetia is an autonomous republic; in the former, South Ossetia (with only 60,000 Ossetians and 30,000 Georgians) is only an autonomous oblast, somewhat lower in status than an autonomous republic. The South Ossetians feared the break up of the union, and sought unity with their northern brothers. The Georgians held that Ossetians only came to South Ossetia in recent centuries (!), and that they should rightfully return to Russia. The Ossetian problem had considerable potential for violence in post-Soviet Georgia.

In northwest Georgia, on a crucial rail link to Russia (crucial not only to Georgia but to Armenia) is the mountainous Autonomous Republic of Abkhazia, where the Abkhazis form only a small minority of 17 percent of the population (with Georgians comprising 45 percent). Abkhazis immediately called for separation from Georgia, and Tlisi authorities feared for the security of the Georgians living there. Also in Abkhazia are Adigei (sometimes referred to as Cherkess), Abaza, Ingush, Kabardians, and Chechens. They are predominantly Muslim, and conflict among these groups has been a common feature of recent political history. These conflicts have centered, however, within the Russian Federation, and as of late 1994, a Russian invasion of Chechnya had begun. Finally, in Georgia, on the border with Turkey, the Adzharis, who are ethnically Georgian but Muslim in religion, pose yet another secessionist threat.

The national scene in Ukraine is even more complex, and perhaps even more "loaded" with historic antipathies. Ukraine has 52 million people and 110 nationality groups: 37 million Ukrainians, 11.35 million Russians, 486,000 Jews, and 440,000 Belarusans. The Kuzbass (originally from Siberia) miners, many of whom migrated to the Donbass mining areas, hardly were aware that they lived outside "Russia." Crimea, which Khrushchev ceded to Ukraine in 1954, is a vibrant Russian tourist area as well as the home of a key "Soviet" naval base. Russians in Crimea have pressed for the creation of "Novorus," an independent republic as part of the Commonwealth of Independent States. In the Transcarpathian region Slovaks, Czechs, Hungarians, Rumanians, Gypsies and Germans live together with Russians and Ukrainians. Transcarpathians have pressed for a special oblast, but issues of incorporation into neighboring republics have also been raised, especially by Moldova and Romania in regard to the strip of land in Bessarabia and northern Bukovina that were given to Ukraine as a result of the Molotov-Ribbentrop pact. Elsewhere in Ukraine Tatars, who were inhumanly uprooted from their native soil in the Crimea, began migrating back to their homeland in the 1970s, and now claim that the

Ukrainians and Russians who live there are doing so illegally. Religious divisions between the Uniate Church (largely Ukrainian in membership) and the Ukrainian Autonomous Orthodox Church (largely Russian), with battles over property rights current on the agenda, cloud the political scene. Less manifest up till now is the conflict between the Uniates and the Ukrainian Autocephalous Orthodox Church (largely Ukrainian). A recent monograph examined the "legacy of intolerance" among religious groups in Ukraine (Little 1991: 5), and the author notes that as the Soviet state "relaxed its oppressive policies toward religion and permitted the legalization of hitherto suppressed churches, members of these churches suddenly find themselves required to confront old antagonisms [which] of late erupted into hostile acts among some of the groups, along with mutual accusations of discrimination and violence."

The remarkable fact in the post-Soviet period is that while both republics were rife with national, cultural, and religious antipathies, potential pogroms were successfully marginalized in the Ukraine, whereas in Georgia national antipathies were the basis for terrorism and war.

In Ukraine, despite a concerted attempt by Russian mass media to stir up national hatreds – virtually all stories reporting incidents come from Russian newspapers and television – the Ukrainian nationalists have been assiduous in policing themselves against their own worst instincts. In the words of Mihaylo Horin, the vice-president of the Rukh, Ukraine's coalitional nationalist party, "The Ukrainian movement Rukh and other organizations, such as the Republican Democratic Party ... have always advocated the view that the Ukraine is the fatherland of various nationalities [who] are not unequal under the law ... We know what happened in Germany in the past: Hitler acted against the Jews ... This also happened in the Soviet Union: Lenin started to act against the landowners ... Whoever uses an apparatus of repression should know: it starts with the suppression of the others – and in the end oneself is suppressed or even eliminated. Thus if we defend the rights of the Jews, Russians, Armenians, and Greeks, we simultaneously defend the rights of the Ukrainian people" (FBIS 911031). Meanwhile, in the Supreme Soviet of the UkSSR, Leonid Kravchuk (first president of independent Ukraine), and virtually all the candidates for Ukrainian-wide elections, have emphasized that the stirring up of ethnic hostility was "inadmissible" (FBIS 910104). But this is more than talk. In March 1991, Russian cadets were counter-demonstrating against a Ukrainian rally for separatism in western Ukraine. A fight quickly broke out. But Rukh "stewards" came to the immediate defense of the Russians, to prevent the creation of martyrs (RFE 910315). A radical deputy from Lviv in the Ukrainian parliament, Stepan Khmara, has tried to stir up all sorts of inter-ethnic violence in order to portray Ukrainians as an embattled people. Despite his wide recognition throughout Ukraine and his impeccable nationalist credentials, Ukrainian political authorities have done everything to marginalize him and restrict his range of potential damage.

Referenda supporting de facto sovereignty in Crimea, both in 1992 and 1994, brought the peninsula to the brink of war with Ukraine. In 1994, the Russian State Duma's Commission on Commonwealth Affairs reported (without corroboration) that Ukraine had deployed 50,000 troops to Crimea, in response to Crimean President Yury Meshkov's bold moves of putting Crimea in the Russian time zone, and putting the Crimean Interior Ministry (and thus the security forces) under his own control. But this crisis, despite the provocative moves by both sides, egged on by elements in the Russian state (including the commander of the Russian 14th army in Dniester Republic), was quickly defused, as the two sides agreed on the existence of two separate interior ministries, and President Kravchuk reiterated that the conflict would be solved only by legal means. In Crimea, the parliament stripped Meshkov of his powers, and the prime minister, S. Tsekov, then Crimea's supreme authority, moderated his views in regard to Ukraine. Both sides marginalized their most fanatic supporters.

Finally, with Ukrainian nationals suffering in Moldova, Ukraine's government looks aside. It fears that if it stirs up trouble by speaking for Ukrainians there, then the Russian, Romanian, and Hungarian governments might well begin to stir up minorities within the borders of the present Ukraine. President Kravchuk frequently raised the specter of Nagorno-Karabakh (RFE 910201). Policing his own people to avoid fanning the flames of historical conflicts was for him a successful strategy. Finally, despite fears of violent religious clashes, the author of *Ukraine: The Legacy of Intolerance* wrote an afterword which reported that as of late 1990, most conflicts had been settled peacefully, even if traditional animosities between churches remain (Little 1991: 73–74).

In regard to electoral violence, it might be noted that Ukraine has a party system quite similar to what Gunther *et al.* (1986) describe as the source of polarized politics in Basque Country. In 1991, more than 100 candidates ran for president (FBIS 911101), with at least four serious contenders. The presidential election was successfully held where the nationalist coalition, Rukh, lost, and a former communist won, and there has been intra-elite accommodation and bargaining since the election. President Kravchuk failed to win reelection due to the economic and social catastrophe that followed in the wake of the Soviet Union's collapse, but his failure was not due to open warfare between nationalists and accommodators. The peaceful election of President Leonid Kuchma in 1994 brought to power a candidate who wishes to accommodate government policies to the expressed needs of the Russian population in Ukraine. Startlingly, this election occurred without stirring up violence between the Ukrainian nationalist west and Russian-accommodationist east.

In Georgia, since the break-up of the Soviet Union, peace has been elusive, both among nationality groups and among Georgian political factions. Electoral politics were played out in an atmosphere of contending armed camps. In 1990, the radical nationalist candidate for the presidency, Gia Chanturia, was nearly killed in an assassination attempt, and at least two people were killed in armed clashes during that campaign. Zviad Gamsakhurdia, who was then considered a moderate with impeccable nationalist credentials, won the election with his "Round Table/Free Georgia" coalition.

Gamsakhurdia quickly lost support among other leading Georgian figures. He had organized the election so that Dzhaba Ioseliani, an art history professor who was leader of the Sakartvelos Mkhedrioni (Knights of Georgia), was not permitted to run. Ioseliani's band of 7,000 recruits, relying on weapons bought from demobilized soldiers who had fought in Afghanistan, established national credibility by fighting Soviet MVD (Ministry of Internal Affairs) troops. But after being marginalized by Gamsakhurdia, Ioseliani mobilized the Knights to overthrow the Georgian president. Even Gamsakhurdia's former allies, disgusted by his erratic rule, soon joined the armed opposition, and a rump group of the National Guard joined as well. In early 1992 the cycle of armed combat led to a siege of Gamsakhurdia's official residence. He finally escaped, but the six-week battle cost then lives of 110 people, and Tbilisi became an armed camp with daily reports of explosions and armed attacks (FBIS 920316).

With regard to nationality groups in Georgia, the South Ossetian Autonomous Oblast was the scene of early bloodshed. Georgian titular authorities denied electoral standing to candidates who preached any form of secession, and this act alone took nationalist Ossetians outside the democratic game. Ossetians appealed to Moscow, not only for the right to field candidates, but to protect them from threats that Georgian would be the sole official language of the republic. Ossetian nationalists began to terrorize Georgian villagers, and Georgians in Ossetia fought back by cutting off all electrical power, in the middle of winter 1991, to Tskhinvali, and by surrounding the city with 15,000 Georgian troops.

Meanwhile, Georgians living in surrounding farming villages began to shoot missiles into Ossetian cities while Ossetians attacked Georgians traveling between farming villages. The Russian (then the CIS) army played an arbitrating role, but the death toll was over 250 in 1991, and there were tens of thousands of refugees. To the south, in Adzharia, a nationalist leader was assassinated in April, 1991, during a demonstration in support of political autonomy. There was a spiral of violence in the making; the old Adzharian elite were then bribing the officers in the army garrisons in order to procure weapons.

The greatest bloodshed for Georgia has been spilled over Abkhazia. In the Stalinist period, the Georgian republic deported many Abkhazis, and those who remained were subject to unwanted Georgianization measures. Their hopes were lifted during perestroika, and Abkhazi leaders appealed to Mikhail Gorbachev, the Soviet head of state, to allow them a higher level of administrative autonomy. The Georgian government was opposed, and there were violent clashes in July 1989. By 1990, Georgian deputies walked out of the Abkhazi Supreme Soviet, giving the Abkhazi delegates the opportunity to declare sovereignty. They were willing to remain part of a federal Georgia, but wanted Georgia to remain part of the Soviet Union, which gave Abkhazis some level of protection against Georgian predation. But Georgia received its own independence, and when its parliament reinstated the 1921 constitution, with no specific mention of Abkhazia, violent conflict returned. The Georgian State Council sent units of the National Guard (which was really a set of private armies, including Ioseliani's Knights of Georgia) which engaged in gratuitous violence, irrespective of the orders coming from the Georgian government. The Abkhazian autonomist movement got military support from other Caucasian national groups, and its guerrillas were able to force a Georgian military retreat from the capital, Sukhumi (Otyrba, 1994).

The return to Georgia of Eduard Shevardnadze in 1992 to serve as head of state gave many Georgians hope for peace. In 1978, while he was serving as chief of the Georgian Communist Party, demonstrations took place on the streets of Tbilisi to protest against restrictions on the Georgian language's official status; Shevardnadze diplomatically gave in to the demands and avoided a possible round of violence. His heroic return to war-torn Georgia from an illustrious career as Minister of Foreign Affairs and pro-democrat in the late Soviet period therefore sparked optimism.

But Shevardnadze could not douse the flames of violence. To be sure, he quickly negotiated a truce in Ossetia. However, Abkhazia remained a nightmare, and only military victory by Russian-supported Abkhazi troops ended open warfare, a war in which about 20,000 people were killed. In 1994, Shevardnadze capitulated to Russia, joined the Commonwealth of Independent States (CIS), and its troops began to monitor the Georgian/Abkhazian border. They were subsequently complemented by a 125-member UN Observer Mission in Georgia (UNOMIG). However, as of mid-1997, a political agreement had not been reached, most of the Georgian refugees from Abkhazia have not as yet been resettled, and sporadic violence along the border mars chances for a political settlement. The situation in the political center is no less incendiary. Unofficial militias remain a threat to political stability. In 1994 Georgy Chanturia, chairman of the National Democratic Party, was assassinated. Worse, assassination attempts on President Shevardnadze in 1995 and 1997 were instigated by former commanders of Georgian security forces (RFE/RL 970101–970630). A culture of violence marks post-Soviet Georgia.

Explaining Ukrainian accommodation and Georgian violence

As was the case with the Catalonia/Basque Country comparison, it would be possible but not fruitful to find the roots of violence and accommodation in the present period in patterns of behavior or social structure from previous periods. In fact, as with the Spanish cases, a powerful story can be told to predict the *opposite* results. The standard national history of Georgia (Suny 1988) points to that country's role, like Catalonia's, as an historic passageway, one in which ethnic and religious minorities could pass through, could integrate socially and culturally, and could operate commercially, without threat to their personal security. And as a passageway between the Ottoman and Russian empires, Georgian elites learned the importance of accommodating to the realities of power rather than fighting for autonomy. The late eighteenth- and early nineteenth-century incorporation into the Russian empire was accomplished without resistance, as the Georgian aristocracy well understood the realities of Russian power. During the Russian revolution, the Mensheviks were the most powerful force in Georgia. But when the Bolsheviks closed in on Tblisi in 1921, the Mensheviks fled the capital city without a fight.

If it would be easy to establish the roots of peaceful accommodation in Georgia, it would be just as easy to relate the story of a militaristic Ukraine, beginning with the arrival of the Cossacks in the fifteenth century. Religious pogroms and inter-nationality wars mark Ukrainian history during World War II. These are not the only stories one could tell of the Georgian and Ukrainian pasts, but they are plausible stories to explain a tradition of Georgian peaceful accommodation and Ukrainian violence. The problem is that in the post-Soviet period, the outcomes have been different from what these stories would predict.

To be sure, in the post-Stalin period, Georgians were far more discriminatory toward minorities than were the Ukrainians. In Georgia, Georgians make up 67 percent of the republic's population. Yet in the 1969–70 school year, they accounted for 82.6 percent of the students in higher education. "National autonomy in Georgia had come to mean," concludes Suny (1988: 304–5), "the exercise of local power against the unrepresented local minorities." Meanwhile, Ukrainians constitute 74 percent of the population in the republic, yet make up only 60 percent of the students in the institutions of higher learning (Subtleny 1988: 531). It might be argued that Georgian discrimination against minorities was a powder keg ignited by the freedoms associated with glasnost. But I don't think this is a significant factor in explaining levels of post-Soviet violence. For one thing, violence in Georgia was as much intra-Georgian as it was between Georgians and minorities. Second, inter-national rancor was present, even prevalent, perhaps even more so than in Georgia, in post-Soviet Ukraine, but it was politically contained.

Contemporary observers of the post-Soviet ethnic scene are more likely to explain the diverse outcomes in Georgia and Ukraine by focusing on Kravchuk's political skill in building coalitions and his sang froid in handling crises in comparison with Gamsakhurdia's exclusionary rhetoric and megalomaniacal ambitions. Other explanations focus upon the Georgians' fear of demographic and regional threat that mobilized them against outsiders in comparison with a more secure Ukrainian environment. While surely not wrong, these explanations have an ex post facto quality to them.

One analyst sees the roots of the present violence in Georgia's unhappy past. Otyrba (1994: 281) explains: "In Georgia one can find examples of all the major causes of ethnic strife in the Caucasus: the legacy of the national-territorial division of the USSR, the problem of the right of nations to self-determination, the tension between federalism and unitarianism, and the frustrations of peoples subjected to repression." While these points are undoubtedly powerful, they do not adequately differentiate Georgia from other republics which made the passage from Soviet to independent rule in a less violent manner.

A more general theory has been proposed that helps differentiate the outcomes in Ukraine and Georgia. Barry Posen (1993b) argues, inter alia, that the principal minority in Ukraine is formed by Russians, whose security is assured by the presence of a neighboring superpower with an interest in their protection. This puts a damper on any provocation by Ukraine and it relieves the Russian populations living there from the need to arm themselves. In Georgia, by contrast, the Ossetians and Abkhazis have no homeland to protect them, and by protecting themselves, they provoke the Georgians. Indeed Ronald Suny (1995), in his description of post-Soviet Transcaucasia, provides data which show that the level of violence in the three Transcaucasian republics is in direct proportion to the size of each republic's non-Russian minority population.

Posen's theory is robust because it defines the domain of relevant cases as situations of "anarchy", with a wide array of cases already documented (albeit only in inter-state relations) by realist theorists. But his theory would not easily explain the high level of peace in Ukraine's Transcarpathian region nor the high level of intra-Georgian conflict in Georgia proper. Nor would it give us any handle on the Spanish cases. I would still not rule out realist theories of national conflict. Those theories and the one I am advancing may well be strong in separate but overlapping domains. Indeed, future research should determine the proper domains of each of these approaches. Rather than compare the two approaches, here I shall seek to flesh out my microtheory, providing a closer look at the two post-Soviet cases.

Microfoundations of post-Soviet nationalist violence and accommodation

Anthropological research of the type reported in the Spanish cases needs to be conducted in order to put the micromechanisms to close empirical scrutiny, and therefore to see if those mechanisms could account for Georgian violence and Ukrainian accommodation in the course of their national revivals. But it is nonetheless possible to give the outlines of a story, relying on those micromechanisms, to make sense of the post-Soviet national scene in Georgia and Ukraine.

Rural social structure

Georgia's rural social structure appears to have maintained the basis for terrorist organization. Ukraine, on the other hand, has become in the past half-century a highly urbanized republic whose small towns and villages could not contain their young men, thus making it far more difficult to create and sustain militant commando groups.

Georgia had a vibrant underground economy in the post-Stalinist Soviet Union. It is estimated to have reached 25 percent of the Georgian gross national product (GNP), among the highest in the Union. A quasi-anthropological study (Mars and Altman 1993) to explain the success of this economy, in the face of strict punishments by communist authorities, pointed to the importance of "network cores" that were constructed from family and business ties by those people who were most successful in this economy. These cores could be successfully and surreptitiously constructed because, in Mars and Altman's view (1993: 548) Georgian village life is still based upon a culture of "honour" and "shame." This culture of honour pushes men to achieve personal economic successes that were not possible in the context of Soviet communism, but it also prevents members of the network from informing on illegal practices to central authorities. The tightness of village networks, it is concluded, helps explain both the motivation and the security of the Georgian underground economy. It is this same village organization that allows for the construction of commando organizations to fight intra-Georgian as well as anti-minority battles in the course of a nationalist revival.

In contrast, the rural social structure of the Ukraine changed immensely in the past generation. Massive rural-urban migration in the 1920s and 1930s were a function of Soviet policies to promote mining and industrial production in the Ukraine (Liber 1992: 49–52). Later, Khrushchev's Virgin Lands project induced 80,000 farmers from the Ukraine to settle in eastern republics. But the rural-urban migration continued, and trends suggest that nearly 70 percent of Ukrainians will be living in large urban environments by the year 2000. As a consequence, the rural labor force in 1965 was 7.2 million; by 1980 it was down to 5.8 million. Subtelny (1988: 528) wryly notes that "on many collective farms it is the weathered old women who provide the main source of manual labor." And this, he argues, has broad cultural consequences (p. 527): "As the role of the peasant in Ukrainian society has diminished, the populism that was the hallmark of Ukrainian ideologies in the nineteenth and early twentieth centuries has also faded. One can even argue that today the concept of the *narod* – in the traditional sense of the poor, oppressed peasant masses – no longer occupies a central place in the political thinking of Ukrainians." The point here is that the number of Ukrainian villages that can produce a nationalist vigilante like Stepan Khmara (a member of the Ukrainian parliament from the strongly nationalist Congress of Ukrainian Nationalists) is small, and the local structures that would enable him to recruit a network of support organizations for commando operations are declining as well.

While rural social organizations have declined in Ukraine over the past generation, the Ukrainian Communist Party grew as fast as any republican party in the post-Stalin period. Khrushchev Ukrainized the party. Oleksii Kyrychenko was the first titular to hold the post of first secretary in any Soviet republic (save Russia itself), and since the Khrushchev period only Ukrainians have held that post (Subtelny 1988: 497). While it remains to be seen whether the UkCP network survived intact through the 1980s, Kravchuk, a leading apparatchik, was able to reconstruct elements of that network and soundly defeated candidates with better nationalist credentials but without the rich organizational ties from the Soviet period. Perhaps being a west Ukrainian with political connections in the east, Kravchuk was able to unify support groups from both regions? In any event, the relatively coherent and partially surviving Communist Party in Ukraine was able to resist power grabs by untested and unstable figures such as Gamsakhurdia who might have been seeking the presidency. The general point is that commando action is less likely when a country-wide party has greater organizational presence than locally based social groups. In Ukraine, this was the case, and local commando actions were successfully policed.

The tipping game

While a precise cost accounting of the Ukrainian and Georgian nationalist tipping games is not possible given the lack of available data, the pattern is similar to what we have seen in Spain. In Ukraine, the *korenizatsia* (nativization) campaign of the 1920s was a great success. While in 1922 only 20 percent of government business was conducted in the regional language, by 1927, 70 percent was conducted in Ukrainian. Schools, media, and cultural institutions followed suit. For example, in 1927 more than half the books published in the Ukraine were in the Ukrainian language and 55 percent of republican newspapers were in Ukrainian (Subtelny 1988: 387–90). These changes laid a basis for Ukrainization of culture in the post-Stalin thaw, where the Ukrainian language became established in cultural life, albeit less so in the heavily Russified cast (Subtelny 1988: 501). And so, the costs of Ukrainizing the society in the post-Soviet period are not so daunting. Even for immigrants, who are largely Slavic, learning Ukrainian, a language closely related to Russian, has relatively low costs. With the national project not-so-threatening to individuals, there is less need for violence to raise the costs of subversion.

To be sure, Georgian prospered in the Soviet period as a language of administration, education and culture (and thus it cannot be compared with the literary and administrative desuetude into which Basque fell in the nineteenth and twentieth centuries). None the less, the costs of accommodating to Georgian cultural hegemony are somewhat higher for a variety of groups than would be the costs for comparable groups accommodating to Ukrainian. Georgian is a Caucasian language, which is a separate family from Indo-European (of which Slavonic, Baltic, Romance, Iranian and Armenian are members). Russians will therefore have a harder time learning it (but only 2.5 percent fewer Russians in Georgia claim to know Georgian than Russians in Ukraine claim to know Ukrainian) (Laitin 1991: 172). Ossetian and Armenian are both in the Indo-European family; their speakers have been adamantly opposed to Georgian language hegemony. Even Abkhazians, whose language is in the Caucasian family, have higher costs adjusting to Georgian. Their language since the 1950s has relied upon a modified Cyrillic script, while the Georgian script is quite distinct. With Georgian being a non-Indo-European language with a non-Cyrillic and non-Latin alphabet, non-Georgians pay a high cost to assimilate. And Georgians who became Russified have similar problems (Hewitt 1990). There isn't sufficient evidence to suggest that any of the violence is related to this sort of accounting, but it has been reported that the Ossetian Popular Front appealed to Moscow rejecting the language measures reported in the Georgian press that would make Georgian the sole official language of the new republic. With only 14 percent of Ossetians knowing Georgian, the proposed Georgian language law presented a daunting challenge. Inasmuch as North Ossetians have done very well in securing higher education in Russia, South Ossetians felt highly discriminated against in Georgia (RFE 910215). Perhaps the combination of low Georgian birth rates and low incentives for minorities to assimilate gave radical Georgian nationalists a sense that the tip toward Georgianization would not occur unless minority groups and anti-nationalist Georgians were intimidated and even terrorized?

Sustaining mechanisms

Georgia has experienced in its recent history a few riveting episodes that have served as a triggering force in the establishment of a culture of violence. In 1956, for example, there was a quiet vigil at a monument to Stalin, one that symbolized disgust with Khrushchev's exposé of Stalin's crimes. The Soviet army came in quickly, killing dozens of young people and wounding hundreds (Suny 1988: 303). Perhaps more relevant, a peaceful prodemocratic demonstration in Tblisi in April 1989 again brought in Soviet troops, and nineteen were killed, mostly elderly women and young girls. After that event, Soviet troops were routinely called the "army of occupation" in Georgian political discourse (RFE 910215). The organization of the Knights of Georgia, which of course required a local social structure conducive to this type of recruiting, grew out of these bloody events.

The war in Ossetia, like the war between Gamsakhurdia and his former supporters, was not determined by history. Georgian authorities saw the Ossetian contacts with Russian authorities in regard to the language issue in 1989 as undermining Georgian sovereignty, and terrorist activities began. A spiral of events followed: the denial in 1990 to Ossetians to run candidates in Georgian elections; and the declaration of the South Ossetian Soviet oblast as an "independent Soviet democratic republic" later that year. Very soon came a tyranny of sunk costs in perpetuating this guerrilla war. When negotiations were proposed by the immediate successors to Gamsakhurdia, a South Ossetian leader found the status quo ante unacceptable, as "too much blood has been shed ... For what? For us to return to the past?" Similarly with Abkhazia: although Otyrba (1994) is correct in his claim that there were historical roots for Georgian-Abkhazian violence, he is incorrect to imply that these roots were any stronger than many other dyads which remained at peace amid the collapse of the Soviet Union.

While it is too soon to say that the mechanisms leading to guerrilla war in Georgia have created a self-sustaining culture of violence, the micro-theory presented herein helps account for that violence. In the late Soviet period a few historically riveting events normalized violence in Georgia. The Georgian social structure, which maintains a strong local base for social groups, allowed for the recruitment of irregular militarized bands in the name of the nationalist cause. This made it easy for political factions excluded from power to challenge Gamsakhurdia through guerrilla tactics. Fear of Georgianization of the entire society, costly for minorities, induced them to defy the Georgian nationalist project. And the realization by vigilantes that it would be irrational for many people who live in Georgia to become "Georgians" in a cultural sense, gave a motivation for nationalist groups to fight against their minorities, rather than bargain with them. These mechanisms all point toward an explanation of how and why the Georgian national project became saddled with violence and terror.

Conclusion

Early in this chapter, the reader was offered a panegyric on the comparative method. A careful reading of this paper, however, should lead one to worry somewhat about its methodological weaknesses. Here in the conclusion – after I have put my best foot forward, and where readers have already seen the bunions – is the proper place to address these weaknesses.

Surely I have propagated a myth of "controlled" variables! Any area specialist can point to scores of stunning historical, cultural, economic, and social differences between Basque Country and Catalonia, or between Georgia and Ukraine. Why did I just focus on the few that my predilections led me to identify? Why do I gloss over the unique and peculiar aspects of each nationalist movement while emphasizing the common? Perhaps causes can be found only in the unique concatenation of factors that are systematically undervalued by the comparative method? In a related concern, why do I assume that the causes of violence in Basque Country are the same as those in Georgia? Perhaps each experienced violence for different reasons, a point that is lost when one accepts the myth of control.

The comparative method has, however, a response to these compelling concerns. The world does not throw up perfectly controlled cases in order to allow political scientists to do better work. Comparativists must continue, Sisyphus-like, to reconfigure their work to better isolate variables they think are important.[2] If the controls are inadequate, the comparativist should design an experiment that has better controls, say between a violent and a peaceful Basque village with the same social structure. We should always be looking for "hard" cases that force us to reexamine our theories. For example, the notion that an indelible memory of violence in the course of a political movement normalizes violence for future interactions may have clear limits, as might be seen from the relatively peaceful Chinese student responses to the horrors of the crushing of the 1989 pro-democracy demonstration in Beijing's Tiananmen Square. The sanguinary hatreds of the Spanish civil war, to use another example, gave communists, conservatives and liberals alike in Spain a sense that their movement for democracy ought to abjure violence. The comparative method should be used, then, to seek out the conditions when sudden and unexpected violence leads to cycles of further violence and when it leads to the coordinated acceptance by all conflicting parties to negotiate peacefully.

Critics can also point out that the sources of violence in the two paired comparisons are not precisely the same. To be sure, in both the Spanish and the Soviet cases there was potential conflict within the separatist regional elites between those wishing to reestablish ties with the center and those who wanted a clean break. But the two Spanish regions did not have serious problems with rooted minority populations not associated with the nationality of the former center, as do the Soviet cases. Nor do the post-Soviet cases have, as was the case in Spain, a reinvigorated center determined to maintain the international boundaries as they existed before the collapse of the authoritarian regime. I cannot claim isomorphism in the pairs.

In response to this criticism, perhaps we should celebrate the incommensurability of the Spanish and Soviet examples, as long as each of the paired comparisons is properly controlled. The fact that research shows similar mechanisms in the two cases of violence and the apparent absence of those mechanisms in the two cases of peaceful accommodation suggests the robustness of the relationship rather than the inadequacy of the design. In fact, highlighting the different contexts in post-Franco and post-Soviet regional politics shows an appreciation for validity. There is no need to ignore different social, cultural, and political contexts by moving to ever higher levels of abstraction. Yet similar mechanisms unleashed in different contexts – as was illustrated in the cases discussed herein – suggest that validity need not be traded off for added generality. Going back and forth between concerns for validity and concerns for generality in the course of a research project makes for good science. Turning potential criticisms on their head, I argue that a common story that helps illuminate apparently incommensurate cases is evidence of scientific success, not failure.

A critical reading of the game model will also lead one to worry about the methods by which actor preferences have been coded. I have claimed here that someone who speaks Basque fluently has a greater interest in the promotion of Basque identity, and will therefore receive a higher pay-off if Basque Country achieves independence. But what about the immigrants to Basque Country who have joined ETA? They are socially accepted by the Basques if they become radical nationalists, and therefore get a high score for joining a violent brigade. These two cases suggest that I can find ex post facto a high pay-off for anyone who becomes an ETA member. These codings therefore have a tautological element to them, as observations on the dependent variable become sources of information for coding on the independent variable.

Indeed, there is an element of tautology in the theoretical presentation herein. One way in which network theorists address this problem is to assume a random or unknowable distribution of preferences (Granovetter 1978; Kuran 1991). Then they can show rapid recruitment into violent movements once a critical threshold is reached. No information on any particular person is necessary. They will say that they can't tell you why Sun Yat-sen, for example, would become the first mover in a nationalist movement. We have no theory as to what is in the minds of social actors. All we can say is that there will be some people a few standard deviations off the mean, that they will be the first movers, and the question is the mechanisms for getting others who are only one standard deviation from the mean to follow.

The problem with this approach is that it gives one little sense of social structure, which is a key to understanding microprocesses. I want to know why it was Sun Yat-sen in China who was the first to form a nationalist movement. I am willing to risk tautology, by trying to figure out what the distinctive pay-off matrices for the early movers are. The key to this research strategy is to develop coding mechanisms for pay-offs that rely on information distinct from observations of subsequent outcomes. This has not been done in the context of the present paper, but it is an area where future research in theoretically attuned comparative politics needs to go. Some network theories (for example, Petersen 1991; Marwell and Oliver 1993) are already making inroads into this problem.

For all its unsolved problems, the comparative method as used in this paper has been able to shed fresh light on the problem of violence and nationalism, and a summary of the results follows.

Violence, terrorism, commando action, and guerrilla war are a related set of tactics that have been employed by groups involved in national revival movements. These tactics have been prevalent in Basque Country from the 1960s to the 1980s, and in Georgia since 1989. In similar national revival projects taking place in Catalonia since the 1960s and Ukraine since 1989, these tactics have played a much more restricted role. Political scientists and historical sociologists who have sought to explain these different outcomes have relied upon variables such as modernization breakdowns, attitudes of the populations, the situation of "anarchy," and ideologies. These macrofactors have been shown to be insufficient for an explanation of the different outcomes.

Nothing inherent in nationalism leads to violence; but since national revivals compel people to make important changes in how they live their lives, violence and terror become an available tool for those supporting or those suppressing the national project. The tool of violence is not historically or culturally determined; it is triggered by factors incidental to macrosociological factors and to the prevailing nationalist ideology.

In light of the gaps in macrohistorical analysis, this paper has taken a different tack. It has relied upon the comparative method to highlight a variety of micro factors that help explain why certain nationalist movements become arenas for terror and others for peaceful bargaining. To be sure, national revival movements challenging relatively weak but tenacious central states provide an opportunity for violence. But there is a wide gulf between opportunity and its violent exploitation.

The gap between the opportunity for and execution of violence is bridged when nationalist leaders can recruit in small villages and towns where there are many social groups whose members are bound by codes of honor. The nationalist group needs also to go through a period of early euphoria, followed by a point at which it becomes irrational for most of those uninvolved in the national movement to join in. This is the point at which terrorist activities come to be seen as a possible way to reinvigorate recruitment. My theory cannot determine whether leaders will actually choose a violent path in order to get past the tipping point. But it does suggest that a stunning success by a rump group of activists, or a bloody attack by forces from the center, may be required before the nationalist organization commits itself to a terrorist course of action. Once such a course of action is chosen, the tyranny of sunk costs and the strategic difficulties for states to make credible security commitments to terrorists who consider leaving their commando units help perpetuate a culture of violence. That I can tell the stories of violence in Basque Country and Georgia highlighting these factors, while juxtaposing the stories of peaceful bargaining in Catalonia and Ukraine where these factors are less prominent, lends credence to the approach.

Notes

This chapter, funded by the Harry Frank Guggenheim Foundation, was originally published in *Archives Européennes de Sociologie*, 36 (1995). Without Roger Petersen's path breaking dissertation (1991), I could not have begun to address the problem posed in this paper. Elise Giuliano provided careful research assistance. Comments on earlier drafts by John A. Armstrong, Assaad E. Azzi, Pieter van Houten, Juan Díez Medrano, Goldie Shabad, Ronald Suny, Arthur Waldron and Joel Wallman are also acknowledged. Leopoldo Calvo-Sotelo kindly arranged for me to present these ideas at the Centro de Estudios Avanzados en Ciencias Sociales, Instituto Juan March. Fernando Reinares, José Maria Maravall, and all the participants at the seminar challenged me to rethink the Spanish cases. For purposes of this reprinting, I have made some revisions due to commentary from Josep Colomer and updated material concerning Georgia, and have linked my ideas about the comparative method to the central theme of the introductory chapter to this volume.

1 Weber (1968: 71, 108, 655, 809–38) discusses rationalization as the process by which a state establishes efficient and orderly rule: a professional civil service, clear territorial boundaries, issuance of a common currency, and establishment of an official language are aspects of rationalization.

2 I mean Sisyphus: even if there are no general patterns, we should continue in our search for them.

3 Mechanisms and structures in comparisons

Roger Petersen

For many central issues of comparative politics, game theory's assumption of rationality is very unrealistic. In my own work on resistance and rebellion, the importance of social norms and irrational psychological mechanisms is so obvious and important that leaving these forces unaddressed would mean forsaking the goal of descriptive validity.[1] At a certain point, hammering a rational framework on to a non-rational reality obscures more than it enlightens. This being said, I will argue in the rest of this chapter that game theory often serves as a highly useful heuristic in approaching many of the most interesting issues of social science. In practical research, the use of game theory forces the social scientist to ask a series of "who" and "why" questions that link mechanism and structure. An explanation wedding mechanism and structure maintains causal specificity while creating the basis for prediction. Such an explanation possesses both generality and descriptive validity.

I will start with some definitions and then list three problems of a mechanism approach: "infinite regress," lack of predictive power, inability to explain aggregate-level variation. Then I will refer to one particular "game" that has been widely used in comparative politics, the n-person assurance game or "tipping model," to illustrate how game theory can link structure to mechanism to help solve these three problems. I choose the "tipping model" because it forms a foundation for some of my own ongoing research. Conveniently, David Laitin's chapter in this volume builds from this research.[2] In illustrating the relationships between structure, mechanism, and game theory, I will take advantage of the presence of Laitin's chapter and analyze it in some depth before turning to my own research. Along the way, I hope that the reader will sense how the application of game theory to important questions in comparative political science often requires anthropological methods.

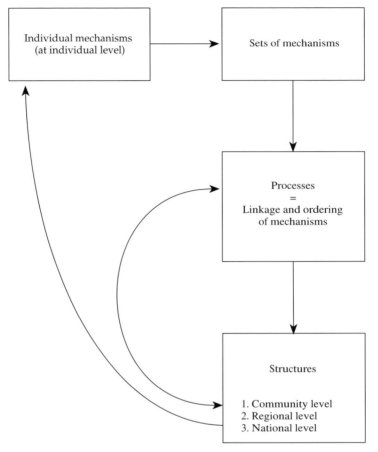

Figure 3.1. Mechanism, process and structure.

Definitions

I will attempt to delineate mechanism, process, and structure with the help of Figure 3.1.

Mechanisms are specific causal patterns which explain individual actions over a wide range of settings. One example was offered in the introduction. An old automobile that is constantly breaking down and being repaired might be retained by the owner despite the likelihood of numerous additional costly repairs due to the "tyranny of sunk costs." Although the optimal choice might be to "junk" the car, the owner refuses rationally to calculate probable future costs because he or she cannot bear the thought of previous repair efforts "going down the drain." The same process might be involved in dysfunctional personal relationships or marriages. One or both partners in a relationship may find themselves continuously dissatisfied, in conflict, and on the verge of breaking up. Rather than ending the relationship, they may choose to remain together and ignore the probability that problems will recur, because they cannot accept the fact that investments in the relationship have been in vain. The "tyranny of sunk costs" mechanism is both general in that it can be applied to a wide variety of cases (cars and spouses) and specific and causal in that it explains why an event occurs. This combination of generality and specificity is one of the benefits of mechanisms. Another benefit is the wide range of behaviors that mechanisms can encompass. Irrational psychological processes such as the "tyranny of sunk costs" or cognitive dissonance reduction are mechanisms, but so are rational adaptation and social norms. Concentration on mechanisms allows the social scientist to deal with realistic actors affected by a complex variety of forces; it forces the social scientist toward causal explanations of increasingly finer grain.

Some studies aim only to create a "laundry list" of relevant mechanisms that help explain a case or a type of event (this is represented by the upper-right box). However, when the scholar orders or links the mechanisms, then a "process" has been adduced.

"Structure" simply refers to relatively slowly changing, relational distinctions. Although structure can be studied at more restricted levels of analysis such as the family or community, structural studies in political science usually focus on macrostructural class and/or political–institutional relationships. For example, what is the relationship between wealth and democracy? Structures produce the broader context within which mechanisms operate. Different broad economic structures, such as capitalism versus socialism, will produce a different set of individual-level mechanisms. Finally, although structures usually change slowly, they do indeed change. Here is where the feedback loop between process and structure comes into play. Process provides explanation for structural change.[3]

Disadvantages of a mechanism approach

Infinite regress

A major advantage of a mechanism approach is fine-grained causal explanation. A counter-argument from those employing variable and/or more purely structural forms of explanation is that ultimate causes can never really be established, so why bother to perform the inefficient task of identifying individual-level mechanisms? King, Keohane, and Verba (1994) go on to describe how a search for an ever more fine-grained understanding of causation can lead to a quixotic quest:

[T]here always exists in the social sciences an infinity of causal steps between any two links in the chain of causal mechanisms. If we posit that an explanatory variable causes a dependent variable, a "causal mechanisms" approach would require us to identify a list of causal links between the two variables. This definition would also require us to identify a series of causal linkages to define causality for each pair of consecutive variables in the sequence, and to identify the linkages between any two of these variables and the connection between each pair of variables. This approach quickly leads to infinite regress, and at no time does it alone give a precise definition of causality for any one cause and one effect. (p. 86)

In the end, the response of King, Keohane, and Verba to the complexity of social and political life is the acceptance of simplification. The three authors conclude: "There is no choice but to simplify. Systematic simplification is a crucial step to useful knowledge" (p. 43). In opposition, some advocates of mechanism approaches believe that complexity requires specificity in method, that too much simplification can take us a step backward from real understanding.

Lack of predictive power

From a social science standpoint, perhaps a larger problem of the mechanism approach is its inability to generate predictions. When one is simply seeking mechanisms explaining a given action, there is no a priori reason to include one mechanism but not another. Therefore, several mechanisms may be operating at a given time, resulting in rampant "overdetermination" problems. Furthermore, unspecified mechanisms may be overpowering the ones we know about. Again, the problems and logic are the same ones affecting prediction in variable analysis, but the level of causal specificity greatly magnifies these problems. Jon Elster provides an illustration in which prediction can be easily made from a variable (price) but could not be made from any single mechanism:

To predict that less of a good will be bought when its price goes up, there is no need to form a hypothesis about human behavior. Whatever the springs of individual action – rational, traditional or simply random – we can predict that people will buy less of a good simply because they can afford less of it. Here, there are several mechanisms that are constrained to lead to the same outcome, so that for predictive purposes there is no need to decide among them. Yet for explanatory purposes the mechanism is what matters. It provides understanding whereas prediction at most offers control. (1989: 10)

Elster holds that mechanisms cannot make claims to generality but must instead be satisfied with "if p, then *sometimes* q" statements.[4] King, Keohane, and Verba might simplify the plethora of mechanisms by combining them within variables that offer higher predictive possibilities. They recognize the loss of causal specificity, but do not estimate this loss as highly as Elster.

Inability to explain aggregate level variation

For some theorists, such as Elster, this inability is not much of a problem. Elster is so wary of the problems of correlational studies and functionalism that he prefers the explanatory advantages of individual level mechanisms even if they remain unconnected to broader theories specifying conditions that help explain aggregate variation. In fact, Elster writes:

Moving from a plurality of mechanisms to a unified theory would mean that we should be able to identify in advance the conditions in which one or the other mechanism would be triggered . . . My own view is that the social sciences are currently unable to identify such conditions and are likely to remain so forever. (1993: 5)

For Elster, social scientists should lower their expectations in the face of the overwhelming complexity of social life. Other theorists, however, take a totally opposite view. Arthur Stinchcombe puts the point bluntly when he states that "Theories of mechanisms are not, in general, useful unless they generate new predictions at the aggregate or structural level" (1991: 385).

Game theory: linking structure and mechanism

Game theory requires a specification of actors, choices, and constraints/ incentives. The set of constraints/incentives can be discussed as the decision structure. The method further requires the specification of a mechanism explaining how a decision results. As a form of rational choice theory, game theory mechanisms must entail rational beliefs and rational evaluation of outcomes rather than social norms and/or irrational psychological mechanisms. Crucially, game theory is strategic, that is, it involves and highlights interdependent decision-making. Game theory's foundational concept is the equilibrium: the set of conditions under which no actor would choose independently to alter its behavior. These conditions may, or may not, be further re-formulated as general laws or connected to laws. Game theory is a method that does not require a commitment to the deductive-nomological form of explanation; it is phenomenological rather than law-like (Little 1993).[5]

It is not difficult to see why this method is widely used in political science. Many of the most commonly studied issues in the field involve strategic decision-making.[6] The study of conflict, central to political science, always involves multiple parties and interdependent actions. Market relations, involving elements of both cooperation and conflict, again entail interdependent choices. For many central political events, coalition-formation, parliamentary voting, electoral competition, and so on, the relevant actors and strategies can be identified, a set of pay-offs established, and an equilibrium deduced. Within this volume, Barbara Geddes employs rational choice games to explain the politics of civil service reform. Miriam Golden analyzes the decision-making involved in labor reduction with the help of rational choice logic and tools. Both pieces are exemplary.

Importantly, the method develops deductive and formal models that specify decision structures under which regularities in behavior should hold. Similar structures should trigger the same mechanisms and thus the same outcomes. When the structures can be identified a priori, that is independently from outcomes, prediction becomes possible. Secondly, the decision structures may connect individual actions to aggregate level phenomena. Through its specification of causal linkages across levels of analysis, game theory can provide individual level prediction from existing aggregate level theory. For those like Stinchcombe, who believe that aggregate level phenomena are the most legitimate focus of social science, game theory provides a way to make theories explaining aggregate variation "more supple, precise, complex, elegant, or believable" (Stinchcombe 1991: 368). Finally, a method that restricts itself to rational micro-mechanisms plausibly linked to observable structures tends to prevent "infinite regress," in practice if not theory. In short, game theory can combine the benefits of a fine-grained causal mechanism approach with the predictive powers of an aggregate-level structural approach.

However, game theory does not seem appropriate for a host of important topics. What about issues which involve very complex or murky sets of constraints/incentives? Or what about events where the salience of non-rational forces, such as social norms,[7] or irrational psychological forces, such as cognitive dissonance, seems too obvious to be ignored? I will argue that even the study of these types of issues might benefit from a game theoretic approach when the action that needs explanation appears to be related to observable social structures. Under these conditions, game theory forces the analyst to ask a series of inextricably linked "who" and "why" questions. The "who" seeks the social structure, the "why" seeks the reasons why changes in structure, or actions by observable sub-groups within that structure, have an impact upon individual behavior.[8]

An example: Laitin's use of the "tipping game"

Within his study of violence in nationalist revival, Laitin employs game theory but does not remain tied to a strict concept of rationality throughout his explanation. In this study, game theory lays down a baseline for coherent comparison and centers the description of process, but it does not prevent the search for other salient mechanisms. I will review some basic concepts of the game that Laitin uses and then discuss how this game is embedded within a less restrictive overall explanation.

Certain concepts involved with game theory effectively link structure and mechanism. The idea of a "threshold" in the "tipping game" is one such concept. "I will act if X percent of others act as well." This is the underlying logic of the n-person assurance game (Sen 1967; Schelling 1985). The n-person assurance, or "tipping", game is ideal in capturing events involving binary choices with pay-offs directly connected to the percentages of others' choices. It seems especially appropriate in explaining rapid switches in mass behavior that result from highly unstable equilibria. Recently, the game has been applied in several forms to explain the massive and rapid turn of eastern European mass populations, thought to be politically quiescent, against the communist regimes that ruled over them (Goldstone 1994; Kuran 1991, 1995; Karklins and Petersen 1993; Bunce and Chong 1990; Lohmann 1992).[9]

The foundation of the "tipping game" is the threshold, that is, the percentage level of participation by a reference group that triggers reciprocation by the individual. Two questions, common to many games, immediately come to mind. First, who is the reference group (X)? Second, why do the actions of this group have this effect? The first question relates to social structure while the second question requires a specified causal mechanism.

Consider Laitin's use of the "tipping game" as an example (see pp. 35 and Figure 2.1). Laitin wishes to connect the strategies of rationally acting nationalists to the linguistic pay-offs of regional populations. Individuals within these regional populations face choices between use of the regional and central languages. Although many individuals develop complex bilingual strategies (using the regional language in one domain and the central language in another), some critical decisions do involve a binary choice of languages. Laitin discusses the important, and binary, choice that parents make in deciding the principal medium of instruction for each child. For this choice, there exists a highly unstable equilibrium, a "tipping point", at which the pay-offs for the regional language equal those for speaking the language of the center. The game predicts a massive and rapid switch to the use of the center's language if this point is crossed.

The use of this game requires Laitin to define the reference group. Here, Laitin's choice of plausible reference group is the regional population as a whole. The game also requires Laitin to specify *why* this group is the reference group and why events within this group (language switch) affect actions of individuals. Laitin specifies four separate mechanisms in connection with percentages of regional language use among the regional group.[10]

1. Status-based "heroic pay-off" up to 25 percent. Along common-sense lines, when low percentages are utilizing the regional languages, the average pay-off for instruction in the central language is considerably higher than for the regional language. However, for lonely poets and philologists, among others, there is a status pay-off rewarded for sacrificing to keep the regional language alive.

2. Status-based sanction beginning at about 45 percent. Those who continue to use the central language despite the rise of the regional language incur a loss of honor.

3 and 4. Economic calculations at 50 percent. These calculations involve the estimate of economic pay-off for learning the regional language, and the estimate of future percentages of regional speakers that will affect both economic and status pay-offs.

The latter mechanism is crucial in connecting language switch to Laitin's central goal of explaining nationalist violence. The game leads Laitin to the hypothesis that nationalists will be most likely to initiate terrorism and intimidation if the gap between language pay-offs begins increasingly to favor the central language at around the 40 percent level. "Language vigilantes" see nationalist violence as an instrument in pushing the percentage of regional speakers to more favorable levels that will in turn trigger both higher economic pay-offs (at 50 percent) for regional speakers and status sanctions against those not switching (beginning at around 45 percent). Nationalists' actions are driven by the position of the equilibria of the game. Notice that there are three equilibria. One lies at 0 percent, another at 100 percent, and a highly unstable equilibrium at about 70 percent representing the "tipping point". Strategically initiated violence drives behavior toward and past that unstable equilibrium.

At one level, Laitin has conformed to the restrictions of game theory. Individuals choose a maximizing strategy according to a specified set of pay-offs. Nationalists choose violence at the optimal juncture. Predictions, based on the identification of equilibria, can be made. At other levels, though, Laitin clearly expands the scope of his analysis beyond the usual range of game theory. The pay-offs incorporate status, honor, and linguistic "heroism", as well as economic values. Laitin also ties in norms, a non-rational force. Importantly, within this game all of the mechanisms and pay-offs are tied to observable percentages of regional language speakers. The benefits of this link between observable structure and mechanisms are clear. First, by grounding his explanation in mechanisms triggered by observable language use, Laitin basically constrains the possibilities for "just so" storytelling that can lead to "infinite regress". There are only so many mechanisms that one can imagine operating between observations of others' language use and individual choice in language use, and Laitin limits himself to four of these. Secondly, the game generates predictions. Laitin's theory can be falsified if nationalist violence is commonly observed at very low or very high percentages of regional language speakers. Thirdly, as Laitin shows in his analysis of cases, isolation of individual level mechanisms does help to explain aggregate level variation. Laitin has created a more realistic story of language use and nationalist violence while still retaining a relatively parsimonious game that can be applied to other cases.

This "tipping game" is only one part of Laitin's explanation, however. It illustrates a middle set of mechanisms. There are two sets of mechanisms that surround this strategic game as told in separate "micro-stories." First, there must be a set of low threshold actors that move the percentage of regional speakers upward. Laitin posits that these actors are created through mechanisms, rational and non-rational, found in dense rural social structures. Secondly, there are a set of mechanisms which sustain violence once it begins. These mechanisms are almost entirely irrational.

The game stands at the center of the entire explanation. Outlining the conditions that precede the game, Laitin's first micro-story explains how dense rural structures help produce low threshold actors necessary to explain original movement in the tipping game. By outlining sustaining mechanisms, Laitin's third micro-story explains why movement within the tipping game is not reversed. The dependent variable, initiation of violence, is predicted by the game. The first and third micro-stories help explain the dependent variable only in connection with the tipping game. Notice how the existence of a game as a baseline allows Laitin to bring in irrational psychological mechanisms without losing coherence. These irrational mechanisms can be specified within the overall process.

Of course, as other contributors in this volume have pointed out, the structure of games can be abstracted and applied to other cases. Games form the baseline for comparison that provides generalizability.

Laitin's explanation can be discussed in terms of Figure 3.1 above. Laitin actually starts with social structure, showing how one particular form of observable social structure, dense and rural, produces a set of mechanisms capable of generating low threshold players. Two more sets of mechanisms are then ordered and specified within the tipping game forming a process. The process, finally, explains structural change in terms of language and organized nationalist cells which in turn perpetuate or trigger identified mechanisms. Here we have a model for the use of game theory in actual comparative research: a game, assuming rationality and identifying equilibria, centering and ordering discussions of numerous and varied mechanisms.

Another example of the "tipping game"

In my own work, I have been trying to understand how rebellion against powerful regimes is initiated and sustained. The substantive material primarily involves resistance and rebellion against Soviet and German occupation in eastern Europe in the 1940s but touches upon the anti-communist rallies of the late 1980s as well. The topic lends itself to the logic of the n-person assurance game. In effect, the potential rebel or protester states, "I will rebel if X percent of the others rebel." The individual's choice is interdependent and can be discussed in binary terms. Moreover, as the demonstrations in eastern Europe in autumn 1989 illustrated, the tipping game's prediction of rapid switch between two strategies seems applicable.

In applying game logic to this issue, however, I discovered that the question of "who" – the reference group that triggers a mechanism – can become exceedingly complex. While Laitin's case featured one reference group – members of the regional population – I came to realize that rebellion and protest could involve the clan, the community, corporate social groups, or some combination. In the analysis of modernized societies, eastern Europe of 1989 for example, the actions of corporate groups (students, workers, Party members) as well as the overall population were most relevant. On this subject, three interlocking tipping games seemed the most realistic model (Karklins and Petersen 1993). In the modernizing societies of the 1940s, on the other hand, the key reference groups were found in the local community in which the individual was firmly embedded (Petersen 1991, 1993). In observing anti-Soviet and anti-German armed resistance during the 1940s, I noticed situations in which one village or community had developed elaborate resistance structures while a neighboring community had no organization at all. It was my hope that through explaining this local variation that I could systematically uncover the mechanisms initiating and sustaining collective violence against powerful and ruthless regimes.

In order to proceed with this study I needed to work at a lower level of analysis, usually the village, and develop a greater amount of detail more common to anthropology than my own field of political science. Here, I wish to show that, even at this level, game theory can serve as a useful heuristic that productively links mechanism and structure. I will briefly review this work and then make some concluding points.

My first set of fieldwork was with Lithuanian emigrés concerning the emergence of Lithuanian resistance to Soviet occupation in 1940–41. During my first set of interviews, I found that most of these emigrés could map out their native villages as they stood on the eve of the first Soviet occupation. They could list, with some confidence, which families had been connected with particular social and religious organizations, the informal circles of economic cooperation, which families and individuals had been most influential in starting organized resistance, and which families had joined or supported the resistance after its inception. Generally, they could even list the number of hectares that each family in the community farmed. The depth of this knowledge amazed me at first. After all, these were events from fifty years previously. However, the families comprising these Lithuanian communities had often lived together for hundreds of years. Even in the late 1930s, social mobility was rather low and local economic and status concerns dominated the lives of rural Lithuanians.

With increasing numbers of interviews and community maps, I was able to begin to create a community-based tipping model (Petersen 1993, forthcoming). First, the logic of the model seemed appropriate: the decision to incur the risks of initiating or joining resistance units could be realistically linked to assurances and pressures connected to the level of participation of reference populations. Not surprisingly, given the nature of Lithuanian society and the Soviet regime's control of information and travel, the most relevant reference populations were the community as a whole and sub-groups within the local community. As with many strategic games, its application linked mechanism and actions within observable social structures. Participation within the community as a whole provided "safety in numbers" (rational calculation); participation in sub-groups triggered different norms depending on the nature of the sub-group; a high percentage of community participation created effective threats.

The next step involved linking observable community structures taken as a whole to the sequence of mechanisms they produce. Community structures could be categorized in terms of existence and size of sub-groups, density, centralization, and so on. They could also be categorized according to the ratio and connection between types of community sub-groups. Space does not permit a full treatment of this process. Instead, I will present perhaps the most stark and least complicated case from actual fieldwork followed by a simplified version of this method.

The first round of data collection primarily dealt with the organization of resistance during the first Soviet occupation of 1940–41. The theory that was emerging was of course based on a tautological relationship between theory and data. Thus, I began collecting new data. I started with a most similar case – anti-Soviet Lithuanian resistance in 1945–52. I traveled to the Lithuanian countryside conducting interviews and mapping procedures similar to those that I had carried out with emigrés in Chicago, Cleveland, and Sioux City, Iowa.

In the summer of 1992 I collected data in a region in southern Lithuania that had been exceptionally bloody in the 1945–50 period. In late December 1944, the Soviets returned to southern Lithuania and the area around the town of Merkine. On Christmas Eve they massacred much of the population of a small village named Klepocai. As the smoke rose from the burning Klepocai, hundreds of people from neighboring villages, many of them youth fearing conscription into the Red Army, fled into the woods to buy time to consider their options. Within a short period of time, many of these refugees had re-incorporated themselves into their communities and many of these communities developed into support networks for the refugee-rebels. In fact, some villages created elaborate systems of underground bunkers that were supplied with food and information by the majority of the community. Buoyed by these local systems of support, a partisan resistance to Soviet rule raged in this area of the Lithuanian countryside throughout the late 1940s. Some of the communities in the region developed elaborate bunker systems to hide their home-grown rebels; often these communities would continue to resist until a significant number of their population were deported to Siberia. Other communities would be ready to support partisans who passed through and might have a liaison man or two, but would not be organized; yet other communities in the same region would try to remain neutral.

As witnessed in the earlier fieldwork, the logic of the "tipping game" pervaded the decisions of many of the interviewees. Again, the community and its subsets were the most significant reference groups. At one level, participation within the community as a whole was producing "safety in numbers"; at other levels, participation within observable social structural subsets could be matched to other specific mechanisms. There were some differences in mechanisms and structure from the earlier period, but no real difference in method. Fieldwork revealed five mechanisms, very similar to those of the earlier period, underlying rebellion: (i) rational adaptation: draft-age youth assessed the resources of their family and village and often decided to rely on them for survival; (ii) "norms of honor": families helped their children despite enormous risk; (iii) social norms of reciprocity: neighbors belonging to common economic work and social groups became involved in the network; (iv) threat: at certain advanced levels of participation, credible threats, implicit or explicit, emerged as a force toward potential non-cooperators; (v) "safety in numbers": the basic logic of the assurance game was operative throughout the process.

After salient mechanisms have been identified, the next step involves creating hypotheses relating observable community social structures to sequences of mechanisms (that in turn explain outcomes). In Laitin's explanation, there was only one reference group and one relevant threshold. Laitin used a relatively simple game to anchor a search for a broader set of mechanisms. Here, multiple reference groups, multiple who-why combinations, complicate the picture. However, the simplest and most common form of the tipping model can still be used as a foundation. All community members are actors in the community-wide "safety in numbers" assurance game. Community members, depending upon their location in community structures, their membership in different groups, their inclusion in certain networks, have different X percent values that help to trigger their decision to participate in resistance. Different subsets of the community population, depending upon characteristics gleaned through fieldwork, can be separated into "early movers" or "late movers", basically assigned rough threshold values. This distribution of thresholds in the most common tipping game again helps guide the specification of a broader set of mechanisms.[11] It helps establish the sequence of mechanisms.

This methodology is not as complicated as it sounds. Imagine that the simple Venn diagram in Figure 3.2 represents the structure of a village in Lithuania in the post-World War II period. The A subset represents draft-age youth, basically early movers with incentives to rebel. Given their desperate position, they will rebel even if no other community members join them. They are the first players, those with a 0 percent threshold that produce the original movement in the tipping process. The B subset represents some social or economic network in the village

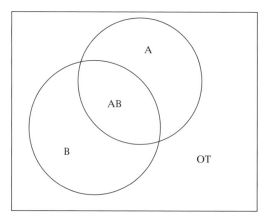

Figure 3.2. An example of the distribution of
thresholds in a tipping game.

with generally higher thresholds. The AB group represents community
members who both belong to local networks and have draft-age sons or
family members seeking support. They will be more willing to accept
less "safety in numbers" and occupy an intermediate position in the
distribution of thresholds. The OT group represents community
members neither belonging to the social or economic network nor
having family members in the woods; presumably they have high thresholds for being involved in dangerous activities with people with whom
they are relatively unconnected.

What sequence of mechanisms could be expected to emerge from
such a structure? The analysis starts with the lowest threshold group in
the community-wide tipping game and works to the highest. The most
likely sequence generating near-universal participation could be hy-
pothesized as the following: (i) draft-age youth (A) calculate support in
family and village; (ii) family members (AB) support sons through
norms of honor; (iii) social and economic sub-groups tied to the youths
and/or their families (B) reciprocate according to social norms; (iv)
threats are made against any non-cooperators (within OT).

This game-centered method avoids "infinite regress". Mechanisms
are linked to observable social structures which are not, in practice,
infinite. Secondly, the method can be used to generate falsifiable
hypotheses. From the simple schema above, three such hypotheses jump
out, each linked to the following observable structural element:
1. The size of A, the first playing subset. In 1945–52, the form of the
hypothesis could be stated as "the higher the number of draft-age males

in the community population, the more likely is the community to reach significant percentages of organized involvement." In the 1940–41 period, subset A would represent membership in certain social patriotic sub-groups, but the principle remains the same, as does the underlying logic. Without this set of early movers, the sequence of mechanisms never begins.

2. The AB:B ratio. Again, the link to the relevant mechanism is clear. AB members wish to help family members (norms of honor) but they also are in normative relationships with other community members who may not wish to be involved. The nature of social pressure and norms of fairness/reciprocity depend upon the AB:B ratio. When this ratio is small, the higher threshold B group may be more effective in resisting the appeals of the AB sub-group; if the ratio is large, the B group will be more likely to feel social or normative pressure to reciprocate.

3. The overall size of the community. This factor relates to the threat mechanism and is especially relevant to the OT subset. Threats rely on monitoring and credible retaliation which relate in turn to overall size. If the size of a community is large, A, AB, and B groups may become involved but they may not be able to influence outsiders.

Furthermore, the link to broader aggregate level theories can be made relatively easily. What explains differences in rebellion among similarly placed nations like Lithuania, Estonia, and Latvia? What explains observed variation among two regions populated by one nation (example: post-World War II Volhynia and Galicia)? The answer suggested here is that this variation might best be explained by differences in local social structures. There are many sociological theories emphasizing centralization, density, and other structural factors that can be linked to the micro-analysis here.[12]

Finally, the method, despite its specificity, does possess a measure of generality. The hypotheses just discussed can be applied to almost any situation in which rebellion primarily forms at the community level. The size of a first-playing sub-group, the size of overlaps, the overall size of the community are general features that can be identified in southeast Asian and Latin American communities as well as in 1940s eastern Europe.

Final thoughts

As should be evident, this research method is time-consuming. Obviously, testing these types of hypotheses requires an immense amount of data as well as time and effort to test. Above all, the method requires the analyst to observe the impact of reference groups on individual action. This necessity entails a good deal of anthropological work either in the field or in the library. Moreover, research will undoubtedly uncover many significant differences in local social structures and a host of aggregate level variables that plausibly have effects at the community or individual level. In order to control for these factors, extensive sets of comparisons need to be made. In my broader work, I make seven types of comparison.

The costs are high, but so are the potential benefits. The inclusion of mechanism and process retains fine-grained causal explanation; the use of identifiable structures allows for generality and prediction. As King, Keohane, and Verba suggest, the causal complexity of the political and social phenomena we wish to explain is enormous. Any methodology used to confront this complexity will employ some form of self-limitation, even if it is not consciously recognized. In a search for mechanisms, this self-limiting process can be rather ambiguous. An experienced and well-read social scientist may be able to identify any number of mechanisms (normative, economic-rational, unconscious psychological) operating during some event. Why choose one set of mechanisms rather than another? Where should the search for causal mechanisms begin? By linking mechanisms to observable structures, game theory addresses many of the problems of a mechanism approach.

Nonetheless, I would not recommend this method unless decision structures are at least partially matched with social structures. For many important issues of comparative politics, this is indeed the case. For the subject of rebellion, individuals need to search for clues in their environment to gauge the structure of constraints/incentives under which they operate. For other subjects, though, the connection between actions within observable social structures and individual action is not so clear. Some actions are so complex with so many mechanisms at play that methods focusing on correlation, or interpretation, are more appropriate.

Notes

1 I realize that many advocates of rational choice theory do not see descriptive validity as an end in itself. We have made a different argument in the introduction and I will not labor the point here. For a discussion of the "reality" of game theory in comparative politics, see Tsebelis (1990).
2 Early versions of my present research are seen in Petersen 1991, 1993.
3 For an extensive discussion of the relationship between process and structure, see Ortner (1990, pp. 57–93).
4 Elster does hold, however, that a mechanism should be sufficiently general

and precise to enable us to locate it in widely different settings. It is less than a theory, but a great deal more than a description (1993: 5).

5 It follows that for many practitioners of rational choice the primary goal is not prediction, but rather the uncovering of mechanisms. James Johnson (1996) makes this point in a forceful response to Donald Green's and Ian Shapiro's *Pathologies of Rational Choice Theory* (1994). I would urge all readers to read Johnson (1996) for a succinct and convincing summary of the explanatory ambitions of rational choice theory.

6 The scope of anthropology is probably wider and is less likely to be so concerned with strategic behavior.

7 Here, I am accepting Elster's definition of norms as not outcome-oriented, and therefore not rational. See Elster (1989: 12).

8 Edgar Kiser (1996) makes some related points in a different context. Kiser makes an argument for the compatibility of sociological narrative analysis and rational choice (Margaret Levi's chapter in this volume can be compared). Kiser focuses on the ways in which rational choice theory accomplishes many of the goals of sociological analysis – delineating temporal sequences, explaining particular events, demonstrating path dependencies – as well as linking action and structure.

9 Oberschall (1994: 84–9) provides a good summary discussion of the importance of assurance in explanations of rebellion/resistance.

10 In an earlier work regarding individual decisions of ethnic minorities whether to enlist in the armed forces, I had developed a similar set of economic and status-based mechanisms (Petersen 1989) which Laitin relies on here. This set of mechanisms may be highly relevant for many situations involving an aura of coercion/co-optation between state and ethnic minority.

11 Laitin's chapter, as he himself points out, does not adequately treat the important issue of threshold distributions. Clearly, the outcome of any "tipping model" is a function of this distribution. Most obviously, if there are no low threshold players the tipping process will never begin. There is a simple, implicit distribution of thresholds in the model. Laitin refers to different social groups with lower than average thresholds – poets and philologists, "language vigilantes" – and then shows how the actions of these "early movers" help to trigger a "mass" with average pay-offs resembling those in Figure 2.1. For many questions, though, a story describing two such groups is insufficient. Furthermore, without an a priori theory linking social structures to the distribution of thresholds, the "tipping game" can easily become tautological and lose any predictive power. The analyst can always find a reason for assigning high pay-offs for the set of early movers. The method then lapses into "just so" storytelling: for any given nationalist revival a story is told of how different social, economic, or political groups held a set of thresholds that happened to trigger one another until a cascading process resulted. The solution to this problem, as Laitin notes, is to "develop coding mechanisms for pay-offs that rely on information distinct from observations of subsequent outcomes" (p. 59). My work directly addresses this problem.

12 I take these up in my larger work. The research of Gould (1993), and Oliver and Marwell (1988) is most relevant.

4 Comparative methodologies in the analysis of anthropological data

Fredrik Barth

Though anthropology is almost invariably characterized in textbooks as a comparative discipline, it is striking how unsympathetic social and cultural anthropologists of different theoretical persuasions are to each others' formal comparative operations, and how little agreement there has been on what might constitute "the comparative method" in anthropology. Yet the explicit discussions and critiques of comparisons that we see within anthropology tend to focus on opposed theoretical positions, or the rejection of the substantive assertions of contesting colleagues, and rarely on clarifying the critical issues that the comparative analysis itself raises. As a result, there has been little movement towards any common standards of methodology for comparative operations. In the following, I will discuss the uses of comparison I have made in my analyses of field materials from the Ok area of New Guinea and from Bali, and reflect on what I see as crucial issues in the uses of comparative methodology on these materials, especially in view of developments in contemporary culture theory.

Zoology and gross anatomy provided early models for comparative methodology in anthropology: in the taxonomies of museum collections and the delineation of culture areas, as well as in the structuralism of Radcliffe-Brown. I believe that unanalyzed templates from these early exercises may still be with us and affect how we pursue our comparisons. The key step in the study of comparative anatomy is to identify equivalent structures, that is, the parts of two different organisms to compare. The criteria for such equivalence rely either on similarities of function (for example, "limbs," "eyes," or "the circulatory system" in two different organisms), or they point to an obtrusive similarity of pattern (for example, a segmented structure and its various modifications between two different organisms, or indeed between the different segments of one organism). Comparison thus involves identifying two forms as "variants" of "the same," which means constructing an overarching category within which the two forms can be included, and compared and contrasted.

Two particular circumstances characterize the study of comparative anatomy, arising from the fact that the operations of comparison in anatomy can be, and archetypically are, performed by dissection and comparison of cadavers on the bench. This fact ensures (i) that the operation of comparison can be done on the empirical objects themselves (that is, the cadavers or organs that are compared and contrasted); and (ii) that there is an inherent correspondence between the operations (dissection) and the nature of the object (a physical body). These principles are maintained even when the dissection is performed on only one cadaver, and the comparison is made to anatomical charts and atlases constructed from the dissection of other organisms: such charts simply stand in for the other object in the comparison, and the actual object of comparison and contrast can if necessary be retrieved and placed beside the object that is being dissected.

Note that when ethnographic comparisons started, these conditions were closely mimicked: two museum collections of "material culture" from two different localities could be placed beside each other on the bench and compared, item by item and feature by feature. But this is no longer true in the comparisons we perform in social and cultural anthropology. It is almost always two or more *descriptions* that are compared, not the described objects themselves: we are comparing anthropological accounts, that is, fictions. It is doubtful that such comparisons can ever transcend the limitations, errors, and theoretical flaws that have been embodied in the descriptions that are the objects of comparison. Many of the explicit comparative analyses in anthropology suffer from this weakness, and HRAF-based comparative work seems to epitomize the difficulties. Thus, the Human Relations Area Files have been constructed from ethnographies of variable and sometimes questionable validity, further transformed as they are reinterpreted and represented through compilation and coding. Since these files are generally used to compare multiple cases and to yield statistical correlations, it has been argued that whatever faulty materials they contain may weaken the correlations that can be discovered, but will neither generate nor obliterate them. Yet this defence of the method may be misconceived: errors in conceptualization, and scholarship generally, are rarely random and often very consistent, since they reflect shared methods and theories within the discipline. The statistical manipulation of such fictions may therefore well produce strong, but empirically quite invalid, correlations. The contrast to comparative anatomy is striking, and arises not from any greater replicability of the anatomists' operations of comparison, but because their empirical objects of comparison are present, subject to inspection, in the very operation of comparison. As long as we social anthropologists are not able to compare the objects of our study, but only our descriptions of these objects or indeed our representations of these descriptions, our comparative method will be seriously flawed. We should try to move the comparative operations we perform closer to the empirical objects we investigate, rather than apply them to such secondary and tertiary materials.

Second, I noted the compatibility of the operation of dissection, employed in comparative anatomy, to the constitution of the biological organisms that it studies. I see it as a major challenge for comparative method in anthropology to ensure a similar compatibility. As long as our objects of comparison are descriptions, the theoretical premises on which these descriptions are based will drastically constrain the comparative operations we can apply. For example, breaking up interpretive or structuralist descriptions into atomized assemblages of traits, and then running cross-cultural statistical correlation tests to uncover linkages between these traits, would seem a very questionable procedure. We must respect the constraints that the theoretical framework and ontological assumptions of a description impose on how that description can be used for subsequent comparative analyses.

Finally and most critically, a crucial difference between the operations of comparison in gross anatomy and in anthropology relates to the constitution and boundedness of the "objects" being compared. Individual organisms provide the most self-evident objects of anatomy, and even body parts and organs are characterized by a separableness and a material substantiality that constitutes them fairly unproblematically as objects of dissection and comparison. The anthropological constructions called "a society" or "a culture," on the other hand, have always presented a more vexed kind of unit; and in view of the persistent critiques that have emerged in contemporary theoretical discourse, the usefulness of such constructs has become increasingly questionable. The lesson must be that we should avoid, if at all possible, conceptualizations that reify "cultures" and "societies" as separate, unitary items of comparison.

These strictures do not, of course, apply to what might be called "comparing models": there is every reason to manipulate model constructs in every possible way, permuting, combining, comparing, and contrasting them, to discover their potentialities and uses. Perhaps we have been careless in not distinguishing these different forms of comparison clearly enough. Comparison to explore empirical objects is a discovery procedure of great power. Applying such a procedure to descriptions we ourselves have authored, and thinking we thereby can discover pattern in the empirical world, is a very questionable methodology indeed.

Does that leave the anthropologist without workable units of comparison, and without valid comparative operations? The time is long overdue when the contemporary theoretical critique of our concepts should force us radically to reconceptualize the role of comparison in social and cultural anthropology; but I believe that careful rethinking will enhance the importance that we give to comparative method in the very constitution of anthropological description and analysis. There can be no doubt that all of our anthropological analyses involve comparisons of ethnographic materials. But I would argue that we can no longer sustain the schematism of distinguishing our analyses of forms "within" a body of field data, and the "cross-cultural" comparisons we perform "between" such units. Indeed, by abandoning this distinction, we also escape some of the difficulties of establishing equivalences, and of only being able to compare descriptions. Allow me to be more concrete, through a discussion first of my New Guinea materials and then of my Bali materials.

Comparative method applied to the Baktaman materials

During my main fieldwork in New Guinea in 1968, I focused my time and attention quite heavily on the single community of Baktaman, varying over the year between 183 and 185 members. The Baktaman were also the focus of my main subsequent description and analysis (Barth 1975). But their world was larger than those 183/185 persons and the territory to which they laid claim, even under the very pristine conditions that obtained at that time; and my participation in their life and activities took me on visits to other, adjoining communities, and put me in contact with a certain number of visiting persons from elsewhere. Thus the relationship network that I hooked into reached considerably beyond the community, and involved a number of cultural differences and differences in physical and social circumstances that were of significance to Baktaman themselves, both spiritually and materially. Without transgressing the boundaries of their world – indeed, so as to participate in more of that world – I could thus extend my attention outside the confines of the traditional format of the anthropological study of a "community," and interest and engage myself in persons and institutional forms that fell outside the physical limits of Baktaman lands, but were part of their world construction.

But I went further than that: in the privacy of my thought and reflection, I also progressively constructed a body of regional knowledge that in some ways became considerably larger than theirs. Besides so to speak accompanying them to the limits of their world and trying to participate in their construction of it, I also interpreted information from other places in the region in a way that one might call multicentric. By that I mean that I tried to come to know other places in the region in the same way in which I was trying to come to know the Baktaman community. This made it possible for me to constitute my knowledge of a slightly larger area as a field of diversity, beyond the limits of a single, unique unit. Indeed, despite the persisting defects in my knowledge of local Baktaman fact and circumstance, I none the less chose to invest some time and effort in exploring this field of diversity: thus I accompanied two patrols over a considerable stretch of land in the Fly and Strickland river drainages, and developed some knowledge of communities far outside the known world of the Baktaman. The survey data I thereby collected – although grossly superficial, unreliable, and incomplete – provided the materials for a first and preliminary paper I wrote on the basis of this field work (Barth 1971).

What was the value to me of such materials? Certainly not that they allowed me to make cross-cultural comparisons between a set of "societies" – places that I had only seen briefly, or heard about, or encountered one or a few members of. I was, on the contrary, adopting a research strategy that I had developed during work in larger-scale societies, namely that of *seeking out diversity*. On earlier fieldwork occasions I had primarily thought of the purpose of this strategy as offering a way to grapple with the problem of representativeness: how to ensure that what might be idiosyncratic or unique features of any particular Kurdish (Barth 1953) or Swat Pathan (Barth 1959) village should not be generalized and inadvertently projected on to other communities in an area. But through that process I had become aware of the analytical uses of variation: how difference, and diversity, can be conceptually transformed into a field of variability, leading progressively to the construction of a set of *dimensions of variation* to facilitate my description of any form I observed. A set of descriptions in terms of such dimensions, in turn, opens a way to analyze how certain features tend to co-vary, that is, may be interdependent or interconnected.

Among the Baktaman, on the contrary, my primary purpose was not to make my description "representative" of more communities in the Fly-Strickland drainage: its focus was on understanding meanings in Baktaman ritual. None the less, a mapping (admittedly incomplete) of local diversity, and the construction of some such dimensions of variation, aided me in observing and describing the particulars of Baktaman ritual forms with greater precision. I was better able to notice and conceptualize forms among the Baktaman by knowing something of how the rituals of closely similar neighbors were indeed different, and by reflecting on what might have been different, or perhaps recently had been different or might shortly become so, in the rituals of the Baktaman. What might be the value of this, fairly weakly founded, perspective on variation? First, it served to inform and sharpen my description and analysis of the forms I could closely observe and document among Baktaman in 1968. Secondly, it served to give me hunches, tentative intuitions, of what might represent the important and foundational features of these Baktaman forms and what might be more trivial, insignificant features representing only a fortuitous historical event or moment in the flux of free variation. If features seemed to be widely shared, or if differences correlated with differences in other features, or seemed to be regarded as salient by Baktaman, I would tend to give them great attention; if not, I would be more prepared to see them as probably less significant.

At the same time, I was also constantly performing "internal" comparisons, as everyone doing fieldwork surely does: how did the several Baktaman ritual performances I observed differ among themselves? How did the accounts of the initiations they had gone through at different times differ as between different Baktaman persons? How were different persons' accounts of the same occasions different? How were other participants' accounts and interpretations of events in initiations where I myself participated as a novice, different between themselves and from what I had observed? Such comparisons were necessary to critique the assertions of people and find my way through the purposeful deceptions and falsehoods that protect a sacred, secret tradition. But in due course, even more importantly, they allowed me to ascertain the actual distribution of knowledge among Baktaman: to map the existing range of understandings, expressions, and experiences.

As far as the comparative operation that is involved, I see no methodological difference between these comparisons of different Baktaman performances and accounts, and the comparisons of a Baktaman performance or account with one from another community, or between two other communities. My uses of them in this particular study were distinct in that I was aiming to construct a maximally sensitive and detailed account of Baktaman initiations, and not of the initiations performed in those other places (Barth 1975). But the methodology of the comparison itself remains the same: I compared each account so as to be clear how they differed from each other, and I looked for systematic co-variation between the forms and interpretations of ritual elements, and features of context: where was the initiation reported to have taken place? at what time, that is, how long ago? what was the social positioning of the informant, at present and at the time of the event? what did I know about the person that might indicate his degree of reliability and willingness to give a true account? and what was his level of knowledge, understanding, and perceptiveness?

Today I would argue even more strongly that these comparisons "within" can no longer be represented as methodologically different from comparisons "between", that is, over longer distances (how long?) and between different institutional contexts (how different?). Working in terms of a modern conception of culture there cannot be one "comparative method" for the longer and more contrastive comparisons (often called comparisons "between cultures/societies"), and another method (what we would perhaps call "close analysis") for the comparisons that we make between different cases and voices within named groups – indeed regardless of whether the named group to which we assign them and to which they might assign themselves is small (183 Baktaman) or large (500,000 Swat Pathans). Recognizing the continuity of variation in culture (Ingold 1993), and the arbitrariness in how we distinguish societies (Barth 1992), the very ideas of "within" and "between" seem to lose their force and usefulness.

This realization later provided the basis for my broader comparisons of initiations from various parts of the Ok region of New Guinea, first presented as a Frazer Lecture in Cambridge in 1983, and subsequently developed in *Cosmologies in the Making* (Barth 1987). I would not be prepared to say whether that study is about comparisons within or between societies, and I do not see that the question is important: the methodology is simply one that makes use of a field of variation for a comparative investigation.

Nor is this comparative method linked to any particular theoretical position, such as the focus on rational decisionmaking and strategies that we see exemplified in many of the papers in this symposium, though it does adopt a perspective that focuses on actors and parameters affecting action. As I see it, the comparative operations in *Cosmologies in the Making* allowed me to establish a set of dimensions of variation by which to describe (i) variations in the connotations of overtly similar symbols in different contexts and places (*ibid.*: 31–37); (ii) variations in the specificity and abstractness of metaphorical readings employed by participants (*ibid.*: 38–45); and (iii) variations in the elaboration of a vision of time and history (*ibid.*: 46–54). A theoretical construction of the process or mechanism of change (*ibid.*: 24–30) could then be tested against these ranges of described variations, but that construction is not derived from the described variations in form: it is introduced as an explanation of why this range, and not another range of forms, has been generated. Thus the comparative operation is both more comprehensive, and more restricted, than we have often thought: while it establishes an existing range of variations in forms, it does not necessarily help you to model the processes that generate these forms. But it does provide the materials to allow you to test and falsify whatever models you construct of such processes.

Comparative operations on the Balinese materials

I had still failed to draw the full lesson from these analyses when I set up my field research project in Bali in 1983. I envisaged something much more like a conventional comparative analysis, as follows: I had found Geertz's 1973 [1966] "Person, time and conduct in Bali" compelling in its depiction of the coherence of status and naming systems, calendars, and rules of demeanor among Bali-Hindus. I had also discovered the presence of some communities of apparently traditional Balinese Muslims in North Bali. These Muslims seemed to offer the opportunity for a very tidy and interesting, conventional comparative analysis: What might eventuate when Balinese become Muslims – that is, change their naming system from the Bali-Hindu forms that Geertz described to (presumably) the Ahmeds and Mohammeds of Muslims; change their Balinese calendars to a Muslim lunar calendar and the structure of time and history that is embedded in Islam – what might then be the effects in the fields of etiquette, the construction of the person, the modes of conduct and demeanor?

As I proceeded with the actual fieldwork, ranging outside as well as within the Bali-Muslim community that Unni Wikan and I had initially chosen as our field locality, I quickly discovered diversity: a multiplicity of differences through North Bali that I attempted in due course to constitute as a broad field of variation. In this case, I could not conveniently focus on particular materials from commensurate initiation rituals in a range of communities, as I had done in the Ok study. The interesting contrasts across North Bali seemed desperately diverse: urban and rural; all degrees of modern and traditional; Hindu and Muslim and Bali Aga; expert and lay; villages with constitutions and custom law specific to each village community; a number of profoundly different conceptual frameworks of knowledge and belief that even a single individual could juggle and shift between (Barth 1989). It took some considerable fortitude to welcome and embrace this riotous field of variation, rather than try to fight it. The outcome after long gestation was the monograph *Balinese Worlds* (Barth 1993). In it, I gave much attention to variations in the social organization of village communities. I also noted the differences between the various kinds of scholars, gurus, experts and wizards that accumulate and deploy knowledge, and the social organizations in which they are lodged. Finally, I tried to describe and compare the positioning of different "ordinary" people in this complex field of cultural diversity.

As in the case of the New Guinea materials, the description of diversity and the identification of dimensions of variation did not of itself produce explanatory hypotheses regarding the processes that might lie behind, and generate, these variations. I believe that it is very important that we recognize that such insights do not emerge as the distillation of the particular form and range of differences, any more than a theory of evolution springs from a description of the different shapes of fossils. It was Darwin's genius that he did not move from a hypothesis of change to a comparative study of the trajectories of change; instead he tried to construct a theory of what were the *mechanisms* of change. Even the closest attention to a field of variation will not allow you to deduce an explanation of what has produced that variation, but as I say in *Balinese Worlds* the observed variation can be used as a provocation to search for one, and a clearly described range of variability is well suited for falsifying theories of what has produced that set of forms.

Thus, ordering a diversity of forms as a field of variation does not in itself induce any theory of process, of possible mechanisms that generate this range of form – though it does cry out for such theories. If not to comparative insights, where might an analyst turn for ideas?

Initially, I would suggest, one needs to reflect on the ontology of the phenomena under inspection: what are the inherent properties of the particular kinds of things that we are concerned with? The diversity that confronted me in North Bali, substantively riotous as the above listing suggests, all seemed to involve differences in the *knowledge* people deployed when interpreting and acting on the world. Thus, the comparison led me to articulate on overarching category – knowledge systems – of which the observed variants could be seen as different cases. Now knowledge, as a modality of culture, is shaped by processes of reproduction and flux: it is taught, learned, borrowed, created and discarded. Presumably, the processes that generate variation across North Bali must therefore be found among those very processes whereby the knowledge of the population is produced and changed, that is, is transmitted, reproduced and modified.

The next step was to go out and observe the events of reproduction and flux in their local diversity: describe them in the necessary detail so I could compare and contrast them, and establish appropriate dimensions of variability to characterize the differences among them. Since the problems should be in principle homologous in any and every tradition of knowledge, I turned to the accounts of sociologists of science for ideas of how such other forms of knowledge are produced and changed. Latour and Woolgar's (1979) *Laboratory Life* argues forcefully that the particular institutional structures, conventions, and contexts of knowledge production provide even the modern hard sciences with the pragmatic criteria which practitioners use to judge the validity of statements and claims in their field, and thereby determine the changing edifice of knowledge. This focus on the criteria of validity whereby different forms of knowledge were judged, on different topics within different circles of Balinese, provided me with the overarching perspective in terms of which different forms of knowledge and knowledge production could be compared and characterized.

A whole range of comparative operations was thereby set in motion. I needed to identify the parameters of power and communication in transactions in knowledge by comparing the ways that contention and discrepant statements were handled and (to variable degree) resolved within each circle and tradition. Beginning with a more standard Weberian search for the sources of authority underpinning the status positions that are found in the different institutionalized traditions (including priests, Brahmins, trance media, wizards, Imams, scholars, schoolteachers, village leaders, ritual experts, mothers, etc., etc.), I then asked what might be the specific and restrictive criteria of validity that were applied within each circle of specialists and participants that produced and used each of these different, particular bodies of knowledge. Descriptions of the arenas, conventions and procedures whereby validity was established in different circles of participants in turn provided models to understand the reproduction, flux, and range of forms of knowledge that were generated in each particular tradition.

Another field of variation, requiring another mode of approach, was that of village organization. The comparison of a number of villages brought out a great diversity in the formal village constitutions whereby village polities are structured. A whole flora of different associations, multiple congregations, descent groups, hamlets, age- or seniority-based assemblies and so on coexist and criss-cross; differently in different communities (Barth 1993: 29–91). Moreover, the native words or concepts for these different groups vary considerably between different communities in the kinds of group or status they are used to designate (*ibid.*: 100).

In this case, I could not construct any limited set of dimensions by which to describe the variation – the diversity of forms was too great, the combinations too multiple. Some patterns are statistically far more common than others, that is, there are a few village types that are relatively predominant. There is also historical evidence that some of these patterns have great antiquity, others are more recent (*ibid.*: 79–80). But to elevate one or another of these forms to represent the norm, the "typical" contemporary North Balinese village, would bring no new insight and might preclude any further analysis of the puzzle. Surely, the fact of persisting diversity is somehow indicative of processes shaping village life and structure.

Comparative method is versatile, and a further step of analysis can be made by reversing its questions, *viz.*: can the disparate forms we are inspecting somehow be seen as *similar*, on some metalevel of description? Posing the comparative task in this form led me to discover an underlying parallelism in how these formal organizations are deployed in the everyday politics of Balinese villages: as a means of subtle but pervasive divisive factionalism within the villages community (*ibid.*: 109–25, 146–56). Comparison aiming at discovering similarities rather than differences thus led to the discovery of a covert commonality of practice underlying a field of riotous formal diversity. This opened the way for a different line of thought, one linking factional and other social patterns to some deep existential concerns that everyday life seems to bring to many Balinese (*ibid.*: 155–6, 286–304, 324–52). Thereby, I was finally able to move one step further in my understanding of how the diversity of village organization in North Bali is generated and maintained (*ibid.*: 352–4). As in the New Guinea study, the comparative operations become very pervasive, but are yet only one of a set of strategies needed to perform the analysis.

The place of comparison in anthropological method

Thus, I am arguing that the template which social and cultural anthropologists use to conceptualize comparative method is too often modeled on an inappropriate schema copied from other disciplines, which illuminates neither the critical difficulties of making ethnographic comparisons nor the true potentials and uses of comparison in anthropology. This criticism can be directed even at the most explicit and exemplary comparative studies in the literature, such as Nadel's (1952) "Witchcraft in four African societies" or Eggan's (1950) *The Social Organization of the Western Pueblo* (cf. also his (1954) discussion of controlled comparison). My view is that we should not think of comparative method as a procedure whereby we compare separately constituted descriptions of two or more cases: we should engage comparison as actively as possible in the analysis of each separate case. Thereby we escape the twin liabilities of reifying our descriptions of social and cultural forms and of comparing those descriptions only, rather than primary materials. We achieve a more versatile, and penetrating, method of comparison by giving careful attention to – indeed seeking out – diversity and variation in our primary materials, whether obtained through fieldwork or by other means. Such comparison across diversity allows us to establish dimensions of variation, thereby establishing the dimensions of our very description of the phenomena we study. The resulting analyses can be utilized in further analytical work from a wide range of theoretical perspectives, but may be particularly useful for building models of process.

5 The role of comparison in the light of the theory of culture

Greg Urban

> It is my opinion that the main object of ethnological collections should be the dissemination of the fact that civilization is not something absolute, but that it is relative, and that our ideas and conceptions are true only so far as our civilization goes.
>
> (Boas 1887b: 589)

The heart of culture

My point of departure in this chapter is the following proposition: comparison is at the heart of culture; culture would not be possible without it. For some readers, this will make instantaneous sense. Others, however, will scratch their heads. Isn't "our culture" what we take for granted? Doesn't it just seem natural – part of the normal order of the universe? Consequently, isn't comparison an unnatural act, one that forces upon us an awareness of the conventional character of what we think of as given? Surely, it has been a key task of anthropology, as part of a larger public debate, to point out to us the constructed character of our world, to unmask as conventional those things we want most to presuppose as natural.

For purposes of this chapter, I take the term "culture" in its broadest sense as that which is socially learned – through imitation, teaching, and inference from observation of others. The question is: how is social learning possible? I will argue that it is possible only thanks to comparison, and, consequently, that comparison is at the heart of culture.

There have been innumerable cases made for using the comparative method to gain certain kinds of information about culture or social structure or human beings or human brains, but, to my knowledge, none has attempted to ground comparison in the very mechanism of culture itself. As a result, none has been able to reason from the absolute necessity of comparison as the foundation of culture to its deployment as a research tool in the study of culture. That lacuna is one that I hope to begin to fill by means of this essay. But it is a rather big lacuna, and one little essay cannot hope to fill even a significant fraction of it. And it is situated in such a way that it abuts on some treacherous problem pits, namely, those concerning relativity and the nature of knowledge.

Let me begin with what anthropologists sometimes call the problem of interpretability. This problem highlights the need for a concept of culture and/or language as something prior to any given empirical experience of the world, but that is essential to that experience. The prototype is the isolated utterance encountered by so many anthropologists upon setting foot in an exotic and little-studied village in some far-flung corner of the earth. The problem is that the anthropologist cannot, at first, understand the utterance. At the same time, manifestly, the "natives" around him or her can. Therefore, or so the reasoning goes, there must be something prior to the empirical experience with that utterance (and it might as easily have been a non-linguistic symbol, such arguments go) – and that prior something must be socially learned, socially transmitted. Hence, that something is culture or language or both.

But in what does that something consist? There is plenty of debate today over the extent to which syntactic structures are hard-wired in the brain. Geertz (1984: 272–75) notes, indeed, that the universal "human mind" is regularly invoked in arguments against relativity. However, even ultra-Cartesian rationalists would hardly dispute that interpretation of a given utterance depends in some measure, at least, upon exposure to other related utterances. One must have had perceptual access to utterances in a given language in order to interpret a present utterance in that language, and, indeed, in order to be able to be said to "know that language." Indeed, if you imagine that an individual in a given social milieu is exposed to just 1,000 clause-length utterances per day (the equivalent of reading perhaps twenty-five book pages or of listening to about forty-two minutes of continuous narration in the oral narratives I have studied[1]), then s/he is exposed to 365,000 such utterances per year. In the one sample study I have conducted thus far,[2] the actual number was 7,230 clauses per day, yielding 2,638,950 clauses per year, a formidable figure for empirical investigation. Such utterances form the objective pool from which an individual constructs and fine-tunes patterns that make interpretation possible.

The interpretive backdrop is made possible in part by comparisons among those objective utterances. To be sure, this is not the kind of self-conscious comparison in which the social scientist is engaged. Social scientists are explicitly remarking similarities and differences, and encoding observations about them in discourse of their own. I will return to this issue later. But they are comparisons none the less. Culture would not be possible without such implicit comparisons. Comparison is at the heart of what it means to learn to interpret socially.

To return to our anthropologist in the village, the rule of thumb has been (since Malinowski's time) that, to do a good ethnography, to really learn to interpret something the way the "natives" interpret it, the anthropologist must spend a year or maybe two or three years living in a community, being exposed to objectively occurring utterances, conduct, material culture, and so forth. Focusing just on utterances, the ethnographer is probably exposed to literally hundreds of thousands of clause-length utterances, and maybe millions. While the initial utterance the anthropologist encounters upon setting foot in a village may be uninterpretable to him or her, after that prolonged exposure the ability to interpret develops. Will the interpretation ever equal that of a "native"? According to the view I am putting forth here, no, probably not. Only if two individuals have had equal exposure can the interpretation in theory be identical. But a corollary is that probably no two "natives" can have absolutely identical interpretations either, since their exposures to objective utterances differ in some measure. Shared cultural interpretability is therefore a matter of degree.

Museums and field research

Anthropologists are surely sick of hearing about the brief debate between Franz Boas (1887a,b,c) and Otis Mason (1886, 1887), into which John Wesley Powell (1887) also entered. The debate has already been discussed by Buettner-Janusch (1957) and Stocking (1968: 155–57; 1974: 1–4; 1994). Yet it continues to be of interest in the light of the current fascination in many different disciplines with cross-cultural comparisons, and it is relevant to the position I am attempting to articulate here. The debate focused on how to organize museum exhibits. Mason argued in effect that, when you classify, you must begin with an idea you have of what you want to compare. You begin with what he called "classific concepts" (Mason 1887: 534). For example, you might compare weapons from different cultures, and so you select the "weapons" from various cultures and place them side by side for purposes of comparison. This is a seemingly straightforward process.

Boas, however, objected. When you are dealing with cultural artifacts, you cannot presuppose that you know what the artifact is, any more than you presume to understand an utterance from a language and culture with which you have had no prior familiarity. What you may be doing in juxtaposing objects via this extractive process is confirming a conceptual scheme that derives from your own culture and seems intuitively obvious to you, but that nevertheless fails to grasp the significance of the object within the culture from which it came. Boas argued that, instead, ethnographic materials should be grouped by tribe or tribal region, so that the objects are presented, insofar as is possible, within their cultural context.

Boas's view makes sense in light of the problem of interpretability as I have formulated it. The isolated "exotic" utterance merely makes obvious the folly of classifying cultural elements based on some preconceived classificatory scheme. (Or does it? This is the issue I will want to be raising). But the problem with Boas' scheme is how to get out of the local area and articulate with other areas. This posed no practical obstacle for Boas himself, since he regarded his position as a methodological one. You begin with the culture-internal comparison as a way of assuring yourself that you have adequately grasped the significance of the cultural element before you yank it out of its context and compare it globally. But this does not solve the theoretical problem. How can we move from the necessity of culture-internal comparison as the basis of interpretability to inter-cultural comparisons? And, from the point of view of culture, what would the significance of those comparisons be?

The problem has become particularly acute in the 1980s and 1990s with the spread of post-structuralism and deconstruction. The objectivity/subjectivity issue was at the heart of Weber's interpretivism, but it mushroomed in significance with Foucault's (1973 [1966]) argument that, if the objective of the human sciences is to grasp how humans interpret the world, then the billiard ball model of reality derived from study of the objective world is inadequate, since interpretation is fundamentally unlike objective phenomena. And if, as Derrida (1986) proposed, there is no anchor for a system of signification, then every such system is equally valid or equally flawed. From what standpoint could a researcher move outward from a local meaning system to compare one with the next and extract general principles? I think there is an answer to this question; it is not simply a rhetorical one. The road of anthropological knowledge does not only lead deeper and deeper into the thicket of local meaning systems.

Let me return to the folly of classifying "exotic" utterances on the basis of a preconceived scheme. I want to give you the background of my own experiences that led me to use the comparative method in connection with certain utterances that I will here classify as "lamentations." I had been living for several months at an indigenous post in the south of Brazil, studying the local language and culture. Upon returning from a field break in Rio, driving into the reserve in my Jeep, I stopped to greet several elderly indigenous women walking along the road. I knew them reasonably well by this point. To my bewilderment, they began to "cry" – and I put cry in quotes here to indicate that that was my interpretation at the time. What was going on? Why were they "crying"?

It is entirely possible that I had actually observed the phenomenon earlier, without knowing it. But now it stood out for me like an uninterpretable utterance. The women were "crying," or so I thought, but it did not make sense that they should be crying in this context. And it was only later that, puzzling over the experience, I recalled the accounts of early travelers (for example, Jean de Léry 1972 [1578]), exploring the coast of Brazil in the sixteenth century. They remarked a phenomenon which they called "tearful greeting" or "welcome of tears."

In studying the phenomenon more closely, I first of all discovered that it had a name in the indigenous language (*zõ*, pronounced phonetically [ðõ], that is, like the "th" in "the" followed by the "au" of "caught," but pronounced with a nasal twang), and that it was a recognizable and perfectly understandable phenomenon to members of the community. I was later able to tape-record instances of the phenomenon, and to study those instances in greater detail. It turned out that *zõ* was more than sobbing or crying, for which the native term *plãl* was used. *zõ* consisted in grammatical utterances articulated with characteristic intonation contours and voice qualities, interspersed with what I came to call "cry breaks." What the connection was between these indices of crying and the phenomenon I was used to calling "crying" (based on my experience growing up in the midwest of the United States) became more problematic the further I delved into the matter. Indeed, it turned out that *zõ* could be employed as a form of greeting, especially when someone returned after a prolonged absence, as when I reappeared in my Jeep after a field break.

The debate between Mason and Boas focused on museums. Mason proposed to organize displays in the National Museum in such a way that "similar" objects from different cultures would be placed next to one another. To follow this procedure, I would have to place examples of *zõ* alongside those of "crying" in the United States, and I would have to label the exhibit something like "Forms of crying in cultures of the world." I would say: "this [playing a tape-recorded instance of *zõ*] is how people cry at P. I. Ibirama in the south of Brazil." Perhaps you can already appreciate what is wrong with this. For me, the problem was that, the more I studied the phenomenon within its cultural context, the less it seemed to resemble what I thought of as crying. My instincts, like Boas', were to plunge deeper into the culture, in order to comprehend the expressive form called *zõ*. I did not wish to snatch the form immediately from its context and align it with others from other contexts. In effect, I wanted to organize the museum – at least at this stage – by grouping objects according to the people or ethnic group from which they came.

What are "cultural objects"?

Cultural objects seem, on the surface of them, to be no different from other objects. They appear to be, first of all, things in the world. As you stroll through the museum, you see such things: a terra-cotta pot with geometrical designs, a swatch of brightly colored cloth, a roughly carved wooden statue. You can also hear such things: a particular instance of $z\tilde{o}$, for example, fleeting though it may be. The sound is preserved – partially at least – by the conversion of sound waves into electrical waves and thence into magnetic waves, which trace physical patterns onto magnetizable tape, from which they can be reconverted into sound by a reverse process, producing a replica of the original sound. Despite this complexity, the sounds are still things in the world, things that you or I or anyone else can behold and comment upon. But are these things, or even the terra-cotta pots, for that matter, cultural objects?

The answer I give is: no, they are not, but they are related to cultural objects. The cultural object differs, first, in being an abstract form of which the thing-in-the-world is one instance, and, secondly, in having associated with it webs of significance. An object can be passed from person to person, but this passage does not constitute cultural transmission. What must be transmitted is the interpretation of the object, including such knowledge as that related to its manufacture and/or use. What kind of object is this physical thing-in-the-world? Where does it fit into a broader interpretation of the world? What kinds of functions does it serve? How is it produced? The transmission of culture does not involve (necessarily) the transmission of conscious answers to these questions. But it does involve transmission of practical or implicit answers. The "natives" are familiar with the thing. They know what kind of object it is, where it fits, what it does, and perhaps how to produce it. They may not be able to articulate this knowledge consciously. But they can manifest it.

Let's look more closely at these things-in-the-world I am calling instances of ritual lamentation. The physical objects contain elements resembling what I learned to call "crying." They contain, occasionally, the "cry break" – the break in the voice that is the essence of what I always called crying. It is a sound whose production can be characterized in terms of articulatory phonetics. Actually, there are several variants of the sound – one involving glottal stops both initially and finally, one involving only an initial glottal stop, and one involving only a final glottal stop. Because I have described these elsewhere (Urban 1988, 1991), I will not go into greater detail here. A naïve coder (cf. Burton and White 1987) would not necessarily correctly pick out cry breaks, but could probably do so with some minimal training. The cry break is an element of physical similarity between what I know as "crying" and the ritual lamentation tradition known as *zõ*. However, picking out stretches of sound containing cry breaks would not allow you to identify correctly instances of *zõ*. Not every instance of *zõ* contains a cry break, and there are cry breaks in natively produced sounds other than those characterized as *zõ*.

If you listen to a sufficient number of instances of *zõ*, you begin to pick out other features. You may notice the regular occurrence of creaky voice – the production of oral sounds with the vocal cords vibrating at a low frequency. You will also notice the articulation of words into lines marked by breath pauses, and you will notice that those lines have a characteristic, if not rigid, sing-song intonation contour, with the pitch gradually dropping. And you may notice that some of the breaths involve a voiced inhalation, where the speaker makes the vocal cords vibrate while inhaling, thereby producing a sound. If you start putting these various factors together, you can begin to recognize, and even to produce, instances of *zõ*.

I want to emphasize what is involved here in the way of cultural learning. It's not sufficient to listen to just one instance of *zõ*. Of course, if you tape-record it, you can convert that one instance into hundreds or thousands of replicas, and listening to those greatly enhances your ability to learn the cultural object. But you will also need exposure to other instances to appreciate the range of variability. Then you will need to observe the occasions on which *zõ* is appropriately produced, and, of course, you will need to know the language to produce utterances correctly, and you will need to know yet another thing – the significance of uttering *zõ*.

You do not get that significance from someone explicitly telling you the meaning. Indeed, if my own interpretation is correct, the significance of *zõ* resides in part in the fact that it is not consciously interpreted through explicit discourse. The point of *zõ* is rather to be a manifestation of an inner state. That inner state is sadness, but it is not just any sadness. It is sadness that is socially appropriate. The significance of *zõ* is not the manifestation of sadness per se, but the manifestation of social appropriateness. *zõ* is thus sharply opposed to the idea of "crying" I learned in the midwest of the United States. There I came to think of crying as something personal, that, preferably, was not to be displayed in public. Indeed, while growing up, other boys would make fun of one, were one to cry in public. Even on occasions where great sadness was felt, my learning emphasized "holding it in." To act appropriately was not to cry, but to make some appropriate, non-tearful, non-whiny statement. You can see now why it is inappropriate, in our museum of sound, to say that "this [playing a tape-recorded instance of *zõ*] is how people cry at P. I. Ibirama in the south of Brazil." So we need to organize the museum, at least initially, along cultural lines. To grasp the significance of *zõ*, we need to understand its place as a cultural object among other such objects at P. I. Ibirama.

At the same time, understanding, especially in the case of *zõ*, can and must come from experience with things-in-the-world, actual perceptible instances. This is true for both native and anthropologist. What makes understanding possible in this case is exposure to actual instances of *zõ*. Because the meaning of *zõ* should not be consciously formulated in discourse, no one can tell you directly what it means, what its significance is. You have to figure it out from your experience with the world. The general conclusion, therefore, is this: interpretation is a function of perceptual access to things-in-the-world from which it is drawn. To give someone a terra-cotta pot is *not* to transmit a "cultural object" to them. The pot, as a thing-in-the-world, may be a manifestation or concretization of a cultural object, but it is not identical with the cultural object. At the same time, to give someone a terra-cotta pot may be to begin to transmit the cultural object behind the pot to them. With sufficient kinds of exposure to instances of cultural objects, the cultural objects themselves are socially transmitted. But the transmission takes time. A naïve observer would not be in a position to appreciate the interpretations that make up the "cultural object" without exposure to the myriad of other things-in-the-world that help to circumscribe and define that object.

Comparison, evaluation, and essentialization

For the people of P. I. Ibirama, comparison outside the boundaries of the local community has been for some time necessary and inevitable. Since 1914 the community has been in constant touch with the outside world, which brings in new experiences, experiences that must be interpreted, allowing them to be assimilated into the native scheme, and, of course, also causing that scheme itself to change. New experiences can result in the transmission of new cultural objects across boundaries. The ethnic grouping, in this case, is not self-contained. Nor was it self-contained even in the preceding 150 years, when, although there were no peaceful contacts, there were hostile encounters with Whitemen. Moreover, there were encounters with other Amerindian groups, and encounters with other bands having what anthropologists considered the same "culture." Such encounters inevitably led to comparison. In interacting with the Whiteman, you might wonder: what is the meaning of shaking hands? how do these people communicate that they are happy to see you?

Some members of the community are, and always have been, anthropologists in this regard. Their experience with things-in-the-world emanating from outside the community boundaries leads them to classify the things as the same as, similar to, or different from those with which they are familiar. This classificatory tendency includes things that might be similar to *zõ*. So the activity, in which the anthropologist engages, of extending a comparison outward from the local community is not a foreign one.

Indeed, such comparisons go back to the earliest experiences of members of this community with classical music, prior to their first peaceful contacts with Whitemen. In the years before 1914, when the Brazilian government was attempting to "pacify" the community, the agent in charge of the government expedition, Eduardo de Lima e Silva Hoerhan, whom I got to know quite well in 1975, hit upon the idea, he told me, of demonstrating his peaceful intentions and noble character to the Indians by playing for them classical music. He had gramophones set up in the jungle that piped out Strauss waltzes. I thought to ask some of the elders in the community, who had been children at the time, if they remembered this, and what their own parents had thought. They responded that they did indeed recall this, and that the elders at the time had cautioned that the hideous screeching was a means by which the Whitemen were transmitting diseases to the people. The youngsters were advised to stopper up their ears with beeswax when within earshot of these sounds. In a sense, of course, they were right. Playing the music was a way of trying to transmit the culture, which in turn would lead to peaceful relations, which in turn would lead to illness and death. While they resisted these particular cultural objects, the contact and illness and death did follow.

The P. I. Ibirama evidence suggests that evaluation is latent in the process of comparison itself, and it is the case that nineteenth-century comparisons, at least, were grounded in an explicit process of evaluation. Social thinkers such as Lewis Henry Morgan (1871), Herbert Spencer (1876–96), and even Emile Durkheim (e.g., 1965 [1915]) used comparison to establish unilinear evolution schemes. Specific cultural objects were examined, for example, kinship terminological usages, in

Morgan's case, and compared with one another for the purpose of showing that some were more advanced than others.

In this sense, the debate between Boas and Mason was not as innocent as it may today seem. The kinds of global comparisons that Mason proposed were typically bound up with evaluations of better and worse, more civilized and more savage, more advanced and more backward. The juxtaposition of "similar" objects from different cultures with one another led to their sequencing, in exhibits in the British Museum, in a unilinear array of this sort. The act of comparison, with its attendant evaluatory moment, seems to bolster political differences in the present, with the most "advanced" cultures occupying the position of greatest power. Comparison was thus in this way, through evaluation, linked to an ideology of superiority and inferiority.

It strikes me as patently false to assume that all comparisons will necessarily lead to that kind of evaluation. After all, the central argument I have been developing since the beginning of this paper is that culture itself would not be possible without comparison. One could not form or transmit cultural objects in the sense I am using that term here. The very possibility of categorization depends upon comparison, and cultural objects are like categories – they are abstract forms of things-in-the-world rather than things-in-the-world themselves. But the comparisons used in establishing those categories are not necessarily themselves explicitly formulated and publicly circulated. It is the explicit kind of comparison that rouses suspicions.

Unless one has been immersed in another culture, and is attempting to take another point of view, the categories used in comparison necessarily grow out of one's own culture. They are (or can become) cultural objects, and, because of this, like all cultural objects, they derive their meaning in part from their interrelationships with other cultural objects in one's possession. Hence, they are part of a cultural scheme – and the comparativist's project, in this sense, is continuous with that of any individual, assimilating new experiences into an existing cultural scheme. As such, they can (however unwittingly) play into existing evaluatory schemes. They can therefore bolster ideologies of inequality.

It is for this reason that the careful culture-internal study of a phenomenon (or set of phenomena) seems such an important prophylactic. How do the practices labeled by the comparativist get interpreted by the people who are said to practice them? To what cultural objects of their own are they related? How are those objects related to one another and to others?

The mercuriality of cultural objects

The brute fact of experiencing other cultural phenomena impels experiencers to compare them to their own cultural objects, just as all internal experiences are subjected to comparisons, such as lead to the establishment of cultural objects in the first place. It would be ridiculous to imagine that anyone could stay entirely inside a given set of experiences, paying attention only to them and ignoring all others. Humans are compelled by an encounter with phenomena to fit them into existing schemes and/or to elaborate or change those schemes.

My own desire for further comparison of the ritual lamentation material was compelled by such experiences. One day I was discussing the cultural object known at P. I. Ibirama as *zõ* with a colleague of mine (Dr. Silver Caiuby Novaes) in São Paulo. She played for me tape recordings of a seemingly similar phenomenon she had noted among the Bororo Indians, about a thousand miles away in western central Brazil. I was struck simultaneously by the similarities and the differences. The similarities were in the form of the things-in-themselves, and also in the contexts of their deployment. Each of the phenomena showed a characterizable line, that is, a stretch of utterance that resembled in intonation contour and otherwise the other utterances making up the instance. However, the line lengths tended to vary, the Bororo lines being longer. Moreover, the intonation contours were different. The Bororo tended to have a much flatter intonation contour than did the people at Ibirama. But both showed the characteristic cry break; both exhibited creaky voice; and both involved at least partially grammatical utterances.

I was subsequently able to obtain tape recordings of Xavante ritual lamentation from Dr. Laura Graham. The Xavante were neighbors of the Bororo, but more closely related linguistically to the P. I. Ibirama community. I studied these materials, and compared them with one another. The Xavante form proved to be more divergent. For one thing, the examples at my disposal showed the lamentation to contain no interpretable sentences. Indeed, most of the lamentation was in vowels, with no actual words (see Laura Graham 1984, 1986). And I found no evidence of the "cry break" in these examples that would so readily link the form to Western "crying." The sounds were produced with creaky voice, but the creak was light, and might well be missed by an untrained, naïve coder. Indeed, the whole phenomenon would probably not be classified together with the P. I. Ibirama *zõ* by anyone unfamiliar with the material, who was listening only to a single instance. Someone from the midwest of the United States might readily mistake it for singing, so melodic is the form.

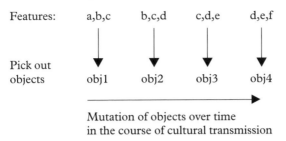

Features: a,b,c   b,c,d   c,d,e   d,e,f

Pick out
objects   obj1   obj2   obj3   obj4

Mutation of objects over time
in the course of cultural transmission

Figure 5.1. The relationship of classificatory features to cultural objects.

Initially, features a, b, and c pick out a cultural object. But as that object mutates over time, the original features serve less and less well to pick it out. By the time it has become Obj4, it is unrecognizable. Thus, pre-determined "classific" features fail to allow us to grasp the trajectory of cultural objects.

Careful study shows, however, that these Xavante examples are similar to the others in their use and significance. Like those at P. I. Ibirama, they could be used in greetings, and, like those at P. I. Ibirama, they seemed to communicate a feeling of sadness, but found a deeper significance in the realm of social appropriateness. By uttering such laments, one conveyed a desire to act properly, to express appropriate grief. And that desire could only be manifested; it could not be talked about.

So we have a problem here. In the large-scale comparative method, one begins with solid "classific concepts." One asks: do these people have a tradition of ritual lamentation? Because the concept is pre-determined, you can only answer "yes" or "no." The concept, if explicitly specified, allows a naïve coder to pick out the phenomenon in any given case. The problem with this, however, is that the cultural object is not as solid as the comparativist's "classific concept." As it is socially transmitted, as it moves through space and time, the cultural object changes its form, takes on a new guise. The object mutates, exhibiting a mercuriality that defies naïve classification, that enables it to slip imperceptibly across the solid boundaries established by the comparativist's concepts. If our goal is to study the movement of culture across space and time, as it passes from one individual or group to another, then we lose the trail of culture if we employ large-scale comparative techniques. I have tried to depict the problem graphically in Figure 5.1.

One of the things we must be able to do, therefore, if we are to study culture and cultural objects, is to modify our classificatory scheme with each new comparison. This is consonant, for example, with the "spiral" comparative method proposed by Lévi-Strauss (1969), in which he began with a myth from the Bororo people of central Brazil, then worked his way outward and around, augmenting and modifying his original structures as he encountered other apparently similar myths. While his stated goal was to discover "brain structures," the method was consonant with that needed to trace the movement and mutation of cultural objects.

The thicket of local meanings

There is a kind of paradox in what I have been suggesting. On the one hand, cultural objects depend for their existence upon comparison. In order to learn socially a cultural object, one must compare instances, and those comparisons lead to a fixing of the cultural object as a kind or type of thing among other kinds or types. They allow one to recognize, for example, an instance of $z\tilde{o}$. Comparison, in this way, leads to the freezing or rigidification of cultural objects, which is a prerequisite to their accurate replication and, hence, transmission. On the other hand, cultural objects, as involving a component of interpretation, are constantly shifting their form. Exposure to new experiences (the empirical starting point for comparison) leads one to change one's image of the cultural object. In this way, as they travel through time and across space, cultural objects transmogrify, modifying their form to such an extent that they become, finally, unrecognizable from the point of view of the original interpretive scheme. They defy preset classificatory concepts. The P. I. Ibirama form becomes the Xavante form of ritual lament. Yet this movement – which results in incessant, restless change – would not be possible without comparison. So comparison produces two seemingly opposed results: the manufacture of fixed classification schemes, and the movement of cultural objects that results in the change that defies those schemes.

The reason for this contradiction appears to be the nature of experiences themselves. If experiences were fixed and limited, there would be little need for comparison. It would be used only to establish the limits and to confirm the fixity. Comparison (ironically?) is less important the more stable the set of experiences. Correspondingly, however, where there is new experience, comparison becomes the crucial method by which the new experience is brought into the interpretive scheme. Bringing that new experience into the scheme, correspondingly, results in changes in the scheme itself. So the motor of the contradiction surrounding comparison is not comparison per se, but rather the experiences being compared.

Nevertheless, empirical research suggests that the human world is, indeed, one in which experience is in flux. We do not find the cultural objects we call "ritual lament" manifesting themselves the same way everywhere, as if we were dealing with a fixed and limited world of cultural forms. Rather, there are variations, and the variations are such that some objects elude our classification scheme as it was originally set up, despite the fact that further investigation shows those objects to be related to the original ones (from which the essentialization developed in the first place) by processes of cultural transmission. And if we probed the matter further, we might trace the evolution of cultural objects into new ones whose form is completely unrecognizable. We might, for instance, find something that has evolved out of ritual lament that we would no longer be willing to call "ritual lament" at all. The tendency to change might defy the very categories of comparison themselves.

Should we conclude from this that comparison is useless in the realm of culture? Geertz (1973: 33–54), in his important essay "The Impact of the Concept of Culture on the Concept of Man," seemed to argue as much, or, at least, that the goal of establishing universals through comparison is futile, even if comparison itself is not. Generalizations, in his words, "are not to be discovered through a Baconian search for cultural universals" (1973: 40). His arguments have led a generation of anthropologists ever further into the thicket of local meaning systems.

But I am not sure that movement ever further (with no looking back) into local cultures is really a necessary, or, at least, the only, consequence of the position Geertz espouses. Certainly, it does not follow from my own line of argument. If cultural objects are mutable, capable of defying the category schemes that enable their transmission in the first place, this does not mean that one stops trying to make sense of cultural objects. The result in the real world, were people to give up on comparison, would be the breakdown of cultural transmission altogether. Confronted with new experiences, one has no choice but to compare those experiences with others he or she has had in the past, even if, as you can now appreciate, the generalizations from such comparisons must be regarded as tentative, never final.

Comparison does not become less important the more you acknowledge diversity and change. It becomes more important. How could you hope to confront that diversity except by comparing your experiences of it? But perhaps the goals of comparison must change. Perhaps we ought not to be asking whether this cultural object is found together with that one, as in the correlationist approach. Or perhaps we ought to be asking not only that kind of question. After all, the cultural objects can always slip through the classificatory net by the process of mutation.

What kind of goals, then, might comparison have instead? It seems to me that one proper goal of comparison ought to be the study of transmission itself. If culture is that which is socially transmitted, then perhaps we ought to be examining the processes of social transmission. How are cultural objects transmitted? What happens to them in the course of their transmission? What are the pathways of movement of cultural objects through space and time? Such questions cannot be answered without the aid of comparison. And the answers will probably not take the form of simple correlations. But they may lead us closer to a theory of culture.

A note on my earlier research

Several conclusions from my earlier research (1988, 1991: 148–71) seem to run against the grain of the position I am putting forth here. First, I observed that there are natural "icons of crying" that can be exploited by a culture in producing interpretable signs of sadness. These include cry breaks, creaky voice, falsetto vowels, and voiced inhalations. A culture can pick up on these and use them in the creation of culturally stereotyped signs, which I have labeled "ritual wailing" or "ritual lament."

A second conclusion is that the cultural signs constituted by assembling the icons of crying (together with other features, of course) function in regular ways cross-culturally. They are meta-emotional signs. In other words, they call up sadness in order that the sadness may "point to" something else – the desire for sociability. The semiotic operation here is not just cognitive. The meta-emotional signs serve to effect the sociability that they point to. In addition to communicating the desire for sociability to others, they kindle that desire in those others, as well as in oneself.

Finally, third, the use of these meta-emotional signs exhibits regularities. For example, ritual laments are used primarily in connection with mourning. If they are used in other contexts, such as greetings, they are also used in connection with mourning. If men engage in ritual lamentation, then women do also, but not vice versa. In other words, there appear to be constraints on the construction of ritual laments as cultural objects.

I continue today to subscribe to these conclusions, which further research has generally corroborated (Briggs 1992, 1993; Chernela n.d.). But how can I maintain them when I have just argued that cultural objects are abstract and mercurial, undergoing mutations over time as they are transmitted? Don't these conclusions, which are of a seemingly universal character, unduly constrain the cultural object, circumscribing its mercuriality?

Well, the conclusions are "universal" in only a very special sense. They represent observations about empirically observable tendencies. The icons of crying can be drawn upon by any culture in accomplishing its goals, but many cultures do not so use them. However, these tendencies do not rigidly determine, in mechanical cause-and-effect fashion, what cultures *can do in the future*. They are tendencies observable in what culture has done in the past. If they constrain culture in the future, this is not because of something intrinsic to culture. It is because of the way human beings are, because of the material that culture has to work with. The possibility remains that culture will find some way, in its seemingly infinite resourcefulness, to surmount the constraints placed upon it.

At the same time, what is intriguing to me about ritual laments is that they are so closely bound up with culture in the sense of social learning, social transmission. They themselves are inventions that are socially circulated. Witness the variation in lament styles from culture to culture, with the variance often fine-grained – differences in line lengths, intonation contours, and the locations of cry breaks and falsetto vowels. But, moreover, and perhaps ultimately more importantly, the styles are inventions that are at the heart of transmission processes. They are communicative and evocative devices, conveying information about the persons performing the lament, but also calling up feelings and frequently, with them, calling up the actual performances, in others who hear them. In studying ritual laments, we are studying one aspect of cultural transmission.

Implicit and explicit comparisons

I have been leaving something out of this discussion, which nevertheless strikes me as critical. This is the difference between *implicitly* comparing, as when you determine whether an experience fits into your interpretive scheme, and *explicitly* comparing, that is, remarking the similarities and differences among experiences or cultural objects. In the latter case, you are, in comparing, constructing another cultural object – the explicit comparison as formulated in utterances or written statements. That cultural object has a life of its own, that may be independent of the cultural objects it purports to describe. What is the significance of this difference?

To answer that question, we might try to answer another: if culture depends upon implicit comparisons, does it depend as well upon explicit comparisons? Or can it do without the latter? Explicit comparisons are a variety of what might be called "metaculture," that is, aspects of culture (or cultural objects) that are themselves about other aspects of culture (or other cultural objects). And it is an empirical question whether we find this variety of metaculture everywhere. Why does someone explicitly formulate a comparison and communicate it to others? Clearly, the communication of the comparison is not directly a part of the transmission of the cultural object(s) involved in the comparison. If one utters, "that was a good telling of the origin myth," the statement itself, if it circulates, is a cultural object that has a life independent of the origin myth. It can be socially learned and socially transmitted. At the same time, the metacultural statement can be part of an attempt to direct the process of social transmission or to alter or maintain the shape of the cultural object itself. It says in effect: "copy this version of the origin myth, not those other versions."

It is not a huge step from explicit but internal metacultural critique to explicit statements of cross-cultural comparison. To say: "this culture is civilized, that barbaric," or "this object represents an evolutionary advancement over that one," is to engage in explicit comparison, but also to formulate or circulate metacultural objects. And those objects are not without practical efficacy. They can be used to direct cultural transmission processes, holding up certain cultural objects as desirable, and disparaging others.

Now I am not so naïve as to imagine that all metaculture (and, hence, also all explicitly formulated comparison) is equally efficacious in maintaining or altering the shape of cultural objects. To my way of thinking, there is a space for a scientific discourse of cultural comparison – and by that I mean a discourse that circulates primarily within the bounds of scholarly communities. Social evolutionary theory was far less problematic within academia than within the public arena. As a discourse for policy-makers, for example, the Comtean social evolutionist slogan "order and progress" became the basis for thinking through a policy towards indigenous peoples (Lima 1991: 240 ff.). We should subject to the greatest scrutiny those explicit comparisons that work their way into the popular imagination. Is the reason for the popularity merely the scientific validity of the comparison? Or does the comparison also feed special interests? And, hence, is the comparison an efficacious form of metaculture, affecting the shapes of the cultural objects it is about?

I do not wish to let myself off the hook. Though my own comparisons are of narrowly scientific interest, not likely to enter into the public imaginary, still they can be subjected to criticism as metaculture. Do they stereotype women, with whom laments are more regularly associated? Do they juxtapose the emotionality of Amerindian Brazilian cultures to the rationality of Western culture? I certainly do not believe that the comparative evidence suggests a stereotype of women. On the contrary, there are cultures in which men engage in ritual wailing, others in which women do not. Moreover, the comparisons do not paint Amerindian Brazilians as emotional as opposed to the rational Westerners. If anything, ritual laments represent a harnessing of emotions for lofty purposes – namely, for the building of societies. Nevertheless, the statements could be misused within a political public context. Consequently, anthropologists, myself included, must exercise vigilance in monitoring the public uptake of professional findings. Moreover, we must critique ourselves to make sure that we are not subscribing to metacultural statements for the wrong reasons, namely, for the interests they serve rather than the culture they reflect.

Anthropology in the past century has been a veritable factory of metacultural pronouncements. Yes, its smokestacks have billowed forth the polluting by-products of its comparisons. Yes, our problem is how to reduce the pollution. But in our rightful indignation, we should not overlook the splendid products the factory has given us, products of stunning beauty and clever utility. For anthropology has played a role not so much in protecting Western culture against intrusion, as in enriching the West by introducing it to the remarkable diversity of cultures on the planet. Among its products are lenses through which new options and possibilities can be seen, devices that liberate us from the constraints of essentialism, and warmers that thaw cultural objects, enabling them to live again.

Even if explicit comparison is not at the heart of culture in the way in which implicit comparison is, we can appreciate its role relative to culture. It is part of an endeavor to gain control over culture. If the tendency to compare grows out of the basic processes of cultural reproduction, the tendency to formulate those comparisons in explicit statements grows out of a desire to bring those processes into the light of consciousness. The statements render parts of culture accessible to consciousness and, hence, consciously manipulable.

And here we come back to the question with which this chapter opened: isn't culture that which we take for granted and, hence, do not subject to explicit comparison? The answer is that some culture is unreflected upon. That culture depends mainly upon implicit comparison for its learning and transmission. But once an element of culture has been challenged, explicit comparisons – reflections upon that element in relation to other elements – can be marshaled to protect or to change it. The scrutinized parts of culture are also culture, and so are the discourses that scrutinize them. Moreover, the former depend upon both implicit comparison (for their learning) and explicit comparison (for their maintenance or reshaping).

Regardless of whether explicit comparison is necessary for culture more generally, I think that it is inevitable in the social world in which we live. Comparison is intimately tied to the processes of the broader culture out of which it grows. With the rise of modern publics, peoples with historically distinctive cultural traditions bump up against one another. The cultural objects they have been transmitting come in conflict and competition. In such an arena, comparative statements are inevitable, and the kind of science that makes definitive statements about the comparison of peoples and their cultural objects is a socially useful science. It achieves a certain authority within an arena in which untutored comparative statements also circulate. It is not coincidental that comparative methods should be spreading throughout the social sciences and humanities in the United States today.

At the same time, because of its seeming social utility, we have to subject its pronouncements to criticism. From the point of view I have been articulating in this chapter, if the comparative method purports to freeze-frame cultural objects, to classify them, and to explain them by reference to correlation or causation, it fails to grasp the essence of the cultural object, which is to be mutable in fine (if not infinitely fine) degrees, changing shape and slipping in and out of classificatory pigeonholes with impunity. I have argued, indeed, that this characteristic of cultural objects is linked to the role that comparison plays in the very foundation of culture. Implicit comparison is the *fons et origo* of both continuity and change. For this reason, a comparative theory that purports to fix cultural objects for all time is inconsistent with the very idea of culture itself.

This statement resonates with that put forth by Geertz (1973). But the conclusion I draw from it is different. For me, as I think for Fredrik Barth (1987) also, the central task of comparison is not to freeze the cultural object. This we share in common with Geertz. But we are also, unlike Geertz, interested in getting at the processes by which mutation takes place. And in this I think that comparison has a significant role to play. We may, indeed, be on the edge of great discoveries, in which issues of cultural transmission, replication, circulation, and diffusion take center stage in a theory of culture. And I believe that such a theory will ultimately prove more true to the facts of cultural variability than one grounded in the correlations or causal relations among multiple putative cultural objects.

Notes

1 In a sampling of Amerindian Brazilian narratives that I have collected the average varies, but about twenty-four clause-length utterances per minute is not atypical. While it is clear that individuals do not sit around and listen to continuous narratives all day long, at least not every day, it is also possible that for some individuals the daily exposure may be several times greater than 1,000 utterances per day.

2 With the help of Mr. Matthew Tomlinson, who kept a voice-activated tape recorder with him for a twenty-four hour period, and who logged his reading during that period. The number of clauses was determined from counts made from the transcriptions and written material.

6 Case studies of contemporary job loss

Miriam A. Golden

Threatened with the bankruptcy of their employer in 1979, a majority of workers in Chrysler plants in the United States voted in favour of substantial reductions in their wage and benefit packages in an attempt to reduce the company's need for workforce reductions. None the less, by so doing, employees tacitly endorsed the subsequent firings of thousands of their fellows. Faced with a similar situation a year later, autoworkers in Turin, rather than negotiating concessions, held out for thirty-five days in a strike against Italy's largest private employer, Fiat, a strike that paradoxically only intensified after the firm retracted its threat to effect forced dismissals and proposed temporary layoffs in their place. At the same time, neighboring Olivetti plants were laying off thousands of employees with the active cooperation of the very same union that was making national headlines with its dramatic industrial action at Fiat.

A year earlier, autoworkers across the English Channel had already conceded that large-scale workforce reductions would be required were British Leyland to recover profitability and competitiveness. Just a few years later, by contrast, British coal miners decided to fight pit closures in a year-long strike that opened in 1984, a strike garnering international attention as the country's most severe and bitter since the General Strike of 1926. Paradoxically, the 1984–85 miners' strike occurred despite repeated assurances from the National Coal Board that no miner would suffer involuntary job loss. Equally ironic was the fact that many thousands more British miners had lost their jobs over the course of the large-scale rundown of the industry that had taken place in the 1950s and 1960s than were under threat of job loss in 1984, but the National Union of Mineworkers had at that time hardly protested. Its acquiescence in that earlier period was also striking compared with the 262-day strike undertaken in 1960 by its Japanese counterpart in the Miike mines, when rationalization in response to the shift from coal to imported oil eradicated the jobs of more than 100,000 miners.

Why, confronting apparently identical threats, do workers and trade unions in advanced capitalist democracies respond so differently? Why do unions sometimes endorse job loss involving hundreds of thousands of their members, whereas on other occasions pitched battles occur over the mere threat of temporary layoffs for only a few thousand? How do we explain variations in the responses of organized labor to largescale personnel reductions?

This study examines the interactions that occur between firms and trade unions in situations of mass workforce reductions.[1] My curiosity about this issue was initially aroused by observing first-hand the thirty-five-day Fiat strike in Italy in 1980, when I happened to be on the scene investigating other aspects of Italian trade unionism in that period (see Golden 1988). Not only were the events under way at Fiat intrinsically dramatic, but they occurred, perhaps somewhat ironically, as Italian trade union officials were almost simultaneously reading newspaper reports of restructuring and job loss at British Leyland that failed to generate sustained industrial action. In the same period, American unions in the automobile industry were aggressively involved in concession bargaining in which benefits, wages, and jobs were all scaled back in a cooperative effort to help bail out a failing enterprise. Thinking comparatively made each particular outcome puzzling. Why did downsizing in today's automobile industry sometimes end in bitter conflict whereas in other cases – cases where workforce reductions were just as extensive and perhaps even harsher on the employees involved – organized labor acquiesced?

Industrial conflict appeared to be an especially anomalous outcome. Almost from the outset, it seemed, Italian union officials engaged in the 1980 strike recognized that they were doomed to lose, at least in the sense of being unable to reverse the company's decision to resort to workforce reductions. Moreover, these same union officials had acquiesced in large-scale temporary workforce reductions only six years earlier, with apparent ill effects, so their sudden hardening of position appeared that much more surprising. The firm, finally, had at the outset proposed firing a large number of workers, which in the Italian context was an unusual and very aggressive move. But curiously the union actually intensified its strike action when Fiat's management withdrew its threat to fire and announced that only temporary workforce reductions rather than permanent redundancies would be effected. What could explain such apparent paradoxes?

To investigate these questions fully, I eventually broadened the cases analyzed to include different industries and a wider array of advanced industrial countries over the whole of the postwar era. The goal was to achieve maximum diversity in the environment, in order to identify common patterns across cases and to analyze characteristics of such interactions regardless of the national and cultural setting.[2] Countries ranged from Italy and Britain to the United States and Japan. Along with the automobile industry, I also included cases from the coal industry, while for the United States, I observed patterns across all manufacturing industries. The research design thus became an instance of a "most different systems" design (Przeworski and Teune 1970).

To account successfully for diverse outcomes across cases, I propose that strikes that occur during large-scale manpower reductions are not – whatever their slogans may suggest – aimed at preventing job loss. Rather, they seek to *defend the trade union organization* during the course of downsizing. I contend that even unions that appear radically to resist market forces accept that there are circumstances in which the enterprise must reduce the size of its labor force. But what no union can accept, I argue, is that the firm take advantage of such a situation to break the union itself. If too many shop floor union representatives are included among those to be let go, or if so much of the union's membership is slotted for expulsion as to jeopardize the very future of the union as an organization, the union responds with industrial action. The aim of such action is to restore the union organization, not to prevent job loss. Strikes over workforce reductions are not, therefore, waged over their ostensible goal. Rather, they are rational, self-interested responses on the part of labor organizations to threats to trade unionism, not threats to workers.

In this paper, I first review some specific cases of mass job loss. Following that, I present the reasoning that underlies the use of game theory in this research and I detail the testable propositions derived from it. A third section offers an initial empirical test of some of the major hypotheses advanced, by examining the extent of strikes over job loss in the four countries – Britain, Italy, Japan, and the United States. A final section resolves the apparent rationality paradox of strikes over job loss.

Some cases of workforce reductions

As I show below, disputes over workforce reductions may sometimes constitute as many as a quarter of all strikes in a country in a single year. None the less, the number of such strikes is inevitably far fewer than the number of strikes that occur over issues affecting wages. The latter almost always constitute the vast majority of industrial disputes in any given year. Despite this, industrial action over job loss often attains a political importance well beyond what the quantitative record alone suggests. Indeed, it would hardly be an exaggeration to claim that politically the most important strikes to have affected the advanced industrial countries in the years since World War II – the strikes whose names are familiar even to the casual observer of industrial conflict and political economy – have been strikes over job loss not wages.

The cases of industrial strife selected for intensive investigation in this study all constituted turning points in the politics of their countries. Some will therefore undoubtedly be familiar even to readers who attend but little to matters involving industrial relations. These strikes occupied the front pages of national newspapers throughout their relatively long durations; they polarized public opinion and threatened premature death to the government in office; they mobilized hundreds of thousands of workers and often almost equally as many police; and they entailed subsequent innovations in national public policy. For the unions that fought them, these strikes almost always ended in crushing defeats, and these defeats marked more general setbacks for the labor movement nationally, setbacks that in all three relevant cases even today affect the strength, militancy, and legitimacy of the labor movements of these countries.

In the longer study from which the current paper is drawn, I examine in detail interactions between firms and trade unions in situations of mass workforce reductions in Japan, Britain, Italy, and the United States. In Japan, I investigate two disputes in the mining industry, both at the Miike mines owned by the Mitsui company. The first, which eventually resulted in a short-lived and partial victory for organized labor, occurred in 1953; the second, which ended in a dramatic defeat, lasted from 1959 to 1960. In Britain, I examine three specific cases: a strike at British Leyland in 1956, again resulting in a partial victory for the trade unions involved, another series of events at the same firm in 1979 and 1980 (events which, however, did not engender industrial conflict), and the strike of British mineworkers in 1984–85, which ended in defeat for the National Union of Mineworkers (NUM). In Italy, I concentrate on a strike at the Fiat works in 1980, led by the Federazione Lavoratori Metalmeccanici (FLM), which labor lost. Finally, in the United States, I survey historical materials relevant to showing why strikes over workforce reductions are exceedingly rare in that country, and why the massive job loss that has regularly affected industry in the years since World War II has almost always been handled with the acquiescence of organized labor.

The disputes investigated here often proved to be of lasting historical significance. The two Japanese Miike strikes were among the longest and most important labor conflicts to have occurred in that country in the postwar era. The second dispute, which ended with defeat for the union movement, also marked the end of the hope for anything other than the enterprise union system that characterizes Japan today. With it, organized labor lost its attempt to secure the recognition of bargaining agents other than employees of the particular firm. If only employees of the firm act as collective bargaining agents, trade union representation is by definition confined to the level of the enterprise. The aspiration to establish national industrial unions along the lines of those found in continental Europe was thereby stifled after the Miike defeat of 1960. Indeed, the national mining federation as well as the country's major union confederation both became involved in the Miike dispute precisely because of the interest they shared in acquiring recognition and legitimacy for national trade unionism generally. The defeat in the Miike mines constituted the final blow to a union movement that subsequently developed along the unique and extremely fragmented enterprise lines with which we are familiar today.

None the less, the events that occurred also heralded important political gains for the Japanese working classes. The plight of the Miike miners catalyzed public opinion, and even though the campaign was orchestrated by the left-wing parties, Japan's conservative government endorsed new labor and welfare legislation that was by international standards quite progressive. Even today, the Japanese welfare state remains, by most comparative measures, relatively underdeveloped. But it took an important step forward in the early 1960s with the passage of new legislation to help displaced miners in particular and later displaced workers more generally. The active labor market policy adopted for coal has since been used for other industries. Active manpower policy has, moreover, proved an important component in maintaining Japan's low unemployment rate, even as most of the rest of the advanced capitalist countries faced increasingly high unemployment in the 1970s and 1980s.[3]

The strike of autoworkers at British Leyland in 1956 also helped catalyze innovations in public policy, although these were somewhat slower in coming than those that followed the great Miike strike of 1959–60. Not until 1965 did the British parliament pass the Redundancy Payments Act, whose main goal was the prevention of industrial disputes over redundancy, largely through the provision of severance payments. At the same time, the 1956 strike had been only one of a series of disputes over workforce reductions that had swept the British auto industry, a series which eventually led the industry as a whole to adopt methods to handle job loss that were less likely to engender industrial conflict. Although autos remained an industry that was relatively strike-prone, disputes increasingly concentrated on wages, and workforce reductions became a less provocative issue.

Even more important to British history was the miners' strike of 1984–85, the country's largest and most serious industrial conflict since the General Strike of 1926. The strike represented a showdown between organized labor and the newly ideological Conservative Party under Prime Minister Margaret Thatcher, and it was a showdown that the union movement lost. Organized opposition to Thatcher's plans for the nationalized industries, to her new industrial relations policies, and more generally to the new Conservative political agenda largely ceased after the defeat of the miners. The British labor movement found itself in retreat thereafter. In the decade following the strike, the trade union movement increasingly adopted policies labeled "the new realism," representing an accommodation to Tory power and to management's newly claimed authority. In the mining industry, too, the strike represented the last (and indeed the only) attempt to use industrial action to prevent the government from moving Britain largely out of the production of coal altogether.

The defeat of autoworkers at Fiat in 1980 also signaled a more general weakening of Italian union militancy. Like the British union movement, in the 1970s the Italian had been highly aggressive, relatively strike-prone, and extremely powerful on the shop floor. Indeed, prior to 1980, the Italian labor movement had arguably been Europe's strongest on the shop floor, as the shop steward movement that had arisen at the end of the 1960s in the Hot Autumn acquired extensive influence over all matters of industrial organization and wage setting. After the Fiat strike, however, organized labor was forced onto the defensive, seeking as best it could to accommodate the economic turmoil of the 1980s. On the shop floor union influence was undermined, as firms sought to regain the authority they had ceded to shop stewards. Europe's strongest factory-based union movement thus found its influence enervated. The Fiat strike was considered a turning point for organized labor, and indeed for the left more generally, one that signaled an overall political shift to the right in the country. Just as the Miike strike of 1959–60 represented the end of the attempt by Japanese unions to construct a European-style nationally based labor movement, the Fiat strike of 1980 represented the end of the attempt by Italian unions to construct a radical, shop floor-based labor movement.

Approaches to the problem

However dramatic and important politically, the industrial disputes reviewed here are part of a class of highly unusual events. Only rarely do firms ignite major displays of labor militancy in the course of workforce reductions. In part because they are infrequent, disputes of this nature are not well understood.

Two additional reasons that disputes about downsizing have not received much systematic scrutiny are probably because they appear to be both difficult to analyze using the standard tools of microeconomics – and hence inherently problematic for economists and students of industrial relations – while at the same time too narrow conceptually to interest political scientists. As regards the former issue, Jon Elster (1989) has argued that collective bargaining generally is too complex to be studied using exclusively the tools of rational choice. One goal of the present study is to show, by contrast, that if we properly delineate the problem to be investigated, the tools of rational choice can be used to produce new and intellectually compelling solutions. Even if all aspects of collective bargaining cannot be understood simultaneously, there is no reason to surrender the attempt at systematic analysis for the entire area of inquiry.

As regards the latter issue, it is true that the problem must be narrowly focused to achieve strong analytic results, possibly more narrowly focused than is traditional in the study of comparative politics. But as William Riker has suggested (1990), a narrow focus to attain a proper solution is a better research strategy than a broad focus that fails to generate conclusive results. Indeed, if Riker is correct, scientific inquiry is more likely to proceed through investigation of what he labels "small events" than those classes of phenomena given by common language ("capitalism," "social democracy," "civilization"). Defensive strikes against job loss certainly fall into the camp of "small events," and by studying some specific instances, I hope to show that these apparently complex, irrational and self-defeating actions can be analyzed within the parameters of a rational choice framework. By narrowing the focus of the phenomena under study, we reduce the trade-off between analytic rigor and empirical accuracy. That is, we can uncover *mechanisms* while still attending to the actual *processes* characterizing events.

A final reason why disputes about downsizing are poorly understood is that standard approaches to the problem are likely to lead to incorrect conclusions. This is apparent if we examine some apparently intuitively obvious – but inaccurate – arguments. Unions, for instance, do not necessarily accommodate temporary layoffs but resist permanent downsizing. Similarly, the nature of the options workers would enjoy were they let go (including alternative employment prospects and the level of unemployment benefits available) does not systematically correspond to union responses to workforce reductions. Likewise, the number of workers threatened by downsizing is irrelevant to predicting industrial conflict. More generally, as all these examples illustrate, union responses cannot be predicted on the basis of a *median voter* model of union behavior. That is, the decisions of union leaders facing workforce reductions cannot be accurately predicted on the basis of the interests of the average union member. Such an approach is typically taken by economists who study trade union behavior. But it is, I argue, misleading to study unions in this way, because union leaders have considerable leeway in making decisions, and their own organizational interests differ from the economic interests of their followers.

What we might call *structural models* of union behavior and industrial relations are also inadequate for the problem at hand. These models, used by both political scientists and economists, examine the impact of structural features of trade unions and the collective bargaining system – such as the degree of internal union centralization, the extent of union concentration, the level of wage bargaining, and the degree of cohesion among employers – on macroeconomic outcomes, including the extent of unemployment, inflation, and economic growth (for an example, see Calmfors and Driffill 1988). This line of argument suggests that where unions, employers, and/or wage bargaining are relatively encompassing nationally, industrial action will be less common (by extension, Olson 1982; Hibbs 1978). Instead, accommodations between unions and employers over workforce reductions should characterize such settings. Conversely, all the countries examined in this study exhibit comparatively decentralized and fragmented industrial relations systems, where industrial conflict occurs with relative frequency and where accommodations over workforce reductions would be less often expected. As a general rule, a structural approach would expect relatively frequent industrial conflict over workforce reductions (and other issues) in all four countries discussed here. This, however, is not the case. In what follows, we see that system-level structural characteristics do a poor job in accounting for the outcomes observed both within and across countries. While the former is hardly surprising – no cluster of system-level characteristics could be expected to account for all the sub-system variation observed – the latter is far more damaging. Some countries with relatively decentralized union movements and fragmented industrial relations systems experience conflict over job loss only rarely, whereas other structurally similar countries experience such conflicts relatively often. Since a structural approach groups these cases together, it does a poor job accounting for the apparently systematic differences among some of these countries.

The inadequacies of conventional approaches in explaining the outcomes of interactions of firms and unions when workforce reductions take place call for developing an alternative approach. This study uses a simple game theoretic framework. Some assumptions that underlie this approach are spelled out in the next two sections. The framework is then used to generate some testable propositions.

Preliminary methodological observations about applied game theory

The use of deductive game-theoretic models for empirical comparative analysis, especially case study analysis, is relatively undeveloped. Hence, there is no body of research on which to call that has developed rules (or even norms) in how to apply rational choice in empirical settings. Rules of evidence for assessing causal statements are generally consolidated across the (social) sciences (for their application to political science, see King, Keohane and Verba 1994). But issues arise in game theory that are peculiar to the study of behavior as strategic interaction involving actors' preferences. In particular, since different conclusions follow from different assumptions about actors' goals (or preferences), determining preferences is obviously a crucial, and sensitive, endeavor. In this section I argue that *asking* actors what their intentions are is often a poor research technique, and that we should instead rely on strong theoretical propositions combined with good case selection.

It may be surprising that the kind of intentional analysis entailed by game theory (see Elster 1983) does not necessarily require actual empirical investigation into the intentions of agents. If anything, in many circumstances, this is both unnecessary and undesirable. The reason, as we shall see in more detail in a moment, is that participants often have strong incentives to misrepresent their goals in these situations. Hence asking them why they did things is likely to confuse and mislead the observer. Instead, a strong research design and proper case selection allow for testing intentional propositions by examining whether the pattern of outcomes across cases is that predicted by the models. At the same time, examining the actual behavior of participants during the course of events is often also an illuminating way to assess their motives.

For the problem at hand, both union officials and company managers have strong incentives to describe their goals in ways that render it difficult to assess them. If, as I claim, unions that engage in industrial action over job loss are really aiming at protecting their own militants, not ordinary workers, it would often be difficult to corroborate this argument by asking union officials if it were true. There are many reasons why union leaders cannot necessarily define industrial action as directed specifically and exclusively at protecting the union's own militants. Such a goal may seem to potential strike participants as unworthy of the sacrifices required. Similarly, the managers of an enterprise may wish to target shop floor union representatives during workforce reductions but may find it politically inopportune to admit this publicly.

There are more general reasons why students of industrial conflict typically find it difficult to assess strike goals on the basis of what participants say about their actions (Hartley, Kelly and Nicholson 1983). In the particular cases I studied, I found considerable variation in how participants described their goals. In Japan and in Britain in the 1950s, union officials often argued that workers should come to the defense of union activists when they were singled out in excessive numbers during workforce reductions in order to defend union organizations that lacked solid footings in the enterprise. In that context, it was apparently appropriate and legitimate to ask workers to make sacrifices in order to build and defend their representative organization. By 1980, this was no longer the case in either Italy or Britain. Workers were asked to evaluate the situations they confronted in terms of what job loss and restructuring would mean for employees, not union organization. Indeed, when I publicly proposed the interpretation of the Fiat strike offered here (in Golden 1989) – that it was aimed at defending union militants, not jobs – Italian union officials who had been involved in the strike seemed embarrassed, and one told me that even if it were true, he certainly could not confirm such an interpretation. Trade unionism no longer enjoyed the heroic profile of its earlier years. In this situation, it becomes mandatory to impute preferences to actors.

The job loss game

A game theoretic model is a simple depiction of an interaction between two or more agents, known as players. Every game has three elements: a set of players, a strategy space, and pay-off functions. In any game, players are assumed to be rational. This simply means that they will try to do the best they can given the circumstances in which they find themselves. What this exactly is, in turn, depends on the preferences each actor holds.

In the longer study from which this is drawn, I examine in detail a number of games between the institutional representative of the firm's employees – the trade union – and the firm's management. Here I lay out the assumptions that drive the models developed there. All of these games begin when the firm, confronting some exogenous shock (such as a change in energy prices), announces that large-scale personnel reductions are required. The games thus open with the decision by the firm that large numbers of personnel reductions are required.

Assumptions of the models

In order to calculate pay-off functions, we make three simple assumptions. These are: that strikes are costly; that firms want to target shop floor trade union activists during workforce reductions; and that unions in turn want to protect their activists. I discuss each in turn.

First, assume that a strike, were it to occur, would be costly to both sides. For the union, a strike is costly because workers lose wages and may need or expect strike funds to be paid, or because the union may lose members if scabs enter the enterprise and work in place of striking employees. For a firm, a strike is costly because it stops or disorganizes production. Firms prefer that industrial relations go smoothly, and that open conflict be avoided. The assumption that industrial action carries costs to both the union and the firm is intuitively obvious and empirically plausible in most circumstances.

Second, assume that when personnel reductions occur, the firm prefers to target union representatives among those to be let go.[4] This assumption is less immediately obvious, and accordingly requires a more elaborate justification. One way for the reader to consider the matter is to imagine how a firm and its employees would confront each other in a kind of pre-organizational state of nature – a situation in which worker organization (both in the particular firm in question as well as in its competitors) did not already exist and in which protective and enabling legislation was absent. In such a context, the firm would prefer to continue dealing with its employees as single individuals rather than an organized entity. The history of early industrial capitalism largely corroborates that the primitive preferences of the firm involve avoiding trade unionism, in that firms in that early period typically tried to discourage the formation of unions.

History, of course, only serves as a metaphor for the game theoretic situation analyzed here. None the less, trade unionism is undeniably costly to a profit-maximizing firm. Just how costly empirically is variable. Using data from the United States, Richard B. Freeman and James L. Medoff (1984: ch. 12) show that where workers are organized into unions, profitability falls. To some extent, this is offset by the contribution union organization makes to the firm's productivity, but whether the losses or gains associated with trade unionism are larger is an empirical matter that varies. The main advantage to the firm in dealing with employees as individuals rather than as a collectively organized body is that organization entails the capacity to engage in collective action (cf. Pizzorno 1978: 278). Without organization, individual workers can disrupt or sabotage production, but strikes as such do not occur, for instance.[5] Incapable of an organized withdrawal of labor power, workers are not collectively able to raise their wages or extract other costly improvements in their benefits and working conditions.

But the most compelling evidence that firms – or at least some firms – would prefer a non-union environment comes from the myriad legislation found across countries belonging to the Organization for Economic Cooperation and Development (OECD) which protect trade unions from employer discrimination.[6] OECD countries generally (although not the United States) have legislation against unfair dismissal, legislation preventing firms from firing union activists purely and simply because of their union activities (OECD 1986: 94). Even in the United States, the Wagner Act provides the right to organize, thereby protecting union activists (Meyers 1964). Such protections for union activists require that firms that remain intent on union busting employ subtler means than firing individual union organizers for no other reason than their union activities.

Mass workforce reductions provide just such a convenient cover for picking off union representatives. When large numbers of workers are let go for justifiable economic reasons, who is to say how many union activists can legitimately be included? Precisely because of the extreme vulnerability of the union during the course of personnel reductions, legislation or collective agreements specifically protecting the organization during downsizing exists in many countries. In fact, the development of seniority rules for layoffs in the United States illustrates that such rules develop endogenously: that is, they develop out of the need to provide institutional protections for trade unions in a context in which picking off union organizers is endemic. Once such rules exist, union-busting during large-scale workforce reductions is no longer a viable option for firms. Thus, where protective legislation or collective agreements exist, we no longer observe firms attempting to discriminate against union organizers when workforce reductions transpire. That we do not observe such behavior does not mean that the firm would not prefer to target activists. The preference remains, but the evidence for it now lies in the rules that prevent it being acted upon. This argument may seem a sleight of hand, but in fact it can be assessed empirically. Cross-national evidence for it, and thus for the realism of the assumption that firms prefer to target union activists in the absence of restrictions on doing so, is provided below.

Thus, in the absence of institutional protections preventing such a move, we assume that management would always prefer to take advantage of situations involving mass personnel reductions to try to disrupt and even to break trade unionism, unless there is too high a cost to doing so. The cost incorporated into the models is that of industrial action itself. Strikes themselves are sufficiently costly to the firm that we assume – in most of the models – that the firm would refrain from targeting union activists for dismissal if it knew that industrial action would ensue as a result.

The third assumption in the models developed in this study is that the union wants to protect its activists on the shop floor from expulsion from the enterprise. Ordinary workers have only to pursue their individual interests, but union leaders have to pursue the interests of the organization itself; that is, they have to act as caretakers for the union or risk its demise. Union officials are the guardians of the institutional needs of the union, of which self-preservation is a prime example. Just as the managers of the firm must worry about profits in the competitive market environment, managers of the union must worry about *organizational survival*, or *organizational maintenance*, in their constant struggle against capital. Indeed, organizational survival may well be thought of as "the central aim of the leadership" (Ross 1948: 16).

An important reason is that, in a democratic context, unions are voluntary associations. Because of this, they are inherently vulnerable to catastrophic losses of power. Members may resign; the firm may refuse to negotiate; the government may withdraw legal recognition of the union or the contracts it underwrites. There is no democratic country in which such threats do not constitute concerns for organized labor. Even where recognition seems secure, a precipitous drop in membership levels or some exogenous change may trigger unexpected aggression on the part of firms that had previously seemed reconciled to dealing with a powerful labor movement.[7] At bottom, capital only tolerates organized labor when constrained to do so, and labor is never entirely immune to organizational threats.

For modeling purposes, we need to translate labor's concern with organizational survival into a maximand; something, that is, that unions seek to maximize and that drives their behavior. In its struggle for survival, the union seeks to maximize the number of shop floor activists it deploys.[8] Perhaps this is in function of the number of members the organization seeks, the revenues it thereby collects, and thus the potential income of union leaders.[9] Nothing so crudely cynical need be the case, however. Shopfloor activists are essential for trade unions to survive and to thrive. "The union participant," a study of shop floor unionism has explained, "is a necessary ingredient without which most local unions could not operate. There must be personnel to fill posts, opinion leaders to inform and stimulate, a cadre to mobilize for the various modes of latent and overt combat" (Spinrad 1960: 244). Seconding this view while speaking directly to the occurrence of mass workforce reductions, another scholar has argued:

> If the management had complete discretion in making the selection [of those to be made redundant], the labor union would be vulnerable insofar as its shop stewards could be made redundant. Shop floor workers would, therefore, become reluctant to become shop stewards. Even though the union structure of officials and members might still be maintained, the activities of shop stewards in looking after the interests of their fellow workers, which is the basis of the union's existence, would tend to diminish. (Koike 1988: 88)

Unions, therefore, value their activists and when mass job loss threatens, their primary concern is to protect their own shopfloor organizations despite the workforce reductions that may occur.[10]

Activists, finally, are hard to find; perhaps the single most common characterization of local unions is the chronic difficulty they experience in stimulating activism and the reluctance of ordinary workers to serve as union representatives (Lipset 1981: ch. 12). Except in extraordinary periods of mass enthusiasm for trade unionism, union organizations are usually hard pressed to recruit shopfloor representatives.

The three assumptions just spelled out underlie the game theoretic models presented in the longer study summarized here. In the next sections, I present the results of the models, results which serve as the hypotheses guiding empirical inquiry for the comparative analysis to follow.

Testable propositions generated by the models

The games that underlie this study generate a number of simple, easily testable propositions regarding the circumstances in which strikes over job loss do or do not occur. The circumstances in which strikes over workforce reductions will not occur are as follows:[11]

- when, for reasons exogenous to the immediate situation (such as statutory requirements or legally enforceable collective agreements), the firm is prevented from targeting union activists during the course of workforce reductions;
- when the union's reputation for toughness is sufficiently secure that the firm refrains from targeting activists, typically because the union enjoys the protection of a well-organized, well-financed national organization.

In the next section, I offer an initial empirical assessment of the basic theory presented here.

A preliminary comparative test of the model

Considerable empirical variation characterizes union responses to job loss. In some countries, organized labor typically tolerates high levels of job loss without industrial action – the United States is a well-known example – whereas in others unions lead strikes over workforce reductions with relative frequency. This section presents some data comparing the extent of industrial action over job loss in four countries. On the basis of the propositions presented in the preceding section, I propose that the main factor distinguishing countries with relatively high (low) rates of conflict over workforce reductions is the absence (presence) of institutions protecting union activists from dismissal during the course of personnel reductions.

This is a coarse-grained argument. It captures the essence of the two propositions advanced above, both of which imply that disputes over job loss occur only when trade union activists are targeted (although not always then). Appropriate comparative data do not exist allowing us to assess cross-nationally more subtle hypotheses regarding the impact of informational imperfections or of exogenous subsidies. As far as activists are concerned, however, existing data permit some general assessments, because some countries have institutions protecting union representatives during job loss whereas others do not, and information on such institutions can be, albeit with some difficulty, collected.

The four countries chosen for analysis offer maximum variation on both strike rates over job loss and the institutional protections afforded union activists on the shop floor. The comparative importance of strikes over workforce reductions is illustrated by the data presented in Figure 6.1, showing the industrial disputes waged over job loss in Japan, the United States, Great Britain, and Italy. The graph shows the number of strikes over workforce reductions as a proportion of the total number of industrial actions in the four economies for every year between 1942 and 1990, depending on data availability.[12] Some idea of the extent of industrial action in the four countries can be gleaned from the following absolute numbers. In 1970 (a year for which data are available for all four countries), there were 5,716 industrial disputes in the United States, of which only 170 were classed as having to do with dismissals. In Italy in the same year there were 4,162 disputes, of which 321 involved dismissals. In the United Kingdom, 123 out of a total of 3,906 disputes involved dismissals. And in Japan, finally, there were 4,441

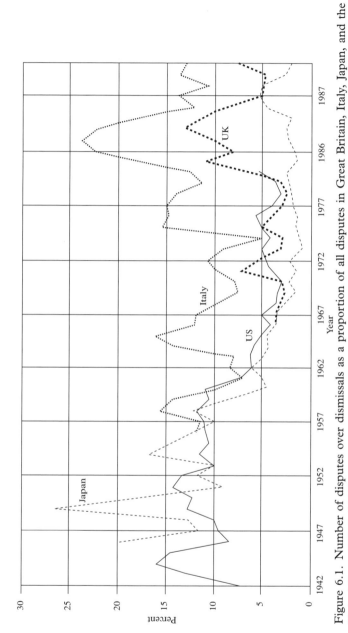

Figure 6.1. Number of disputes over dismissals as a proportion of all disputes in Great Britain, Italy, Japan, and the United States (1942–1990).

Sources: For Japan, Ministry of Labour, *Year Book of Labour Statistics* (Tokyo: Ministry of Labour, various years). For Italy, Istituto Nazionale di Statistica, *Annuario di statistiche del lavoro* and *Annuario statistico italiano* (Rome: ISTAT, various years). For Great Britain, Department of Employment, *Employment Gazette* (London: HMSO, various issues). For the United States Bureau of Labor Statistics, *Bulletin* (Washington, D.C.: Government Printing Office, various issues).

disputes, only 100 of which had to do with dismissals. In absolute as well as relative terms, then, disputes over workforce reductions were frequent in Italy in 1970, whereas the other three countries all had far fewer such industrial actions.

Examining the data over time, the figure shows that the proportion of strikes over workforce reductions was greatest in Japan in the 1940s and 1950s. The Japanese peak of 1949 is unmatched by any of the other three countries, although Italian proportions after the mid-1970s are also quite high. There, the proportion of industrial disputes caused by issues involving job loss rose immediately after the first oil shock in 1973–74 to more than 15 percent, and has stayed above 10 percent for every year since 1975. Even in the 1950s and 1960s, however, Italian unions exhibited a relatively high propensity to strike over job loss, and the proportion of disputes classed this way was often more than 10 percent.[13] In the United States, by contrast, rates were relatively low even in the 1940s and 1950s, and have never gone above 10 percent since 1961.[14] Britain, finally, exhibits very low rates of disputes over workforce reductions throughout the 1960s and 1970s,[15] while in the 1980s such conflicts have become relatively more frequent, sometimes exceeding 10 percent of the total.

The theory advanced above proposes that institutional variations in the protections accorded shopfloor union activists should correspond to these variations in dispute rates across countries. Strike frequency over job loss should vary according to the extent to which shopfloor union activists are protected during large-scale personnel reductions. The following sections offer country-by-country discussions of this hypothesis.

Japan

Japan is an especially interesting case because strikes over workforce reductions were common in the 1940s and 1950s but became quite rare after that. After World War II and throughout the 1950s, disputes over workforce reductions were frequent, comprising more than a quarter of all strikes at their peak in 1949, for instance. In 1960, however, the number of such conflicts tumbled to under 10 percent – indeed, in most years after that, to less than 5 percent – where it has consistently remained until the present.[16]

The theory presented above predicts that the decline in the frequency of strikes over workforce reductions in Japan parallels the development of institutions protecting union activists. And this is largely the case. In the 1940s and 1950s, Japanese firms exercised complete discretion in selecting those to be expelled during workforce reductions. Even after the end of the Red Purge in 1949–50, which constituted a direct attack on labor's right to organize, enterprises continued to single out union activists throughout the 1950s, systematically attempting to weaken unions affiliated with what had become Japan's major confederation, Sohyo, and to promote "second" unions. In these disputes over workforce reductions, at least during the first half of the 1950s, "union activists were *always* the target of discharge" (Fujita 1974: 354, emphasis added). As Kazuo Koike writes:

> Prior to the mid-1950s when layoffs were more common, if the number of volunteers [for layoffs] did not meet the quota, managements [sic] would make the additional selections, usually choosing older workers (45 years of age or older), those with poor attendance records, and those who were "less efficient." The last item, in particular, tended to be used to lay off active union members such as shop stewards. (1983: 49)

Even in the 1980s, another scholar could write that "There is no established rule or agreement on dismissal like the 'seniority' principle in the U.S.A. Therefore, management also uses these dismissal methods in its attempts to weed union activists from its work force" (Shigeyoshi 1984: 5).

Workforce reductions still occur in Japan, and in large numbers. But after the 1950s, unionized workers were largely protected from them with the development of what is called "lifetime employment," guaranteeing job security to unionized employees. Indeed, Koike has argued that after the long and costly strikes of the 1950s, firms "have since become very cautious in their selection of the workers to be laid off" (1983: 49). Taishiro Shirai too notes that, because disputes over workforce reductions in Japan have been especially costly, firms have learned not to trigger such strikes (1968: 330). In the 1970s, for instance, when recession resulted in noticeable numbers of layoffs, "Management was careful not to resort to the nomination of candidates for redundancies, but maintained instead a system of advertising for volunteers" (Koike 1987: 91). The same had been true when workforce reductions were required even in the years of labor shortage in the 1960s (Ujihara 1974: 160). As a result, trade unions have tended to cooperate in workforce reductions affecting their members since 1960. Firms have stopped targeting union activists – indeed, union members altogether – in workforce reductions. This has allowed unions to gain stability on the shopfloor. No longer threatened when workforce reductions take place, unions no longer mobilize their members to oppose such reductions. Industrial disputes over job loss largely ceased in Japan once firms no longer targeted union activists in the course of large-scale personnel reductions.

United States

In the United States union militants enjoy almost complete protection from expulsion from the firm thanks to seniority arrangements (Abraham and Medoff 1984: 90). Seniority orders job loss according to when one was hired, with the most recently hired the first to be let go. In this context, disputes over job loss are extremely rare since union representatives tend to enjoy more seniority than the average worker. Moreover, as the theory presented above would lead us to expect, as seniority arrangements have become virtually universal in the years since World War II, the incidence of disputes over workforce reductions has fallen even further. This is true despite the fact that American firms resort to layoffs with considerably greater frequency than firms do in Europe or in Japan (Moy and Sorrentino 1981). The American data verify that the frequency of layoffs does not by itself necessarily engender frequent industrial conflict.

Italy

Italian unions also enjoy seniority provisions when redundancies occur. A 1965 agreement between the country's three union confederations and management bodies stipulates three criteria to use in the event of permanent workforce reductions (*licenziamenti*): the technical-productive requirements of the firm, seniority, and the family responsibilities of the employee (Ventura 1990: section 6.4). Temporary layoffs, however, are entirely unregulated, since the courts have ruled that the provisions regarding redundancies are not applicable (Scognamiglio 1990: 447; Ventura 1990: section 6.8). Moreover, Italian firms have used temporary layoffs to the almost complete exclusion of permanent workforce dismissals since legislation was adopted in the 1970s allowing public funds to be used to subsidize the costs of temporary layoffs to the firm (Padoa-Schioppa 1988). As the hypothesis presented above would lead us to expect, the incidence of industrial action over workforce reductions has grown in Italy with the increasing number of institutionally unregulated layoffs that have taken place since the first oil shock.

United Kingdom

In Britain, finally, there is considerable variation in the institutional protections afforded union representatives during the course of workforce reductions. Seniority – there called "last in/first out" (LIFO) – although the single most important ordering device for workforce reductions, is applied considerably less frequently than in the United States. While it may be true that it constitutes "the most widely used method for choosing who in a slump will be made compulsorily redundant" (Oswald and Turnbull 1985: 82), results of a 1984 survey of enterprises found that LIFO constituted the basis of selection in fewer than half the cases involved (Millward and Stevens 1986: 221). Corroborating this, the results of a 1985 mail survey of the thirty-one largest unions affiliated with the Trades Union Congress (TUC) found that only 28 percent of the twenty-five unions responding reported that LIFO proved of principal importance in the selection of the redundant (Booth 1987: 405–06). Seniority, the author concludes, "does not appear to be of primary importance in the management of redundancies in Britain, . . . an interesting contrast to the US experience" (Booth 1987: 409). When seniority does not obtain, management exercises discretion in the selection of those to be dismissed. Given this, it is not surprising that British rates of conflict over discharges have fluctuated considerably in the years for which data are available, comprising more than 10 percent of the total number of strikes in the latter part of the 1980s (when job loss in Britain rose).

Conclusions

This preliminary four-country analysis corroborates that industrial action over job loss is most likely to occur not where job loss is most frequent – by all accounts, the United States – but instead where institutional protections for union representatives on the shop floor are weakest. This constitutes prima facie evidence in favor of the realism of the assumption that firms prefer to target union activists during the course of large-scale workforce reductions, provided statutory or other restrictions preventing them from doing so do not exist. These protections are most secure where seniority provisions regulate layoffs or where union members are virtually exempt from layoffs altogether.

Heroic defeats, rationality, and job loss

Disputes over workforce reductions often seem marked by a kind of irrationality, as though the actors involved had to know that their efforts were doomed from the outset. This is true, for instance, of both the 1980 Fiat strike and of the 1984–85 strike of British mineworkers, and to a somewhat lesser extent of the 1959–60 Miike strike. The appearance of irrationality attached to these events is a function of the union's ostensible primary goal during the disputes – namely, achieving the withdrawal of the threat to discharge large numbers of employees. Were this the principal motivation of the strikes in question, the union leaders involved would indeed be pursuing doomed efforts. In all of the strikes investigated in this study, union leaders seemed to know from the outset that manpower reductions, even if only temporary, were inevitable. In *none* of the disputes examined were workforce reductions avoided (although sometimes the number of employees affected was reduced). This is hardly surprising. In any market economy job loss is inevitable in some circumstances. Unions must acquiesce in changes in manpower requirements, even if acquiescing in workforce reductions does not necessarily entail accepting the original terms and conditions established by management. In the United States, for instance, where layoffs are common, negotiations between labor and management regularize the conditions under which workforce reductions occur. Often unions are able to improve the outcome in both quantitative and qualitative terms. None the less, job loss is endemic to modern market systems.

Despite this, the unions involved in the disputes mentioned above often articulated the public goal of preventing workforce reductions altogether. The interpretation advanced in this study argues that such a goal was not actually the primary objective behind the union's behavior. Instead, these disputes are better understood as aimed at issues of organizational maintenance – more precisely, the protection of shop stewards in most cases. With this as their goal, these strikes can be reinterpreted as instrumentally rational courses of action. That in some of the cases considered in this study the union officials involved lost the battle to protect their own organizations does not mean that defeat was inevitable. Instead, union decision makers underestimated their chances of success.

In both the Fiat strike and the British miners' dispute of 1984–85, the rhetoric of conflict focused primarily on the attempt to save jobs. "No firings!" was the union's slogan in the Fiat case, "No pit closures except through exhaustion," the NUM's. Workers were mobilized largely around the goal of preserving jobs. In Japan too the Miike union in 1959–60 was typically depicted as clinging to an unrealistic understanding of the workings of the market economy. Its reaction to the threat of workforce reductions was usually understood as an attempt to prevent manpower reductions entirely.

None the less, comparative evidence shows that the desire to preserve jobs, however deeply felt among employees and among union officials, is not enough to spur a union organization to undertake a costly industrial dispute. In Britain, for instance, even as the NUM mobilized the country's miners against pit closures, thousands of employees in the manufacturing industries were losing their jobs thanks to large-scale restructuring. In the case of British Leyland, the country's largest domestic automobile producer, thousands of men were threatened with job loss, much of it concentrated in regions already marked by relatively high unemployment. Yet the unions organizing BL's autoworkers failed to undertake concerted industrial action to try to prevent workforce reductions.

Nor can it be said that the economic threat facing British mineworkers was substantially worse than that confronting their counterparts in the auto industry – if anything, the reverse was the case. In neither instance were forced redundancies at stake. The National Coal Board had repeatedly promised that no miner would be subjected to involuntary job loss even with widespread pit closures. At British Leyland, too, large-scale workforce reductions were effected virtually without any forced dismissals. Finally, the financial compensations attached to work-force reductions were actually greater for mineworkers than autowor-kers. The threat of job loss was not experienced more severely by miners than by autoworkers and the potential hardships for those let go were not more serious for the former than for the latter. Yet only the former trade union engaged in industrial action ostensibly aimed at preventing job loss.

British evidence thus shows that the extent and intensity of the threat of job loss is a poor predictor of union reactions within a single country. The same is true across countries. In Figure 6.1 we observed a relatively low number of strikes in the postwar era around issues of redundancies and layoffs in the United States. Yet comparative research reveals that workforce reductions are much more common in the United States than in Europe or Japan (e.g. Moy and Sorrentino 1981). The frequency of workforce reductions is thus also a poor predictor of union responses.

Once we reinterpret disputes that occur in situations of workforce reductions as aimed at issues of organizational maintenance and not at preventing job loss, these disputes no longer appear instrumentally irrational. In two cases reviewed above – the 1953 Miike strike and the 1956 dispute at the British Motor Corporation – the unions involved secured written agreements protecting their organizations in the event of future workforce reductions. Thus, it is feasible to achieve such a goal. Even though in both cases large-scale workforce reductions were carried out as planned, these strikes were victories for the organizations involved.

In the three other cases sketched above – the 1959–60 Miike strike, the 1980 Fiat strike, and the 1984–85 NUM strike – the unions failed to secure the organizational protections they sought. At Miike, the activists originally slotted for expulsion were all forced out of the firm, a second union established and the original union largely displaced by it. At Fiat, workforce reductions were carried out on the basis of lists drawn up exclusively by the firm instead of using rotations as the FLM had insisted. In the NUM case, finally, government policy towards the coal industry has remained largely unaltered, hundreds more pits have been closed and the union's membership drastically reduced. The likelihood of the NUM merging with a larger body has become extremely high as a result of the organizational shrinkage that it has endured.

In all three cases, however, there is good evidence that the union organizations involved lacked critical information necessary to evaluate accurately the likelihood of success of industrial action – success, that is, in relation to securing organizational protections, not preventing job loss. It was the absence of full information that engendered defeat once these strikes were under way. In the Miike case, the union under-estimated the speed with which the Mitsui company would be able to establish a rival second trade union and underestimated as well the appeal that the new organization would exercise among Miike miners. At the same time, the union may have been unaware that the company would successfully secure agreements from its competitors not to take over its markets during the course of the dispute. For all these reasons, the unions involved underestimated the ability of the firm to hold out during the strike. Had the financial and organizational pressures on the firm been greater, it is possible that Mitsui would have had to capitulate on the issue of firing union activists, as it initially seemed the firm was prepared to do. Had that occurred organized labor could have won the strike – not in the sense of preventing workforce reductions, but in the sense of preserving the trade union organization.

In the case of the British miners in the mid-1980s, organized labor also lacked critical information indicating that its chances of success were poor. The NUM overestimated the likelihood of blackouts during the dispute because of an absence of current information on the require-ments for coal of the electricity industry. In addition, the union under-estimated the police preparation that had been undertaken prior to the dispute, thereby overestimating the likelihood that the union could roll the strike through Nottinghamshire and keep many more miners from working than proved the case. For both these reasons the NUM seriously overestimated the effects the strike would have on the British economy generally, effects that could plausibly have led public opinion to force the government to call new elections, as had occurred in 1974. Had this transpired and had new elections taken place, it is possible that a Labour government would have been elected, a government that would then have altered Britain's energy policy and possibly substantially reduced the number of pit closures over the subsequent decade.

The 1980 Fiat case is the most difficult to evaluate. The union knew of the firm's productivity problems and knew too of the firm's commitment to reduce costs. The union also had information regarding the likely reactions of the rank and file to a strike, and especially the kinds of divisions that would probably surface. For these reasons, the union should have anticipated defeat. But even though the FLM had good information on the feelings of the Fiat rank and file about industrial action, union leaders seem to have radically underestimated the extent to which a noticeable segment of Fiat's employees would actively oppose industrial action. The FLM was completely unprepared for the display of anti-union and anti-strike sentiment among Fiat employees that occurred. It was at this point that the union quickly capitulated, relinquishing any hope of securing protections for its militants in the course of mass workforce reductions. Again, the absence of full and accurate information – in this case, information on the reactions of employees who did not support the strike – explains why the union lost its attempt to protect its own organization during workforce reductions.

On the basis of this evidence, I would argue that the goals of all three strikes were realistically conceived, and industrial action an appropriate course of action with which to pursue them. These goals involved securing protections for union militants and activists. The decisions involved occurred on the basis of the best information available. This proved inadequate. In these three cases, an absence of critical information meant that the unions involved overestimated their own capacities to secure agreements protecting their own activists. On this issue they were defeated.

Notes

1   The terminology associated with mass workforce reductions is not consistent cross-nationally (British and American usage differ, for instance), historically, or even in one country in one period. American usage is especially confusing and ambiguous (Oaklander 1982: 187). British usage is superior, since it distinguishes temporary layoffs from permanent workforce reductions, which are referred to as redundancies (Gennard 1982: 107; Lee 1987: 20). I will consistently use the term "layoff" to refer to a temporary separation of the employee from the workplace, one carrying with it the likelihood of recall. "Firing," "dismissal," or "redundancy," will all be used to refer to permanent, forced dismissal, one where the worker's job has ceased to exist. In speaking generally of "workforce reductions," I deliberately fail to specify how these reductions will occur. Options include layoffs,

firings, natural wastage and attrition, incentivated and early retirements, and so forth. For operational convenience, I define mass workforce reductions as those involving at least 10 percent of the workforce (specified at the plant, division, or company level), although any particular threshold is only a matter of convenience.

2   Cases could only be selected in contexts of democratic stability, however, where unions are allowed to organize and represent workers collectively. This necessarily limited me largely to the postwar OECD countries.

3   The importance of active manpower policies in keeping unemployment low in the 1980s has been noted by Layard, Nickell and Jackman (1991: 62–64 and 472–73).

4   I interchangeably refer to these persons as shop stewards, union representatives, activists, and organizers.

5   So-called wildcat strikes may occur even in the absence of trade unionism. But these are unlikely to be frequent, protracted, or even very compact. Regular, cohesive, and protracted industrial action requires organization.

6   One must avoid fallacious reasoning here. Saying that the existence of protective legislation cross-nationally shows that all firms actually want to union bust is akin to arguing that because all countries have legislation against theft, everyone actually wants to steal. Yet theft would probably be considerably more common without legal protection against it. The historical record suggests that union-busting would too.

7   A good example is Sweden, once heralded as representing Western Europe's most notable case of pacific class compromise. After 1983 Sweden's peak management association began disassembling the collective bargaining system so favored by labor, eventually causing a collapse of centralized bargaining and a concomitant widening of wage differentials (see Hibbs and Locking 1995 on the latter; Pontusson and Swenson 1996 on the former). In the early 1980s the conservative-led coalition government attempted (unsuccessfully, as it turned out) to dismantle Sweden's so-called Ghent system for the distribution of unemployment insurance, which has unions administer unemployment insurance, and has been a critical component in Sweden's exceptionally high unionization levels (see Rothstein 1992). If even Swedish employers can turn so aggressive, so can employers anywhere.

8   In studies of trade unionism, setting a maximand for organized labor remains an unresolved issue. The classic debate between Arthur Ross (1948) and John Dunlop (1944) turned on the maximization issue, with the former unwilling to identify a maximand. Whereas Ross contended that a focus on the political processes of trade unions, and especially on the importance of organizational survival for the leadership, was essential, Dunlop – and with him most later economists – was more concerned with specifying an objective function for the union. As Henry Farber (1986) suggests, however, it may be possible both to attend to the political processes of unions and to specify a clear objective function. By identifying the maximization of shopfloor activists as the goal of the organization, I seek to do just this.

9   Farber (1986: 1079–80) discusses some relevant difficulties in devising a satisfactory theory of the objectives of union leadership. Maximization of

membership is sometimes used, but this is generally operationalized as maximization of employment because of an implicit closed-shop assumption; that is, it is assumed that those employed automatically become union members. This assumption is inappropriate for most European countries, however. Maximizing the number of shop floor activists seems a way to cover both closed and open shop situations. Where there is no closed shop, recruitment depends critically on activists; thus, the leadership may be assumed to maximize the number of activists in order to maximize members. Where there is a closed shop, the leadership may be assumed to maximize activists in order to maintain a wage advantage over non-union settings in order to retain the inframarginal worker.

10 This does not mean that unions do not want to make the conditions for ordinary members who are subject to workforce reductions as good as possible. Where their own organization is not under threat, unions consistently try to reduce the numbers involved and to improve the terms and conditions of expulsion. But where their own organization is subject to threat, the union strives to protect itself first.

11 In the longer study from which this paper is drawn, I also elaborate propositions about when strikes over workforce reductions may occur. I omit these here, since they are not easy to follow without examining the actual games.

12 The standard measures of industrial disputes are the number of strikes, the number of participants, and the number of hours lost. While these data are generally available for the four countries, for Japan the only strike data that are regularly disaggregated by cause are for the number of disputes. It is therefore not possible to analyze other aspects of industrial action over workforce reductions in Japan. For this reason, I restrict the analysis to an examination of the number of strikes over workforce reductions as a proportion of all strikes in each of the four countries.

13 Italian data on strikes by cause are available only since 1956.

14 Data on strikes by cause are not available for the United States after 1981. However, even in the 1970s the proportion of disputes concerning job loss remained consistently less than 5 percent.

15 Data on the cause of industrial disputes in the United Kingdom are available only since 1966.

16 This pattern mirrors the general pattern of industrial conflict in Japan. Strike propensity generally was high in the 1950s (higher than most other advanced capitalist states), and remained so until the mid-1960s, after which it declined such that by the late 1970s Japanese strike rates were lower than major Western European countries, with the exception of Germany (Hanami 1984: 206; Korpi and Shalev 1980).

7   Defining the contours of an Islamic reform movement: an essay in successive contrasts

John R. Bowen

Anthropologists' stock in trade is the fine-grained knowledge of the local: how things happened in a particular place and time, how people thought and felt about those events. But increasingly central to the discipline are phenomena of world scale: ideologies of development, broadly diffused television programs, international religious movements. Many anthropologists now focus on how people reshape these (and other) international phenomena in their own social lives, and argue that what appears to be the homogenization of world culture is better seen as many processes of appropriation and reinterpretation.

The broad scope of these social processes poses new challenges to anthropological methods. For the comparative study of Islamic religious forms and movements, for example, what is the appropriate strategy? Older methods of regional comparison, long established in the discipline (see Johnson 1991 for a survey), focus attention on regional social and cultural traits and away from the religion's cross-regional reach; usually Middle Eastern social institutions are compared (see, for example, Keddie 1972). A two-way contrast between widely differing cultures, such as that of Morocco and Java explored in Clifford Geertz's *Islam Observed* (1968), highlights broad cultural contrasts but downplays the processes by which ideas and institutions are differentially transmitted and shaped (see also Lindholm 1992).

It may be that the gap between the international scope of these topics on the one hand, and the cultural detail of specific, local social forms on the other, is too wide to be bridged with a single set of comparisons. One answer is to focus on processes of diffusions and migrations themselves, as in Michael Fischer and Mehdi Abedi's (1990) study of how Iranians create new communities of (and debates about) worship and cultural identity in Iran and in the United States, or in Pnina Werbner's (1988) studies of Muslim communities in Britain.

Another answer to the global/local challenge is to focus on the processes by which particular social forms have been historically differentiated. The comparative study of colonial policies is one promising avenue for this kind of research, as when Allan Christelow (1992) compares the different outcomes of French policies in Algeria and Senegal, focusing on the preexisting differences in the roles played by religious judges, and the consequences of those differences for municipal politics. Starting from the Muslim side is William Roff's (1987) analysis of the contrasting ways in which movements adapted "Wahhabi" ideas to particular circumstances in the nineteenth century.

I argue here for the advantages of a multistage comparative approach, in which a case is subjected to a series of successive contrasts, each at a different level of generality and each pointing out different aspects of the ways in which Islamic religious practices are shaped. This method does not lead to an explanation of all the phenomena concerned – indeed I see it as mainly useful in providing the richest possible understanding of one society's religious forms. It suggests, first, which elements are locally specific and which are more widely distributed and, secondly, which mechanisms of differentiation may be of general scope.

I begin by examining religious forms and religious change in one society, the Gayo of highland Sumatra, Indonesia. Reformist leaders working in this region have adopted certain strategies, developed particular rhetorics, and highlighted certain beliefs, chosen from larger conceptual universes. They have done so with the particular contours of Gayo society and the previous practices and ideas of Gayo men and women in mind. Contrasting the Gayo movement with other movements, near and far, throws into sharper relief the nature of those choices by pointing to the paths not chosen. A contrastive analysis thus underscores the sensitivity of religious phenomena to social and cultural features.

Most of the 200,000 Gayo speakers in Indonesia live in the central highlands of Aceh province, on the northern tip of Sumatra, bordered by the Acehnese on the coasts, and with the Batak and Minangkabau peoples further south. The Gayo have been Muslims for centuries, probably since the seventeenth-century reign of Iskandar Muda. Dutch forces invaded the area in 1904 and ruled until Japanese conquest in 1942; Indonesia became independent after a long struggle between 1945 and 1950.

Islamic reformism grew out of the melting pot of people in the new town of Takèngën in northern Gayoland. Traders and teachers from elsewhere in the Dutch East Indies came to settle in the town, finding there a new class of Gayo merchants and civil servants, who had to learn what was beginning to be called Indonesian in order to speak with them. Beginning in the 1930s, a group of Gayo religious teachers returned to their Sumatran homeland from schooling elsewhere in the Dutch East

Indies and began to urge their fellow men and women to purify their religious activities of non-Islamic elements. These teachers emphasized the unique authority of the Qur'ān and hadīth, and associated themselves with the general movement for religious reform popular throughout the archipelago and in the Middle East. The reformists were opposed by other Gayo teachers, who affirmed long-standing religious practices and the authority of prominent religious scholars of the past. These divisions between reformists and traditionalists continue to animate discussions in the highlands today (Bowen 1993a).

Local self-differentiation

The first contrast to which I wish to point is one which has motivated the reformists themselves, namely, that between traditional village religious practices and what they took to be correct Islamic practice. To examine this contrast is thus also to trace a process by which the reformists defined the goals and strategies of their campaign. It underscores the important general feature of cultural analysis that members of a society engage in comparative study in order to learn and to change their culture, and that one stage of an anthropological study is to analyze those comparative processes (see Urban, chapter 5). Elsewhere (Bowen 1993a) I have tracked the reformists' own analyses of religious contrasts over a series of religious practices, from worship to healing to the observance of major feast days. Let me take one feast day observance as an example of how reformists constructed a local set of emphases in dialogue with older practices.

All Muslims, one can safely say, recognize as normative the observance of the annual Feast of Sacrifice (Arabic *īd al-adhā*), which commemorates the willingness of the prophet Ibrāhīm to sacrifice his son at God's command. God's command to sacrifice to Him and to Him alone is contained in the Qur'ān in chapter 22 (verses 34–38) and again in chapter 108. The collection of reports of the prophet Muhammad's deeds and statements (the hadīth) specify how Muhammad carried out this command during the month of pilgrimage.

Each year upwards of one hundred Gayo undertake the pilgrimage, and in the highlands, during the holiday period, Gayo often talk about the sacrifices the pilgrims are carrying out in the city of Mina simultaneously with their own. In the largely traditionalist village community of Isak where I have done most of my work, households sacrifice various kinds of animals: chickens, ducks, sheep, goats, or water buffalo. Just prior to cutting the victim's throat, the sacrificer dedicates the animal to one or more relatives, who receive religious merit from the sacrifice. Who actually cuts the throat is not of great importance; a man may delegate the job to someone else.

The sacrifice is carried out in the name of the household. Women as well as men speak of "their" sacrifice, and couples decide jointly on a list of people who will receive its merit. In the case of a buffalo, the beneficiaries usually include parents on both sides, and daughters as well as sons. Widows also carry out sacrifice (without being socially redefined as men), and when a wealthy female trader in Isak sacrificed a buffalo, others tended to speak of it as her sacrifice, not that of her husband (who was also part of the household).

Following the sacrifice households host ritual meals, called *kenduri*s, where, depending on whom you ask, blessings, or merit, or just prayers are sent to the spirits of the deceased. These ritual meals are central to many events in the highlands and elsewhere in the archipelago. In Isak, during each of the four years when I was present for the *īd al-adhā*, three or four households each sacrificed a buffalo and sponsored a village-wide *kenduri*, where men and women chanted Qur'ānic verses and statements in praise of God far into the night. These special kenduri were intended to send extra merit to the host's ancestors. Recitations please God, say villagers, who then relieves the torment of these ancestors. (The number of guests times the number of repetitions yields the overall benefit.) The learned man who leads the guests in chanting will have been given a list of the people to whom the merit should be transmitted; he then embeds these names in a long prayer (sometimes saying the names very softly), thereby directing the evening's merit to the intended beneficiaries. These sessions are also held after the death of any adult in the community.

Not only do the words sent to God generate spiritual benefit for deceased relatives, but the sheep or buffalo that has been sacrificed by a household also provides a future material benefit. On judgment day, the persons named as sacrificial beneficiaries will be able to ride on the animal to the place of judgment. Only one person can ride a goat or sheep to the Meraksa field, but seven can ride on a buffalo. A buffalo sacrifice thus provides the opportunity to bring together parents, children, and grandchildren on the back of the afterlife vehicle, and if they had the resources most Isak households would stage a buffalo feast sometime during their lives.[1]

Gayo reformists consider most of these practices to be anathema. Ritual meals, where the underlying assumption is that the event sends merit to a spirit, violates the general reformist idea that one can only benefit from one's own actions. "Did you not hear the words of God,

'People shall have only as they have labored'?" concludes one popular Gayo poem aimed at ritual meals.

The ideas that sacrificed animals give one merit, and that they provide a vehicle in the afterlife, are not so clearly contrary to general reformist thinking. (Indeed, a scholar especially influential among highlands reformists, Hasbi ash-Shiddieqy, argues that sacrifice generates merit for the sacrificers (n.d.: 24).) But town reformists sought to distinguish their own interpretations and practices as clearly as possible from those of the villagers. In part this was because townspeople's identities were based on their rejection of the past and their embrace of the new; in part it was because of their own religious convictions.

Certainly religion was the main idiom for, if not the entire substance of, townspeople's work of differentiating themselves from villagers. Town friends told me on many occasions of how villagers remained in "pre-Islamic days" (*jaman jahiliya*), evidenced by their reliance on *kenduris*. And because notions of ritual efficacy, tied to ritual meals, were so central to the village ritual complex, reformists have worked to rid town observances of any public linkages among killing, eating together, and merit-making. Their efforts are not direct deductions from international reformist teachings, but strategies for ritual reformation motivated by the desire to distance themselves from village, "heathen" practices.

In 1989 I observed the celebration of the Feast of Sacrifice in a modernist stronghold in town. When asked about the purpose of the ritual, Baléatu residents invariably referred to God's command in the Qur'ān to follow the example of Ibrāhīm. (Villagers, by contrast, usually mentioned the importance of providing a vehicle for the afterlife.) For these modernists, to follow the example of Ibrāhīm means to adopt his attitude of selfless and sincere devotion, *ikhlas* (Arabic *ikhlās*). One scholar explained that one receives merit from the sacrifice only if it is done with the proper intent, "for the sake of God and not for a worldly reason." He called the notion that the sacrifice becomes a vehicle for the afterlife "amusing."

In recounting the story of Ibrāhīm, Baléatu narrators emphasized his prior decision to give something away in devotion to God, not the moment of sacrifice itself (which would bring up village ideas about the purpose and result of sacrifice). The killing of the goat or other animal was sometimes left for someone else to perform, privately, effectively downplaying killing and eating in favor of other public events: street parades, congregational worship, and chanting in the neighborhood prayer-house.

Town people did eat in the prayer-house, but referred to the meals as "eating together" and never as *kenduri*s. Friends of mine gave away food on the feast day, and mentioned prominently the invitation given to town orphans to eat in the prayer-house as proof of the event's real character. The meal was about self-sacrifice, and not about creating merit. (The fear of mistaken understandings of what the eating means sometimes leads to extreme reactions. I recall one teacher who reacted in horror when cookies were passed around a classroom after he had delivered a homily to the students about the meaning of sacrifice.)

Town religious practice has thus developed in part as a reaction to prior models of sacrifice. Because villagers emphasized ritual meals and the efficacy of the sacrifice itself, town modernists avoid any association between the killing of the sacrificial animal and eating together. The value of selfless sacrifice is instead underscored.

Now, it could be said in objection to this argument that even though this was so, all reformists in the Muslim world may have been led to this particular set of emphases. I thus will need to look at the ways in which this feast day has been observed in other settings, and do so below. But let us hold in mind for the moment the self-differentiation mechanism discerned here as a candidate for a general mechanism by which people create religious forms. This mechanism is analogous to Gregory Bateson's process of "schismogenesis," by which people (typically, couples) become more different as part of an interactive process of self differentiation. It is also equivalent to the process identified by Claude Lévi-Strauss by which neighboring societies invert myths as they borrow them, so as to make clear the cultural boundaries between the two social groups. This mechanism will lead one to look for strategies and rhetorics in which reformists exaggerate their differences with existing practices in order to make as urgent and compelling as possible the need for people to follow their lead.

Social frameworks for reformist cultural forms

This first level of contrast, the negative one of differentiating the movement from existing practices, is complemented by a second level, the positive one of adapting the forms of religious change to existing social frameworks. That which must be changed becomes the polar opposite of the correct path; that which may be left as is becomes the conditions and context for change.

In the Gayo case this social context emerges most clearly in contrast to that of the neighboring lowland Acehnese peoples. Gayo modernists led, and continue to lead, dual lives. In the town they learned from, and worshipped with, men and women from elsewhere in the Indies, and so developed a supraethnic religious culture in which they used Arabic and Indonesian languages and shared the goal of national independence (Bowen 1993a). But these same men and women also maintained ties with their villages of birth; many returned to those villages, where they urged fellow villagers to mend their religious ways.

This particular social framework gave a distinctive stamp to highlands modernist culture. Gayo modernists, then as now, participate in village social life, but they also aim at reforming established rural religious practices from within. In order to reconcile their religious reformism with their village social allegiances they carved out a distinct religious sphere of activity, one in which people of diverse backgrounds could participate (in town life), but which would also allow for the continuation of older cultural activities and social ties (largely in villages).

Gayo modernists thus have underscored the contrast between matters of religion, where one must follow scriptural norms, and all other matters, where, in the words of Muhammad, "you know best your affairs." This position has allowed them to urge practicable reforms in village religious life without calling for the abandonment of other social practices, something neither they nor their audience would have welcomed.

The Gayo stance has led them to accent certain features of the general modernist position over other features. In order to mount the strongest possible attack on certain village ritual practices, they have emphasized the scriptural constraints on interpretation rather than the process of independent reasoning (*ijtihād*), which elsewhere has been a hallmark of modernist rhetoric. Gayo modernists frequently and vehemently denounce all innovation (*bid'a*) in ritual affairs. Secondly, they have emphasized the boundary between religious ritual (*'ibādāt*) and the rest of social life, focusing on reforms of the former, rather than claiming that a particular set of religious orientations should guide all activities. By contrast, in many other societies, "reason" (*aqal*) has been developed as such an all-purpose religious value. Finally, seeking to reshape the individual worshipper's religious practice and not to create new forms of society, Gayo reformers have emphasized the direct, unavoidable link between the subjectivity of the individual worshipper and the reception of the ritual act by God. Only worship done with the right intent counts in God's eyes.

In order to change the ways in which less educated Gayo understood religious ritual, modernists created an entirely new genre of poetry, one that in its formal features as well as in its content underscored the separateness of religious matters from secular ones. The poetry embodies the particular highlands mixture of socioreligious emphases: a separation of religious from merely social, and a focus on the individual's practice. Most poems feature one or more lines of Arabic scripture, followed by an elaboration of the scriptural message in Gayo verse – possibly a unique juxtaposing of languages and styles within the Islamic world. It underlines the scriptural dependence of religious understanding and addresses a Gayo-speaking audience. It was generally sung by local poets, some of whom were also popular singers in other genres. The poetry soon became a highly popular performance genre.[2]

In these poems modernists stress the importance of forming and holding the correct intent, a task which requires remaining attentive, having faith, and correctly formulating, to oneself, the act's religious purpose. They argue that intent is necessary to create any religious merit, and that, therefore, one cannot create merit for others. From this proposition they eliminate from the sphere of religious activity ('ibādāt) practices that were (and still are) important to many Gayo, including reciting verses for the benefit of the deceased.

Once they have narrowed the field of permissible ritual action to exclude certain older practices, modernists then ask: what are the conditions for worship to be effective? Here modernists refocus the question of efficacy on the worshipper's subjectivity rather than on the social conditions surrounding the event. The poems attack three specific elements of an older subjective stance toward worship: ignorance, blindly following other people's teachings, and following Gayo norms rather than religious ones.

In one poem, for example, after stressing the importance of knowing and intending one's actions, the poet introduces the voice of an ill-informed person who disclaims any need to study scripture:

> Me, grandpa taught me just so.
>   Straying from scripture? Don't worry, teacher.
> For grandpa also read the Qur'an, recited the Prophet's life,
>   memorized Arabic.
> As for me, no need to learn religion,
>   just follow grandpa's legacy.
>
> The worship prayers I just keep short;
>   keep them brief, never long.
> If it's accepted, then it's accepted;
>   if not what can I say about it?

Poets frequently used sarcasm; reformist teachers were known for their shrill voices and incessant nagging at people to change their ways. The sarcasm and shrillness stand out markedly against the background of usual Gayo indirect approaches toward rebuking and advising others, and were aimed at interrupting the normal social fabric and etiquette so that it could be replaced by something else. Gayo modernists did not seek to construct a city on a hill, but to reform the behavior of villagers and townspeople without removing them from their social context. They did so by insistently drawing them back to scripture, underlining both the Arabic source and the vernacular gloss, and on the basis of these truths assaying villagers' behavior in the religious sphere.

I have argued so far that Gayo modernists focused on narrow religious reform rather than broader societal issues at least in part because they retained a strong identification with their villages even as they became actors in a new religious sphere. The town of Takèngën became a multiethnic center for modernist thinking, and thus encouraged both the development of a transethnic formulation of religious concerns and early alliances with nationalism. Yet because Gayo reformers continued to be deeply involved in village affairs, they focused on transforming village religious life. This set of social commitments led them to carve out a distinct religious sphere for reform, and this sphere defined the limits of public debate.

This line of argument emphasizes the role of social ties in channeling religious reform strategies in one direction rather than another: the particular intentions, strategies, and rhetorics of actors, the issues they chose to emphasize, and the ways they formulated and expressed their ideas so as to influence various audiences. This analysis would imply that other strategies, and other background social situations, would lead to differing religious forms.

Even microvariation within a region can produce different strategies for (and cultural forms of) conversion. Take the neighboring Acehnese people. This contrast is particularly telling for the frequent cultural contacts between the two peoples, especially in religious affairs, and the development in both societies of a modernist Islamic consciousness in the 1920s and 1930s (Siegel 1969). The social context for religious modernism in lowland, northern Aceh differed from that in the highlands in two major ways. First, the context was all-Acehnese. The most important organization was not the pan-Indonesian Muhammadiyah but the Aceh-specific association of religious teachers called PUSA (Persatuan Ulama Seluruh Aceh, All-Aceh Ulama Association), led by a future governor of Aceh, Daud Beureueh. Modernist imaginings thus primarily concerned a new Aceh rather than Aceh's place in a new Indonesia.

Secondly, modernists developed their social critique in terms of the opposition of village life to a larger world outside the village. "They appealed to men to act not as villagers but as Muslims; to the 'ulamā' [religious teachers], this meant forgetting traditional social identities"

(Siegel 1969: 74). This opposition was also strongly linked to opposi-
tions of gender and religious values. Whereas most Gayo men remained
in their villages throughout their life, even if they went away for a brief
period of study, most Acehnese men spent years away from their village
at study or work, in all-male settings. Women, by contrast, were at the
center of village life, remaining in their natal villages after marriage,
receiving houses from their fathers, and managing rice fields. Men felt
themselves treated by their wives as children when at home; the high
divorce rates of the area followed from these tensions. Male religious
spokesmen identified women with emotions and desires, *hawa nafsu*,
which the properly religious (male) individual must transcend through
the strengthening of reason, *aqal*. Men could best develop reason and
control passions away from the village.

The Acehnese social fabric in which modernism developed was thus
one of a male/female opposition within an ethnically specific framework.
Acehnese modernists sought to transcend village life rather than, as in
the Gayo highlands, reforming it. They did so in the idiom of struggle:
for self-mastery through worship, and for economic success through
individual labor, both in some sense a continuation of the earlier
struggle against the Dutch through war. These struggles involved
individuals, joined in "mechanical solidarity." A powerful image of the
properly religious society was found in congregational worship, where
all Acehnese worshipped side by side and in precisely the same way
(Siegel 1969: 262–75). The social and political importance of this
image led provincial leaders to feel particularly threatened by particular-
istic, inward-looking, local forms of worship (Bowen 1989), which held
much less social import for Gayo leaders.

The earlier struggles as conceptualized by *'ulamā'* were embodied in
the poetry of holy war. The epic of the Acehnese war, the Hikayat Prang
Sabi (Story of the Holy War) relates the journey from this world to the
next (Siegel 1969: 74–77; 1979: 229–65). Arabic scripture also appears
here, and, as in Gayo poetry, it is foregrounded against the background
metrical scheme (Siegel 1979: 261). Here, too, scripture has an "un-
varying message" to convey (*ibid.*: 263). But scripture serves not as a
source of correction for wayward villagers, as in highlands Gayo verse,
but as a source of promise, of the reward that awaits the fighter in
paradise.

From the 1930s on, Acehnese religious forms looked at the possibility
of creating a new society on earth rather than in paradise. These new
forms of religious persuasion include sermons and newspaper articles.
They emphasize, not the reform of village life in a strictly demarcated
religious sphere, but the building of a new society on socioreligious

principles. If Gayo modernists stress the boundary between religion and the rest of society, their Acehnese counterparts emphasize "the idea of society as a manifestation of *ibadah* [religious duty]" (Siegel 1969: 116). Acehnese modernist writings point to the tone that worship gives to all of life, not the reform of specific acts (as in the Gayo poetry). They portray Aceh as a once and future glorious nation, in which struggle strengthens reason, and reason orders men in their actions (*ibid.*: 119–33).

The tone of the earlier poetry and the later sermons and articles is redemptive, future-looking. These forms take men out of their current social surrounds and turn them toward a future promised society. The dominant metaphor is an awakening from sleep, not the interruption of current social practices. And it is a message that is directed at men, not women. Thus Gayo modernists urge their fellow men and women to transcend ethnic identity in favor of a scripture-based life in their village surrounds; Acehnese modernists urge their fellow men to transcend village identity in favor of an ideal Acehnese unity of supra-local male individuals.

Most-different cases: Indonesia and Morocco

So far we have explored two fine-grained contrasts within the province of Aceh. By contrasting village and town practices with respect to one particular ritual, the Feast of Sacrifice, certain features of Gayo modernism appear more understandable, including the strong desire to avoid any association between the observance and feasting. Reformists sought to differentiate their true path from the mistaken behavior of old by accentuating the differences in the religious sphere. This comparison suggested a mechanism of self-differentiation that may have greater generality.

By contrasting the paths taken by reformists in the highlands with those taken in the Acehnese lowlands, the specific qualities of each emerge more clearly, and to some extent these qualities are accounted for by contrasts in social institutions. Reformers took account of these social differences in choosing their emphases and in developing new forms of religious poetry to convey the new messages.

But confining our analysis to one province, or even to the archipelago, may mislead us into taking some elements of Gayo reformism as universal, disconnected from cultural specificities. A feature that is characteristic of, say, Indonesian Muslim life will only appear as such when Indonesian religious forms are contrasted with others in a different culture area. Such a maximal contrast will point up a separate kind of mechanism, that of cultural fit; that all other things being equal, Muslims will tend to interpret religious prescriptions in ways that fit with regional cultural ideas. Certain elements of the Feast of Sacrifice, for example, are shared by Gayo villagers and town modernists alike. Women are active participants in the rituals. They may perform sacrifice. They are members of a household unit that is directly involved in the activities: in the villages, when they gather together for a ritual meal (and in images of the family, holding hands, being saved because of their wise decision to sacrifice animals to God); in town, when the family gathers for tearful confessions of their shortcomings and of their love for each other. These elements of female and family involvement are also found in other Indonesian societies and in the writings of Indonesian religious scholars. For example, the possibility for women to carry out a sacrifice on *īd al-adhā* is explicitly defended by the influential modernist scholar Hasbi ash-Shiddieqy, in a work on the Feast of Sacrifice (n.d.). Are they generally true of Muslim societies, or specific to Indonesia? Or to a wider belt of Asian Muslim societies?

One would not even see these elements as noteworthy were one not to explore further the way in which the Feast of Sacrifice is carried out elsewhere. At this point our question shifts once again, from how the same reform movement was differentially developed in the highlands and lowlands of Aceh province, to whether or not certain features of a specific ritual are part of a worldwide Muslim tradition or whether they vary across cultural regions. For this question we can appropriately start by searching for the maximal contrasts, the differences that will aid us in constructing a field of possibilities. As it happens, we can begin with Morocco, at the other end of the Islamic world, recently studied for its forms of sacrificial ritual practice by M. E. Combs-Schilling (1989).

Here, in contrast to the family-oriented practice and ideology found in Indonesia, patriarchy is accentuated through ritual. Each year on the feast day the king, who claims descent from the prophet Muhammad, publicly plunges a dagger into a ram's throat, reenacting Muhammad's ritual practice and underscoring his tie to the Prophet. Combs-Schilling (1989) argues that the sacrifice also reaffirms patriarchal power in the family and embodies a notion of male fertility. After the king has accomplished his sacrifice, male heads of household throughout the kingdom follow suit. Each publicly kills a ram, the size and virility of which is commented on as a measure of the man's own virility. In village and town settings, the other men of the household stand erect to witness the sacrifice; women and children are either absent or in the background, seated. Women play only the role of passive observers to the sacrifice; after the killing they may dab some of the victim's blood on their faces to "share in the power of sacrifice" (1989: 231).

This public enactment of patriarchy accords with Moroccan cultural assumptions about the opposition of male reason versus female passion. More generally, the fixed male/female opposition is just one instance of the belief described by Lawrence Rosen (1984: 47–59) that one can read from social characteristics of persons to their attendant mental states. The Moroccan view asserts that persons have essential differences in their mental characteristics, depending on such critical social differences as gender and place of origin. This theory underpins not only gender segregation and patriarchy, but also legal processes of determining a reliable witness (*ibid.*).

This maximal contrast brings out two major cultural differences between Morocco (and perhaps other North African societies) and Indonesia (and perhaps other Asian societies). The first is the salience of the killing event in the former, but not in the latter. Whether on Java, coastal Aceh, village or town Gayo, Indonesians downplay the act of killing in favor of other aspects of the ritual. Because this contrast appears to be primarily cultural, rather than a function of social frameworks or of religious interpretive positions, it probably is less likely to become a matter for debate in either cultural area. It also tinges all other aspects of the ritual, including the second axis of contrast, that of patriarchy's greater or lesser centrality. As Combs-Schilling emphasizes (and others support her account), the ritual is publicly, officially interpreted in Morocco not just in a gender-segregated way (as one would expect to some extent in coastal Aceh) but in such a way as to underwrite the domination of women by men.

The contrast between Moroccan and Gayo (and some other Indonesian) ritual practices thus points toward broad cultural contrasts that also shape, differentially, the way Muslims interpret scriptural commands. This maximally broad contrast is especially important in preventing us from assuming that particular features observed in one place are true of Muslims generally. Thus, elsewhere (1992) I drew on precisely this contrast to criticize the assumption that Islam contained an essential patriarchy, visible in the ritual form of the Feast of Sacrifice. Combs-Schilling had claimed that the Feast of Sacrifice was inherently patriarchal, not only as practiced in Morocco but in its essential form and interpretation, and that it was indicative of the inherent patriarchy of Islam. By viewing the public form of the Moroccan Feast of Sacrifice as a synecdoche for all of Islam, her analysis eliminated the possibility of alternative, culturally specific elaborations of Muslim tradition.

But it turned out that even within Morocco one finds such alternatives, some of which, as with Gayo modernist self-differentiation from villagers, appear to be constructed in explicit distinction to the public, state-backed patriarchal form of ritual. Abdellah Hammoudi (1993) describes observances in a village near Marrakesh, where women play a ritually central role in purifying the sacrificial victim. They also gather its blood not just to share in its power but for use over a long period of time to guard the home and to combat illnesses (1993: 91–92, 197). Moreover, over the longer ritual cycle (found in parts of Morocco, Algeria and Tunisia) the Feast of Sacrifice is followed by a series of carnivalesque processions and masquerades in which characters representing women, Jews, workers, and other figures flaunt sexuality and, in classic ritual-of-reversal fashion, violate the sanctity of the sacrifice by wearing the skin of the sacrificial victim (1993: 16). The masquerade highlights the social contradictions between classes as well as those between male and female. These representations of otherness and of social contradiction "give the lie to that rigor of purity that the sacrifice tries to impose (despite the feminine ritual that accompanies it and timidly contests it) and unveils the rigor of the real" (1993: 248). Stressing the resemblance to European forms of carnival, Hammoudi argues that these rites are part of the overall process by which Moroccans made Muslim sacrifice their own (1993: 16).

The publicly patriarchal character of sacrifice and the explicit links to the Ibrāhīm myth, emphasized by Combs-Schilling, are also documented by Hammoudi. But these public forms now appear as pronouncements that disguise the activities and counter-representations made by women, and in this respect resemble men's pronouncements of the social links established through marriage as studied in Algeria by Pierre Bourdieu (1977: 30–71). Moroccan ritual activity, at least in some places, is not the unambiguous proclamation of patriarchy but a structured combination of official patriarchy and other forms, either domestic (such as the henna preparations for the victim) or interstitial (such as the masquerades). In these offstage events the socially necessary activities of women gain voice.

Together, the Moroccan and Gayo cases show how Muslims have shaped a particular set of ritual duties in sharply contrasting ways, with cultural foci that do not derive in any direct way from Islamic scripture, but rather are the products of adapting, elaborating, and transforming scriptural and other elements in directions that make sense locally. The contrast with Morocco might suggest a similarity to Clifford Geertz's *Islam Observed*, but it differs in its point of departure. Geertz began with the contrasts between Javanese and Moroccan cultures, especially with regard to mysticism and authority. The analysis therefore led him to underline those cross-cultural differences. The contrast here began from a religious obligation that Muslims recognize and seek to fulfill in Morocco, Indonesia, and elsewhere. The emphasis is less on global cultural typifications (Moroccan or Indonesian styles) than on the diversity of ideas and forms within as well as among Muslim peoples.

The kind of analysis illustrated here seeks to build up a richer understanding of what appear to be similar phenomena through a series of successive contrasts. Moving up levels allows us to find similar mechanisms governing differentiation within and across cultures should they exist. Perhaps the association between the social separation of men and women, on the one hand, and a religious opposition of reason to passion, on the other, is one such mechanism. It might explain both differentiation within Indonesia and differentiation between most Indonesian societies and most Middle Eastern societies (cf. Lindholm 1992). As emphasized by Greg Urban and Fredrik Barth (both this volume) no compelling reason leads us to assume that differentiation within cultures is governed by different mechanisms from that shaping variation across cultures.

Indeed, the Morocco/Gayo contrast points to a further caveat: the emphasis on male/female differences is not to be taken as essentially characteristic of one culture in contrast to others. It has been made the basis for public Moroccan performances, but it also is central to Acehnese notions of religion, as we saw earlier, for very different reasons. Recall that Acehnese notions of male "reason" and female "passion" were socially supported by a strong separation of men (who travel) and women (who remain in villages), a separation that was then projected on to the religious plane. Acehnese did and do draw from many of the same Muslim texts as do Moroccan advocates of patriarchy, and perhaps in both cases gender separations have led to similar religious interpretations. However, other cultural ideas (for example, about patriarchy, and the determination of person-characteristics by social origins) differ sharply between Morocco and Aceh. Political ideas do as well: Acehnese ideology diffuses authority across religious and other leaders; Moroccan ideology focuses authority on royal power (Munson 1993).

In this maximal frame of contrast within which we have been working we would eventually wish to point to many other ways in which Muslims have reworked the Feast of Sacrifice: for example, the Iranian displacements of the moral and political message of the sacrifice on to the martyrdom of Husain at Karbala (Fischer and Abedi 1990: 166–68), or the new understandings of the distribution of the sacrificial meat that have emerged among Pakistanis in Britain (Werbner 1988). These and other cases (for example, Holy 1991: 36–39) would enrich our under-standing of the range and limits within which the ritual has varied. The goal of this further exploration would not be general rules about when the ritual is observed in one way, and when in another, but rather an increasingly broad *and* fine-grained understanding of why Muslims in certain places have created certain ritual forms.

Notes

1 Similar ideas about the use of the animals as vehicles on judgment day are reported for Aceh in the nineteenth century (Snouck Hurgronje 1906, I: 243) and for Java (Woodward 1989: 86).
2 See Bowen (1993b) for an extended account of this genre.

8   Producing an analytic narrative

Margaret Levi

> Of course the method of presentation must differ in form from that of
> inquiry. The latter has to appropriate the material in detail, to analyze
> its different forms of development, to trace out their inner connection.
> Only after this work is done, can the actual movement be adequately
> described.
>
> Karl Marx, "Afterword to the Second German Edition," *Capital*: 301

Democratic governments have a strong interest in promoting behavioral
consent, compliance with the demands of government that is freely
given. Behavioral consent lowers the transaction costs of governance by
reducing the need for monitoring and enforcement, but it is also a sine
qua non of democracy. Without a considerable degree of consent, a
regime is not, by definition, a democracy. But how do we know consent
– or its absence – when we see it? Compliance is an incomplete
surrogate. People comply for all kinds of reasons: fear of sanctions from
governments or other citizens, economic returns, altruism, and ethical
commitments that are rationally and strategically implemented.
Although standard rational choice offers models of variation in compliance based on tangible incentives and sanctions, rational choice theorists generally fail to capture the ethical elements in the citizen's decision
to behaviorally consent, particularly when the costs to the individual
appear to exceed the benefits. As with studies of voting and some forms
of collective action, standard rational choice accounts offer more guidance to understanding why people do not cooperate than why they do.
Rational choice has an especially difficult time – and, according to some,
should not even try – accounting for why people pay taxes when there is
little likelihood of being caught for nonpayment; why recipients of
welfare and unemployment insurance report earnings higher than a
certain amount; and why young men volunteer to risk their lives in war.

In *Consent, Dissent, and Patriotism* I draw on rational choice theory to
develop a model of the conditions under which citizens will give or
refuse their consent. Contingent consenters are rational actors in the
sense that they are strategic and calculative of costs and benefits, but

152

they are also ethical actors seeking to do the right thing. *Contingent consent* is a citizen's decision to comply or volunteer in response to demands from a government *only if* she perceives government as trustworthy, she is satisfied that other citizens are also engaging in ethical reciprocity, and she calculates the costs of compliance as bearable. The first two conditions are necessary conditions; the third increases the percentage of contingent consenters.

A trustworthy government is one whose procedures for making and implementing policy meet prevailing standards of fairness and which is capable of credible commitments. In both contingent consent and contingent refusal to consent, the assessment of the actual policy can make a difference. However, I am assuming that in most cases citizens are willing to go along with a policy they do not prefer as long as it is made according to a process they deem legitimate, and they are less willing to comply with a policy they like if the process was problematic.

Ethical reciprocity refers to the norm of contributing one's fair share as long as others are also doing their part. Contingent consenters are strategic but ethical actors; they want to cooperate if others are also cooperating. They wish to be fair, but they do not wish to throw their contribution away. Thus, ethical reciprocity is distinct from social pressure. The first is a matter of both ethics and tit-for-tat; the second is a question of selective incentives.

An assessment of costs and benefits also influences the decision to comply, but they are not the only consideration of contingent consenters. Even when short-term material self-interest would make free riding the individually best option, the contingently consenting citizen still prefers to cooperate. However, if the costs of compliance become too high, then a cost-benefit calculation will probably trump other considerations.

My empirical aim is to determine how much of the compliance we see in democracies might be attributed to contingent consent. Contingent consent is only one source of compliance (see Figure 8.1). Analytically, citizens may also comply because they are opportunistically obedient and calculate only the individual costs and benefits of the decision. There are some additional reasons for compliance, of course,[1] but these are the two of interest for this chapter.

In order to investigate the extent of contingent consent, I consider variations in volunteering for military service during both peace and wartime over the past 200 years in six countries; Australia, Britain, Canada, France, New Zealand, and the United States. During the nineteenth and twentieth centuries democratic governments expended considerable resources on constructing armies and ensuring that they

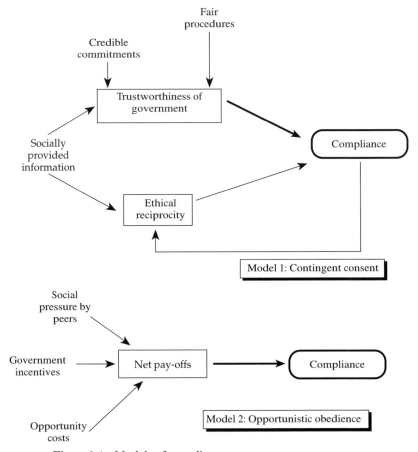

Figure 8.1. Models of compliance.

have popular support. I am particularly interested in how democratic governments have encouraged young men (and, more recently, young women) to serve willingly and even enthusiastically and why that behavior seems to vary over wars and across countries.

The link between theory and hard empirical research is emerging as a major rational choice enterprise, particularly in economic history and comparative politics. Recent criticism of rational choice (for example, Green and Shapiro 1994) argues that it has failed to explain much of anything. Wrong though this is, there is a grain of truth in the critique. Rational choice has yet to demonstrate satisfactorily its empirical power. There has been more emphasis on the development of formal theory than on how to use formal theory in the service of explaining actual events and choices. On the other hand, the richly detailed accounts provided by the best comparativists and historians tend to lack a theory that makes it possible to generalize from the cases or even compare other cases. One possible solution is the creation of analytic narratives,[2] accounts that respect the specifics of time and place but within a framework that both disciplines the detail and appropriates it for purposes that transcend the particular story.

An analytic narrative requires an explicit demonstration of the formal structure of the argument, elaboration of the story in which the theoretical puzzle is embedded, and, finally, consideration of how to put the theory at risk. Theory by itself will not suffice, nor will a stockpiling of details. It does, however, require of those whose lifeblood is archival and field research to invest in the development of formal theoretical skills. Such scholars, among whom I include myself, often use a mode of inquiry that appears distinct from their mode of presentation. This does not, however, make us inductive theorists, at least in the conventional sense. The work is still informed by a deductive model, and its end result should be an even better deductive theory as well as an explanation of the particular empirical puzzle under consideration.

Reliance on deductive theory[3]

To study contingent consent, I begin with a deductive model that generates some testable, or at least observable, hypotheses. Then, to the extent possible, I evaluate those hypotheses with case studies, linked by theoretical concerns rather than by time and place. However, the deductive model with which I start the investigation and the one that motivates the presentation of my findings are not the same. Rational choice, with its microfoundations in the aggregation of individual decisions, informs the inquiry and aided me in developing the general model of contingent consent, but the explanatory theses often grew out of the empirical research. This, of course, raises a question at the outset to which I will return later: having developed the model in the process of exploring the data, how can I then claim an independent confirmation of the data? Before turning to this thorny problem, however, let me first consider the constraints on my investigation created by my initial commitment to using rational choice as my principal road map.

I first deduce a short list of "fundamental utilities" (also see Scharpf 1990: 484–85). Given that one utility function is far easier to model than more, my preference, when possible, is to posit one fundamental utility. In many cases, by considering what is of central concern about the person or persons being studied, one can then deduce what is the most likely utility function. For example, if one is investigating people buying and selling, maximizing wealth seems a reasonable assumption. If one is researching peasants in risky environments, maximizing security has some appeal. If one is writing about the choice of policies by rulers, maximizing revenues to the state is one possibility (Levi 1988) and maximizing security in office another (Geddes 1994). Obviously, the assumption of a fundamental utility radically simplifies the world and the people within it, but, if done with attention to the problem, it simplifies the world realistically and usefully.

Clarifying the utility function is not enough given that individuals make choices within constraints. Thus, the next step is to specify those constraints. The deductive model provides a road map through the morass of detail. I then use this road map to specify the actual institutional arrangements that give precision to the constraints operating in the time and place under investigation.

From the combination of the utility function and the constraints, I can then theorize the likely choices and outcomes of behavior. For example, in *Of Rule and Revenue* (1988) I argued that the reason why the Roman Senate of the late Republic maintained the institution of tax farming, even when it was demonstrably corrupt, had more to do with the relative bargaining power of potential publicans than with the transaction costs of creating a capacity for state revenue collection. I drew on my more general "theory of predatory rule" to deduce the factors and propositions relevant to the investigation of this very particular instance. In *The Fruits of Revolution* (1992), Jean-Laurent Rosenthal demonstrates how wealth-maximizing individuals failed in their efforts to improve water control (or did not even try) in pre-Revolutionary France when property rights were ambiguous and authority dispersed, but that the change in institutional arrangements clarified both property rights over water and judicial/administrative authority in a way that facilitated water management after the Revolution. Rosenthal's account of pre- and post-Revolutionary France offers a solution to a puzzle in French history and a model for understanding the conditions for effective irrigation and drainage elsewhere. He does this by drawing on a more general theory of the factors that inhibit or facilitate economic growth.

In *Consent, Dissent, and Patriotism* (1993) I face a somewhat different problem. Citizens qua citizens do not necessarily have a single purpose; the institutions of government tend to order the preferences of rulers but not of citizens. To put it another way, the citizen's utility function is complex and has a number of arguments, including personal wealth-enhancement and, for many, some concern with duty and the promotion of the general welfare. I assume that those who are most likely to contingently consent are strategic actors who wish to contribute to the collective enterprise. However, as with the choices of rulers, the choices of citizens also reflect constraints. For citizens, those constraints are the costs of compliance (or noncompliance) and the likely behavior of others.

Case studies

Having engaged in the first step of deductive theorizing, I then turn to the empirical study. As a consequence of the detailed investigation, I inevitably refine my model. Seldom do the data speak neatly to the model I have devised. Moreover, the material itself suggests solutions that I had not previously considered but that are consistent with the general theory from which I initially derived my propositions.

Data collection[4]

Many of the problems that we find interesting theoretically are not susceptible to statistical analysis. In my investigation of contingent consent, I chose to consider issues of compliance with military service rather than taxation or welfare rules, issues initially of more interest to me. I believed – and still believe – that I was able to get more systematic evidence on the variation in behavior in this sphere than in other policies constitutive of citizenship.

Military service is an important area of citizenship in which it is possible to observe relevant behavior. Even so I encountered some serious obstacles in my research. First, the statistical data were not as available as I thought they would be. No country has kept comparable or complete statistics over time on who joins up and who does not, and cross-country comparisons have proved difficult at best. Moreover, whole years and sets of records are missing. A fire in the St. Louis depository that held all the US draft records is one kind of reason. More arcane is the account of a small fire that destroyed relevant materials from World Wars I and II in the Australian War Memorial. The representatives of the British government operate under strict rules of secrecy concerning a very large amount of military-related material, and they uphold those rules rigorously. The Australian government operates with a greater openness. The problem arose because in the Australian War Memorial were records that the British had deemed secret and the Australians had not. The British resolved the problem, or so my reliable source tells me, by planting a mole archivist in the War Memorial. This mole lit a small fire in the relevant stacks and then disappeared.

The second obstacle was the accessibility of data even when there is reason to believe they are not missing. Having spent weeks meeting people who could introduce me to people who could give me a proper introduction to the head archivist at the Service Historique de l'Armée de la Terre at Vincennes and then spending days clarifying with her precisely what I needed, we discovered that the relevant material had, but a few years before, been transferred from the central to *departement* archives. When I returned the next year with further and different inquiries, a new archivist was in place. He listened to my questions and then had a young soldier usher me into a private room. The soldier set several file folders on my desk and permitted me to photocopy as much of the material as I wanted. I photocopied it all. Who knows what I will one day need and if I could ever locate those files again?

The British had a very different sort of access problem. They, like most of the countries in my sample, operate with a rule that closes records on military personnel for up to fifty years after the relevant war. However, when I asked about personnel statistics from World War I, the military historian in charge of the records informed me that, one, they were not aggregated, and, two, the only way I could get access was to get permission from each recruit or his closest living relative to look at the individual attestation papers. I concluded that even the National Science Foundation would consider the cost too high for what might prove a very low return on the investment.

Data problems led me to investigate the model by means of case studies rather than some large cross-national, cross-historical time series analysis. I must admit, however, that this was not my only motivation for doing case studies. There are still relatively few attempts to use modern political economy to provide sustained analyses of comparative political behavior in actual concrete settings. For both area studies specialists and historical macrosociologists, case studies have been the major form of research and communication. Although case study work – in both sociology and political science – may correct the lack of adequate detail common to broad comparisons, it usually fails to offer adequate causal mechanisms. This makes generalization problematic. Part of my aim is to use game theory and some of the theory developed in the new economic institutionalism to overcome this limitation in the case study approach. I am hardly alone in this enterprise, of course. The names of Robert Bates, Avner Greif, Jean-Laurent Rosenthal, and Barry Weingast, my collaborators in the *Analytic Narratives* project, come instantly to mind, as does the work of my political science collaborators in this book, Barbara Geddes, Miriam Golden, David Laitin, and Roger

Petersen. Others engaged in similar undertakings are Elinor Ostrom and George Tsebelis.

The reliance on case studies posed a third obstacle to my research, particularly in Australia, Canada, and New Zealand. These are countries with very small populations and very long histories of European colonization. Consequently, the secondary literature is spotty. On some issues it is very good, on other issues non-existent. This is in marked contrast to France, Britain, or the United States, in which so much of the history has been mined in great detail. Given the breadth of coverage I am trying to achieve, a paucity of secondary sources sometimes proved a real handicap.

Making incommensurate data commensurate

Although I engage in little of the way of standard statistical analysis, I am still engaged in the act of comparison. Throughout my cases, I am comparing behaviors that may bear the same label but that are either measured or constrained differently. Let me make this more concrete.

In one of the chapters of *Consent, Dissent, and Patriotism* I investigate variation in conscientious objection in three countries, the United States, Australia, and France, over three wars – the two world wars and Vietnam for the United States and Australia, and the two world wars and Algeria for France. Both the United States and Australia had statutes that made conscientious objection legal; France did not but none the less labeled certain acts of noncompliance as conscientious objection. In all three countries what was measured as conscientious objection was largely determined by the definition of the individual who engaged in the act, but the acts themselves were different. In the United States and Australia, the measurement was of those who registered as COs, those whom the courts certified as COs, or both. In France, it was of those who refused to wear a uniform or carry a gun and cited reasons of conscience for their refusal. Thus, throughout the chapter I had always to make clear the objects of comparison and my justifications for the basis of comparison. The reader may disagree with my choices, but I hope to have given her enough information both to agree (or not) and to come up with an alternative criterion.

In another chapter I consider government reliance on such practices as substitution and commutation, means by which a citizen can escape the draft by paying another to take his place or by paying the government a fee in lieu of service. France, up until approximately 1870, and the United States during the Civil War, permitted these forms of "buying out." However, the rules that regulated the practices were different across time and across provinces and states. There was, in fact, no obvious way to make the data commensurate. I used the data illustratively as indicators of who used substitution and commutation and at what price, and I focused my analytic attention on the politics that produced the changes in the rules. The variations in the institution of "buying out" rather than its statistical variations became the dependent variables of the chapter.

In the study of conscientious objection, the attempt to make the data commensurate revealed the effects of the rules of the game on behavior. In the study of "buying out," it revealed the effects of political and economic behavior – and norms – on the rules of the game. In both, it helped clarify what was, and could be, the object of investigation. The effort to make incommensurate data commensurate has another advantage as well. It is also useful in making a non-question out of what appears to be an empirical puzzle. The Irish and Scots disproportionately provided enlistees for the Victorian army, but the percentage of recruits of Scottish and especially Irish nationality declined significantly over the course of the nineteenth and the early twentieth centuries when measured against the percentage of their populations within the British Isles (see Figure 8.2). I discovered this fact in my own readings of the *General Annual Returns of the British Army* and then found it referred to in several important histories of participation in British military service (Hanham 1973; Spiers 1980; Fitzpatrick 1989; Floud, Gregory and Wachter 1990). At first glance, it seems that the decline in Irish participation in the British military is a nice indication of a change in contingent consent; after all, it correlates with a rise in Catholic Irish nationalism. However, the variation over time disappears when one controls for the decline in the percentage of Irish males in the British male population (see Figure 8.3).

This analysis of the data makes it hard to prove that the shift in Irish volunteering was a case of contingent refusal to consent, despite considerable narrative evidence that suggests such an interpretation. In this instance, then, the process of ensuring that the data at one point in time are commensurate with data in another point of time eliminated, rather than revealed, a dependent variable. It solved one part of an historical puzzle by showing how it was not such a puzzle at all – or at least not in the form it originally appeared.[5]

The analytic narrative

The detailed investigation of comparative materials offers a source of fresh insights about the initial model. Having started with behaviors that

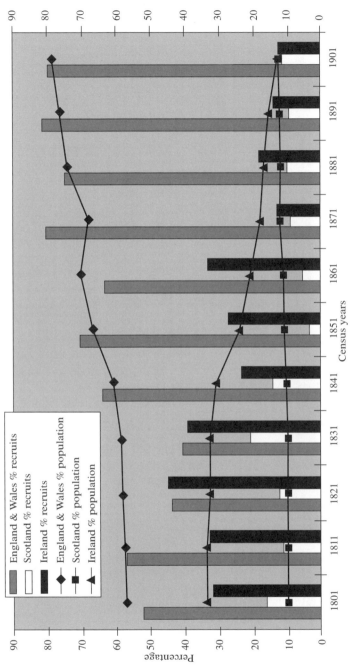

Figure 8.2. Recruits in the British army by percentage of nationality.

Sources: Floud, Wachter and Gregory 1990: 91, Table 3.4, for 1801–1901; Spiers 1980: 50, Table 2.6, for 1830–1912.

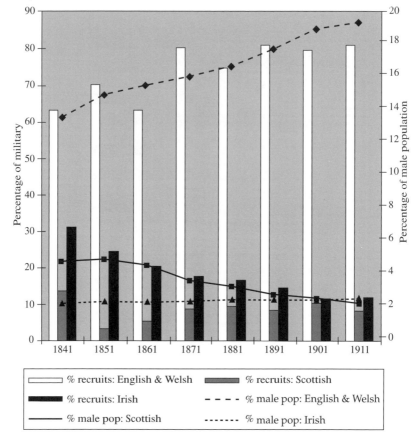

Figure 8.3. Percentage of male population in the British military by region of country.

Sources: Flora, Kraus, and Pfenning 1987: Vol. 1, p. 51; Spiers 1980: 50, table 2.6.

seem inconsistent with a rational choice model, the comparative cases generate ideas about how to explain these behaviors. Although the research involves a lot of "soak and poke," it remains constrained by questions generated from the initial deductive framework. Even more constrained is the presentation of the findings. Each case is a narrative in the sense that it tells a story and often a story of a unique situation. However, by generating a formal model, even the schematic game on which I rely, and then deriving the comparative statics the game

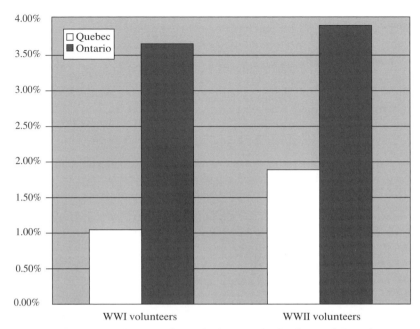

Figure 8.4. A comparison of volunteers in Quebec and Ontario, World War I and World War II.

Sources: Granatstein and Hitsman 1977: 160. All figures are rounded to the nearest one-tenth of a percentage point.

suggests, I am able to generate not only the hypotheses I believe to be compelling but also those I hope to falsify.

Again, let me be concrete. Canada during the world wars presents two distinct puzzles. First, what accounts for the variation in responses of the francophones and anglophones to government demands for military service? Using the two largest provinces, Quebec and Ontario, as surrogates for francophones and anglophones, respectively, there was much more resistance to conscription in Quebec than Ontario. Moreover, young men in Quebec volunteered at a much lower rate than young men in Ontario (see Figure 8.4).

The two models of compliance described above generate competing hypotheses for this variation. Either the inhabitants of Quebec faced a different incentive structure from their neighbors or they were less likely to consent willingly. Investigation of available data suggests that the differences in economic standing, marital status, and several other tangible economic factors were insignificant between the provinces (Levi 1997: ch. 6). However, a statistical analysis, in and of itself, is indeterminate; there are simply too many factors at play and the figures are too aggregated. An analytic narrative provides more compelling evidence for an interpretation based on contingent consent.

The second puzzle is the difference in timing of government conscription in the two world wars. During World War I, the government imposed conscription despite the opposition. During World War II, the government refrained from imposing conscription until very near the end of the war, and it was able to do so then only because of a successful plebiscite in 1941 in which the Prime Minister asked of the public:

Are you in favour of releasing the Government from any obligations arising out of any past commitments restricting the methods of raising men for military service?

In this case, as in most of the cases I describe in *Consent, Dissent, and Patriotism*, there appears to be a common game, a legislative policy game[6] that restricts the military service rules a government can enact and effectively implement. The establishment of policy in an electoral system can be modeled as a simple extensive form and nested game in which a government policy-proposer (a chief executive or minister), G, moves first and chooses a policy from among its menu of policies. The legislature, in the form of the median or pivotal legislator, L, moves second either to accept or reject the policy. Influencing the decision of the median legislator is, first, his or her political ideology and, second, his or her estimate of the response of the electorate. Given these preferences and this structure of the game, the policy proposers will pick and the legislators approve the policy that is most likely to appeal to the pivotal voter. This will be the equilibrium outcome.

Three factors will affect this equilibrium: the extensiveness of the policy demanded by government, the expansion of the franchise, and changes in norms about what constitutes a fair policy. Changes in what government actors perceive as the necessary numbers who must contribute and the necessary size of their contributions will shift government priorities and alter the trade-offs. Expanding the franchise changes the identity of both the pivotal legislator and the pivotal voter. An electorate composed only of nobles has a different range of preferences and values than does an electorate that also includes the bourgeoisie, which is different again from an electorate composed of the entire set of adult citizens. Finally, there may also be a change in the standards that the median legislator and voter use to evaluate policies. One line of argument I pursue in *Consent, Dissent, and Patriotism* is the extent to which changes in democratic institutions also change democratic norms, particularly conceptions of fairness.[7]

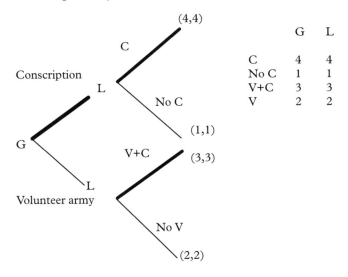

Figure 8.5. Large demand game 1.

Thinking about the process in this way produces comparative statics. The equilibrium outcome reflects the preferences of the pivot, but the preferences of the pivot change in response to: external threat (or ambition) and, thus, the demand for troops; composition of the effective electorate, and prevailing standards of fairness.

The case of Canada is one of high demand by the government in a system of male suffrage in World War I and universal suffrage in World War II. However, the women's vote is not what made the difference, given that the electoral split had a cultural rather than gendered basis. Francophone voters would always be the minority when their views conflicted with voters, as they did on the question of conscription. Many francophones believed conscription was unfair when Canada itself was not under attack, and they doubted the fairness of the treatment of their young men in an English-speaking and anglophone-dominated military.

In circumstances of high demand and relatively full suffrage, the pivot will prefer conscription to the choice of a volunteer army (see Figure 8.5), *ceteris paribus*. However, the existence of significant opposition may alter the outcome. If the opposition is strong enough, it will change the locus of the pivotal legislator and make volunteering the outcome. If the opposition is strong but insufficiently strong to secure its preference for a volunteer army, it may win concessions in exchange for its support. If it is weak, government can simply ignore it. The game tells us the preferences but not the clout behind those preferences (Figure 8.6). It

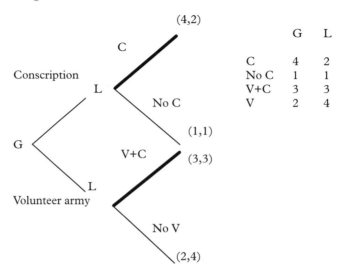

Figure 8.6. Large demand game 2 (with opposition).

does emphasize, however, the strategic quality of the choices; the choice of each depends on the probable choices of others.

This is, of course, another way to state the importance of pressure politics. However, what the theory of contingent consent offers is some insight into the reasons for opposition to conscription and what the formalization offers is a means to discipline the narrative. The formalization aids in the identification of what information is necessary to explain the outcome, and the subsequent appropriation of the details produces refinement of the explanatory propositions appropriate to the specific historical instance of the general phenomena represented by the game. Considerably more material is collected than is presented and on a far larger range of issues than can actually be discussed. However, without a limiting analytical framework the resulting explanation is ad hoc.

One piece of information the analytic narrative demands is the intensity and extent of opposition, but this is an obvious question for which one does not require the apparatus of the analytic narrative. Information that might not have been collected without the combination of theoretical modeling and formalization has to do with the effect of francophone opposition on the anglophone majority. Anglophones acted strategically. They did not commence World War I with enthusiasm for conscription, for they believed enough Canadians would volunteer to fill the ranks of the wartime army. Their reasons for choosing a conscription policy appear to have had more to do with the desire to ensure that the francophones do their part than with the level of demand for troops. By making conscription a legal requirement, the anglophones could compel equality of sacrifice from the francophones. Anglophone preferences, reflected in the pivot, enabled the prime minister to enact the policy he sought.

Mackenzie King, prime minister during World War II, may have preferred conscription, but his strategic calculation was different from his predecessor's. Moreover, he faced a legislative pivot less willing to conscript. Aware of the history of francophone riots and other forms of intense negative response to the imposition of conscription in World War I, the prime minister and legislators suspected that the costs of imposition might be higher than the benefits. They implemented conscription only when they believed that the government could find needed troops in no other manner. Moreover, they engaged in considerable groundwork in the francophone communities of Quebec and elsewhere in Canada before actually compelling service.

This short exposition of a particular analytic narrative once again substantiates the importance of a theoretical model to make sense of and make more compelling statistical findings. It reveals the importance not only of detailed investigation of the case but also of the role that can be played by game theory in generating, organizing, and illuminating the detail. Game theory, as this example indicates, demands knowledge of history; otherwise, it is difficult to make sense of the choices actors make, informed as they are by the actions of others in the past. Strategic decisions are based on calculations of what others are likely to do in given circumstances, and often it is history that informs those calculations, especially when self-interest can promote several alternative courses of action.

I am neither alone nor pioneering in using game theory and other formal models both to generate explanations and to constrain the narrative. For example, Elinor Ostrom (1990) among others uses game theoretic logic to consider the conditions under which local communities will devise solutions to common pool resource problems. Ostrom started with a list of the solutions derived from game theory, and all the solutions she discovers fit with one or another of the abstract solution concepts. None the less, by appropriating the detail, she discovers a whole range of rules and enforcement mechanisms she had not previously imagined. In his work on the institutional foundations of economic development, Greif (in progress) explores the history of Genovese commerce in the late medieval period. In the process, he discovers experiments that failed as well as those that succeeded in establishing secure property rights. On the basis of these findings, he is able to refine the model with which he began to make it more explanatory of the particular case, more general, and more realistic.

Analytic narrative builds on the work of positive political theorists and economists, especially game theorists, who have made considerable progress in uncovering the logical structure of many political economic problems. The new economic and political theory clarifies what factors are causally important and what junctures are critical. One of its major contributions is the folk theorem, that is, the demonstration that there is no unique equilibrium in a wide variety of interesting strategic situations. Having specified the preferences of individuals who must interact with each other in order to produce an outcome, formal theory can identify the range of available organizational structures or choices strategic actors might make. However, where there are multiple equilibria, it cannot tell us which structure or outcome will in fact emerge. The new economic institutionalism provides some guidance. Norms, institutions, and technologies narrow the choice set and often create a unique equilibrium outcome. Once in place, they may create path dependence, which in turn eliminates many potential equilibria in the future.

Norms, institutions, technologies, and path dependence are abstract concepts. The new economic institutionalism tells us what kinds of phenomena to look for to give these concepts substance. For example, the explanatory power of this approach is enhanced by the identification of institutions that promote credible commitments (see, for example, North and Weingast 1989) and cultural beliefs (Greif 1994). The theory on its own does not tell us much about either the origin, content, or form of the institutions and beliefs that produce and sustain an equilibrium. To get at these factors, we need to turn to the specifics of the case. We need to offer a narrative that links the theoretical concepts. For example, to understand francophone opposition to conscription in Canada requires knowledge that there is a norm of noncooperation with the federal government. The origins of this informal rule are past experiences, reinforced by government representative institutions that make francophone legislative victory nearly impossible. Thus, francophones came to distrust anglophone government promises and developed a rule, in the form of a norm, to protect themselves from the worst effects of government defections from its promises.

Kreps' important article on corporate culture (1990) offers a good example of the problem of explaining an actual result by relying only on deductive theory. The formal model leads him to expect and search for mechanisms that support trust among players as a means to reduce transaction costs. A hierarchical organization in which the hierarchical superiors possess a reputation for trustworthiness provides such a mechanism. Reputation can be effective in securing contracts and promoting relative efficiency even where there are likely to be unforeseen contingencies. For reputation to reduce transaction costs, there must be long-lived parties transacting with each over an infinite period and some guiding principle for dealing with contingencies not covered by the contract. Kreps uses Schelling's notion of focal points to argue that what maintains reputation is a corporate culture that provides both the necessary principles for decision-making and a means to communicate those principles to both hierarchical subordinates and other decision-makers. However, when hierarchy will be the organizational structure and which principles will compose the corporate culture requires case by case specification.

There is, thus, an interpretive aspect to the enterprise of analytic narratives, but the interpretivist insistence on meaning and intersubjective understanding often creates an overemphasis on specificity that obscures the commonality among cases and places. The insistence of rational choice analysts on revealed, constant, and exogenous preferences permits generalization by identifying the important differences in constraints among cases. However, this variant of rational choice begs the questions of the role and origins of norms and of how norms change. Political economic theorists are just beginning to address endogenous preference formation. The best work, such as Greif's or Laitin's or Putnam's, is linked to a detailed knowledge of the case and not just to a formal theory. An explanation of actual field or archival data requires an elaboration of the actual norms or institutions that are providing the focal point for strategic action, of the concrete junctures at which path dependence is begun, and of the tangible mechanisms that sustain the resulting equilibrium and path. Otherwise, it is analytics without a narrative.

Testability and robustness

Having told the story and offered an explanation are the first two of three important aspects of the presentation. The next step is to make the explanation offered in the qualitative inquiry convincing. Most rational choice theorists seem to feel that they have succeeded when they have demonstrated the plausibility of their account. Even more satisfying would be compelling support for the superiority of the explanation and indications of its generalizability. This is achieved by considering the theory in the light of alternatives, ensuring that it meets the constraints of a formal model, and/or exhibiting its robustness. Most of us use but one of these means; in the best of all worlds, the scholar does all three.

A major challenge posed by and to analytic narrative techniques is the problem of observational equivalencies. The same data can be "read" in two different ways. Different analyses produce different explanations of the same phenomenon. In some cases, the explanations are non-complementary. For example, government expenditures on welfare go down, and fewer people demand welfare benefits. Is this because fewer individuals need welfare or because many poor people doubt that they will qualify and so do not bother asking?

Observational equivalencies can also be complementary. Illustrative is Ferejohn's (1991) contrast of the Whig, interpretivist, and rational choice (or neo-Whig) accounts of parliamentary elections in early Stuart England. In my own work on conscientious objectors, when the costs of becoming a CO go down and the ideological reasons for opposition increase, there is a rise in applications for CO status. Are both concerns equally applicable, or is one dominating the other? In both of these examples, attention to the meanings the actors assign to actions supplements the rational choice account and provides a fuller explanation.

The most common approach to demonstrating the superiority of an explanation is to test it against alternative explanations. This demands identification of data that arbitrates among competing accounts. Even when done relatively well, consideration of competing accounts is only partially satisfying, however. First, most of us have gone to some lengths to document the plausibility of our arguments by showing their fit with the facts. To do justice to someone else's argument requires a nearly equal amount of space. The other hypotheses seldom get equal weight, no matter how good the attentions of the scholar; generally, the strategy is simply to show the inconsistency of the alternative with certain key pieces of evidence. Secondly, there may be no extant alternative explanation. Does this require the author to construct one out of whole cloth? Thirdly, social science may benefit here from the model of science, in which it is incumbent upon the author to make the strongest case possible for her position and incumbent upon the critic to tear it down or present a more satisfying theory.

Another means of providing support for a theory is through formalization. Formalization helps put a theory at risk by constraining the logic and clarifying the key variables. Formalization promotes rigorous argumentation and structures statistical analysis. It does not improve our capacity to do statistical analysis of questions for which the statistics are not adequate, but it can improve our capacity to identify the factors that must be present, the necessary causal relationships, and the mechanisms that link them.

The third means to provision of compelling support for the explanation is through consideration of out-of-sample cases. Thus, the presentation often ends with a discussion of cases not tied to the original empirical investigation and source of insight. For example, in my recent work on military service, I conclude my own researches when young men join the military. If my argument is robust, it should also explain a variety of other instances in which compliance with government policy is at issue. This led me to consider research done by others on soldier compliance with officers in the French military during World War I (Leonard Smith 1994), variation in compliance with government policies in Australia and the United States, and tax evasion throughout history (Levi 1988).

The concern with robustness and testability marks the presentation as well as the inquiry. In most work in history or comparative politics, the explication of the case or cases under investigation is sufficient. For analytic narrative, equally important may be the extent to which the model generalizes to other cases. The deductive approach facilitates the development not only of particular theories that explain the particular case but also of general theories with a wider applicability. This is harder to do with inductive approaches. It is not all that easy with deductive theory. Given the complexity of the social world and the limits of our techniques of understanding, the best we can do at this point is probably some version of Coleman's "sometimes true theories" (Scharpf 1990: 484).

Conclusion

> There is no royal road to science, and only those who do not dread the fatiguing climb of its steep paths have a chance of gaining its luminous summits.
>
> Karl Marx, "Preface to the French Edition," *Capital*: 299

I end this essay as I began – with Marx. His aim was to uncover the general laws of society. Mine is a far more modest but none the less daunting project. I wish to develop a model that explains actual behavior that we commonly observe. The process of developing the model requires both deductive reasoning and empirical investigation. The process of explanation requires making the model more precise and then using it not only to tell a story but also to identify the aspects of the story that produce focal points among the multiple equilibria and that determine and sustain the paths a particular society or group takes. The process of identifying what we commonly observe is at the heart of this enterprise. It often involves bringing into the light what we did not notice before. It certainly involves reinterpreting what we see. Having a testable model of contingent consent, for example, demands learning how to read compliance and noncompliance as political expressions of contentment or discontent with government and its policies.

To offer up compellingly a model such as contingent consent requires an analytic narrative that informs both the inquiry and its presentation. Exposition of all the detailed material appropriated is dissatisfying as explanation or narrative, but its collection is essential for refining and specifying the model. Once the model is clear, then analytic narrative is both possible and preferable, that is, if the aim is to help build "the royal road to science."

Notes

1   For example, compliance may result from strong moral views or habits that make individuals indifferent to the personal costs of the action. See Levi 1997 for an elaboration.
2   This is a term that defines the approach taken by Robert Bates, Avner Greif, Jean-Laurent Rosenthal, Barry Weingast, and myself in our joint book (1998).
3   This section draws on Levi 1991.
4   This section draws heavily on the introduction to *Consent, Dissent, and Patriotism*.
5   There are still issues of Irish participation that become evident during the controversy over the introduction of conscription in Britain in World War I.
6   Barry Weingast suggested this game to me.
7   If such changes do occur – and I believe they do – then they will alter the preferences of the pivot and, thus, the policies proposed by the government actors. For example, in the chapter on "buying out," I argue that neither the demands on government nor the extension of the franchise provides an adequate explanation of change in the views of the median on commutation and substitution. The emergence of democratic norms seems a necessary component of the explanation. On the other hand, who could and was likely to vote influenced when – and if – the governments of Australia, Britain, Canada, New Zealand, and the United States introduced overseas conscription in World War I.

9   Political consciousness on Boa Ventura: 1967 and 1989 compared

Allen Johnson

On the basis of research conducted on a Brazilian *fazenda* in 1966–67 (Johnson 1971), I formulated a hypothesis concerning the emergence of class consciousness among tenant farmers in a highly class-structured society (Johnson 1975). Recent restudies in 1988–89 offer the opportunity to evaluate that hypothesis in the light of twenty-two years of significant change in the Brazilian political economy. In this paper I will illustrate the value of long-term research (field studies of the same community over many years) as a type of comparative research capable of generating and testing hypotheses of theoretical and practical importance.

I will show that the tenant farmers' political consciousness – that aspect of thought and belief relevant to political action – has changed substantially during a quarter-century of change in Brazil at large, in a direction that partially (but not entirely) confirms my original hypothesis. I will also argue that, in speaking of a change in political consciousness, we are not so much speaking of the transformation of one belief into another, as of a shift in the weights assigned to the elements of a complex of interrelated, sometimes contradictory, beliefs.

The theoretical problem

During my original field research on Boa Ventura in 1966–67 I lived for a year among forty-five households of peasant sharecroppers (*moradores,* or "tenants") who raised subsistence and cash crops on land provided by a wealthy absentee landlord, in return for which they provided the landlord with shares of their harvest or days of labor as their "fund of rent" (Wolf 1966: 9–10). As I came to know them well, I became increasingly aware that they did not express the resentment and desire for political change that I had assumed would naturally accompany their extreme poverty and the many insults they experienced as occupants of the lowest rungs of an extremely class-stratified society. With very rare exceptions, the heads of household with whom I became well ac-

173

quainted did not view the landlords they knew as class enemies, despite
a prevailing view among social scientists at that time that the landlord
was "the most important social enemy of the peasants" (Quijano 1967:
306). Furthermore, although Boa Ventura is located in the interior of
Brazil's northeast, only a few hundred kilometers from the Atlantic
coast, no one expressed any interest in or much knowledge about the
dramatic political events surrounding the *ligas camponesas* (peasant
leagues) that had only a few years earlier struck the coast. Such was the
political force of the ligas camponesas that they were a major factor in
the military coup of 1965, which severely repressed them (Ames 1987:
160).

To the contrary, the *moradores* of Boa Ventura were most interested in
forming personal (patron-client) ties with landlords, not only their own,
but also those on neighboring fazendas. Rather than chafe broadly at the
injustice of class society, their focus narrowed to the comparative
generosity or stinginess of particular landlords. Not only were they not
resentful of their dependence on patrons, they actually viewed dependence as a source of strength (cf. Hutchinson 1966: 18). To distinguish
it from "proletarian consciousness," I named the viewpoint of the
tenants "client consciousness" (Johnson 1975). Whereas proletarian
consciousness is a true class consciousness where the workers recognize
that their solidarity is a potent weapon in the struggle to achieve a
greater share of the political (and economic) pie, client consciousness is
not class consciousness at all. It is, in fact, a kind of opposite: clients
orient themselves toward powerful class superiors to whom they pledge
loyalty in exchange for largesse.

The patron-client relationship orients the worker to the landlord for his greater
personal security. Since the landlord has limited resources, each worker is
automatically in competition with every other worker for his favors ... Most
landlords use this fact to encourage loyalty and thereby to reduce the amount of
passive resistance and small-scale cheating which peasants are prone to exhibit
... Thus, in a socio-economic environment which leaves the poor man without
land or security of any kind, the patron-client relationship offers a degree of
security unavailable by any other means; the price he pays is a loss of
independence, which in this setting is also a gain, and an increased isolation
from his fellows, who are as poor and weak as he is. (Johnson 1975: 14)

The tendency of client consciousness to encourage an isolating competitive relationship with fellow tenants, in contrast to the political inter-
dependence and mutuality of interests implied by proletarian
consciousness, is illustrated in Figure 9.1.

In order to understand this empirical finding, I had to reexamine
certain theoretical assumptions with which I had entered the field. In

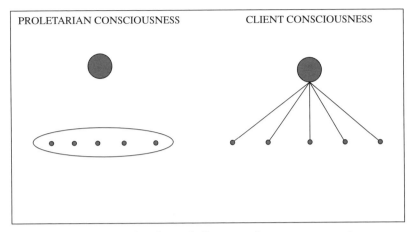

PROLETARIAN CONSCIOUSNESS   CLIENT CONSCIOUSNESS

Figure 9.1. Proletarian and client consciousness compared.

keeping with the tendency to assume a pervasive class conflict between peasants and landlords, theorists saw peasant revolts and uprisings in the past as very common events and as evidence for a simmering class rage poised for periodic expression (Wolf 1969: xii–xiii; Feder 1971). Class inequality in Latin America was regarded as obvious injustice, in the face of which peasants were thought to be too intimidated by upper class military and police power to express their profound but inchoate political opposition (cf. Wolf and Hansen 1972: 149–50). In many cases peasants were described as politically powerless victims of oppression, submissive and deluded by a religion that "nourishes the 'culture of silence' and contributes to a politics of despair" (Forman 1975: 55, 71, 219).

Such analyses had failed to prepare me for the viewpoint of the tenants of Boa Ventura. However accurate the literature may have been as a description of the objective class position of Brazilian peasants, it was still ethnocentric and could not serve as a model for the tenant's client consciousness (which I will describe in more detail in the section beginning on page 180). The prevailing theory did not address the rationality of peasants' understandings of the political economy and how best to serve their own self-interest within it. There was an implicit assumption that if peasants did not see the landlord as their social enemy, they were mired in false consciousness (cf. Lipset 1985: 50). But even if that were so – and I would deny that it is – the fact remains that peasants act on their own political consciousness, not ours.

Part of the problem was that by viewing peasants from a distance and in the abstract, as by definition the obvious victims of social injustice, theorists failed to recognize that tenant farmers, like humans everywhere, are actively engaged in evaluating their self-interest and formulating their understandings and their political activities to reflect that evaluation. Because their politically relevant actions do not conform to theoretical expectations of mass protest and revolt does not mean they are engaged in a "nonpolitics" (Forman 1975: 146) with no relevance to the greater political economy.

In fact, the political ideas of the tenants of Boa Ventura in 1967 were a complex mix of partly contradictory ideas. While they accepted their dependence on patronage, they also spoke proudly of their contributions to the landlord's wealth, through their labor ("the strength of our arms"). They would refer to themselves as *"os pobres"* ("the poor") and view the rich as having all good things, and they sometimes went so far as to point out that landlords did not seem to do much work to earn their great rewards. They knew that state power enforced unequal access to land and other resources, yet admired powerful patrons and sought their protection. They spoke of the need to treat the landlord with respect, yet told jokes and tall tales in which landlords and other elites were humiliated and ridiculed (Johnson 1997, 1998).

A problem for the social scientist confronted with such a complex set of beliefs is to specify the conditions under which one belief or another will be actualized into one form of behavior or another. Even use of the dichotomy of *ricos* and *pobres* in everyday conversation is not itself evidence for true class consciousness. Marx, and most students of class conflict since, knew well that the cultural construction of class inequality may take the form of a class awareness, or "consensus," that acknowledges and labels differences in wealth and status yet is a far cry from the "revolutionary class consciousness" that seeks radical political change (Morris 1979: 37).

The specific goal of this paper is to test a hypothesis concerning the conditions under which "client consciousness" and clientage behavior became converted into "proletarian consciousness" and such associated behavior as peasant syndicates, labor unions, or mass protest and political action (Johnson 1975: 15). Given that peasants on the northeast coast had only a few years earlier (1959–64) participated in the kind of political movement implied by class consciousness (Forman 1975: 183–8), whereas peasants of the backlands had not, what could explain the difference? Briefly, my argument was that agrarian society in the backlands of northeastern Brazil, with its comparatively distant center of national power – evidenced by a lack of legal protection for the rights of tenants and a complete absence of social security benefits and accessible public health services – left local elites as the only sources of security impoverished tenant farmers could hope for.

Patrons were sought-after sources of credit, charity, and protection from arbitrary actions of potentially exploitive class superiors such as merchants and policemen. The previous owner of Boa Ventura, who had sold it just prior to my arrival in 1966, had been such a patron, a wealthy man of esteemed family and such personal eminence that he had served as both general in the army and police chief of the state capital. He acted both as a benefactor who provided free medicines and milk to families with sick children and as a local strong-man who strode around the fazenda with a Colt .45 in a hip holster and insisted (for example) that amorous youths marry the girls they had made pregnant. So loved was he by the tenants of Boa Ventura that more than 90 percent of those householdeads interviewed in 1966–67 said they preferred him over the new landlord and wanted him back. As one tenant put it, "when he left the fazenda, people even cried."

Yet this old landlord had required a higher rent (i.e., shares and labor) and was more authoritarian than the new one. Why this loyalty to a member of the old guard? The answer is that he was more protective than the new landlord: he provided credit to tide families over temporary shortages, medicines and other health care for the ill, and patronage in dealing with such outside institutions as police and hospitals. From the tenants' perspective, his higher rent was an insurance premium, and the new landlord's reduced rent was a cancellation of the insurance policy.

In fact, the new landlord could be seen as a representative of a more capitalist way of operating, just as the old landlord could be understood in light of a more feudalistic/paternalistic system of landed wealth and noblesse oblige. In discussing this transformation at earlier periods of history, Wolf had commented: "What is significant is that capitalism cut through the integument of custom, severing people from their accustomed social matrix in order to transform them into economic actors, independent of prior social commitments . . ." (1969: 279).

I would modify Wolf's comment slightly, to point out that people were always economic actors, in the sense of evaluating their options and making choices, but the rules of the game had changed: landlords could no longer be counted on to observe their customary obligations. Wolf goes on to argue that, with capitalism, not only are tenant farmers and other rural poor cut loose from patronage, the patrons themselves are displaced by new forms of power:

[Capitalism] mobilizes economic resources and renders them amenable to new forms of allocation and use; yet in so doing it also cuts the tie between these resources and any connection they may have had with traditional social prerogatives and political privileges. It proves a powerful solvent of the integument of power, exacerbating tension not only through its own action, but freeing also tensions and contradictions previously contained by the traditional system of power. As the economic resources of chiefs, mandarins, and landed nobles become subject to the movement of the market, their claims to social and political command are increasingly called into question. Many of their inherited titles end up on the auction block. (Wolf 1969: 283)

In Wolf's sense, the transfer of ownership of Boa Ventura was a moment in the historical transformation of a rural economy toward greater integration to national and world capitalism.

Hence, my original hypothesis (Johnson 1975: 16):

Proletarian consciousness and group action among rural workers in Latin America are creative responses to the breakdown in paternalism which necessarily accompanies the widespread transformation of rural society from its traditional, pre-industrial form to a modern, industrial-capitalist form. Where paternalism is strong, proletarian consciousness will be weak, and vice versa.

Galjart (1964: 21) and Hutchinson (1966: 17) had made similar arguments, although they saw peasant unions and syndicates as simply transferring the search for patronage from landlords to union leaders, rather than the true transformation of political consciousness that I predicted in my hypothesis.

My argument was similar in part to that being developed contemporaneously by Julio Cotler (1978: 73–74):

La relación de clientela se basa en la subordinación de una serie de individuos, de distinta posición social, a un jefe capaz de ofrecerles diferentes tipos de bienes y servicios, de acuerdo a su capacidad de movilizar recursos políticos en favor del caudillo. Esta relación de intercambio asimétrico se caracteriza por su naturaleza interpersonal, con el consiguiente efecto de diluir las identificaciones de los intereses de grupos, insistiendo, en cambio, sobre los estrictamente personales.

[The client relation is based on the subordination of individuals of different social positions to a patron capable of offering them different kinds of goods and services according to their ability to mobilize political resources on behalf of the patron. This asymmetric exchange relation is intrinsically interpersonal, with the consequent effect of diluting the identification of group interests in favor of strictly personal ones.]

Cotler (1968) described the relation between rural patrons and clients as a *triangulo sin base*, a triangle without a base. As in Figure 9.1 above, any pair of tenant farmers forms a triangle with the landlord at the apex, but the absence of a solidary link between the two tenants means that the triangle has no base.

Many changes are potentially likely to enable the formation of solidary links between formerly atomized dependent peasants: wage labor, contact with union activists, education, populist political activity (Handelman 1975: 48–61). My view was that change in peasant political consciousness happens *specifically* in response to the landlord's changing self-interest and political outlook. With the increasing rationalization of the Brazilian economy, landlords would seek to transform their relations with labor from the old, quasi-feudal patron-client relationship into an employer-employee relationship where the landlord's responsibility to labor was to pay wages and nothing else. Providing subsistence opportunities and social security benefits would increasingly seem like a waste of money and resources to landlords who would rather use their scarce lands exclusively for cash-crop production to meet the opportunities of Brazil's growing economy. As landlords lost interest in patronage, tenants would find them decreasingly satisfactory sources of security and would turn to political activism to preserve what they could of their families' security. It would be the changing political economy of Brazil, therefore, that would weaken the tenants' loyalty to landlords and other local elites and strengthen their sense of the value of class solidarity for achieving political goals.

Theoretically, my hypothesis assumed that political consciousness at any moment in time is but a subset of all the beliefs and knowledge that subjects have of the political economy and their place in it. Given that tenant farmers could at one moment criticize the landlord and in another praise him, say in one context that dependence was humiliating and in another that it gave them strength, hold that the poor are powerless and yet have bargaining power, their political consciousness at any point in time would emphasize only some of these beliefs over the others. In 1966–67 their emphasis lay on the advantages of dependence on patronage. To put it another way, their relevant behavior indicated that they had selected from the available pool of beliefs and knowledge a subset that could be called client consciousness, in the manner in which many cultural beliefs undoubtedly come to hold sway:

Individuals may be exposed to a variety of beliefs or behaviors, evaluate these alternatives according to their own goals, and preferentially imitate those variants that seem best to satisfy their goals. If many of the individuals in a population have similar goals, this process will cause the cultural variants that best satisfy these goals to spread. (Soltis *et al.* 1995: 475)

Some of the fumbling reasoning out of which my original hypothesis emerged – especially the idea of peasant rationality – has since received eloquent exposition and development (Scott 1976; Popkin 1979). Key has been recognition that to understand political consciousness we must pay close attention to the experiences and expressions of those whose political consciousness we wish to understand.

How else can a mode of production affect the nature of class relations except as it is mediated by human experience and interpretation? Only by capturing that experience in something like its fullness will we be able to say anything meaningful about how a given economic system influences those who constitute it and maintain it or supersede it ... To omit the experience of human agents from the analysis of class relations is to have theory swallow its own tail.

... In place of simply assuming a one-to-one correspondence between "objective" class structure and consciousness, is it not far preferable to understand how those structures are apprehended by flesh-and-blood human actors? Class, after all, does not exhaust the total explanatory space of social actions. Nowhere is this more true than within the peasant village ... Neither peasants nor proletarians deduce their identities directly or solely from the mode of production, and the sooner we attend to the concrete experience of class as it is lived, the sooner we will appreciate both the obstacles to, and the possibilities for, class formation. (Scott 1985: 42–43)

Political consciousness on a Brazilian fazenda: a comparison of two points in time

Longitudinal comparison as a research strategy

My purpose here is to explore change on Boa Ventura between 1967 and 1978 as an example of the anthropological tradition of "controlled comparison" (Eggan 1954; cf. Nadel 1952; Johnson 1991). The idea of controlled comparison is to examine two communities that have much in common, in order that specific differences between them may be more confidently explained. For example, when Nadel compared the Nupe and Gwari, who were virtually identical in all aspects of society and culture, he found that Nupe fear of witchcraft practiced by women was more intense than was that of the Gwari. When he found a "concomitant variation," that Nupe women were much more active in trade and commerce than Gwari women, he believed he had an explanation for the differences in witchcraft fears, since strong and independent Nupe women were more frightening to their men than were the more traditional Gwari women to theirs. It is significant that he subtitled his paper on this subject, "An Essay in Comparison."

The present example may also be considered a case of such controlled comparison. It is possible to specify with much confidence the significant changes that have taken place on Boa Ventura and in its environs between 1967 and 1989, while holding most other relevant variables constant: the fazenda remains largely the same in size and function; the landlord and most of the *moradores* remain the same. Dramatic changes in the commercialization of the northeast, therefore, and in the social security system, may be confidently related to changes in consciousness, both for moradores and for the landlord and his family.

In this sense, the comparative study of a single community at two points in time is a case of controlled comparison, and is thus a "subgenre of comparison," as Bowen and Petersen put it. Indeed, researchers who have done long-term anthropological research generally view it not only as a means to generate hypothesis, but to test them as well (Foster *et al.* 1979: 9–10, 109–11, 325). For this reason, longitudinal comparison may also be considered a kind of natural experiment: the two categories (comparison and experiment) are not mutually exclusive.

There is an important difference, however, between a bench science experiment in a Petrie dish and a longitudinal comparison of sociocultural change. In bench science, the goal is to reduce a hypothesis to two variables: one independent, the other dependent. In a natural experiment like longitudinal comparison such reduction is not possible, nor is it desirable. Sociocultural change is generally systemic, in the sense that a number of variables change together. In the present example, tenant political consciousness, landlord political consciousness, tenant population size and density, land-use patterns, labor costs, technology, market prices, agrarian reform, retirement benefits and public health are all changing in a patterned way that cannot be reduced to a bivariate hypothesis-testing experiment. It is the change in the *pattern* that is theoretically interesting, and the fact that the pattern is changing in predictable and understandable ways adds much plausibility to the analysis. We cannot criticize the study on the grounds that a single variable may be changing in a chance, random manner: a whole cluster of variables is covarying in a definite direction that makes sense. The result may not have the precision and reliability of bench science, but it has great plausibility (validity).

Longitudinal comparison of Boa Ventura: 1967–1989

In the light of more than twenty years of change on Boa Ventura – based on research in 1966–67, 1982 (Caroso 1983), 1988 and 1989 – I would judge that my original hypothesis was about half correct. The change I predicted in the economic self-interest of the landlord has come to pass, and with it the rapid fading of patronage. On the other hand, I failed to anticipate a compensating response from the Brazilian national center, which has provided social security and health benefits that I could not imagine in the interior northeast in 1967 and has forestalled the emergence of revolutionary class consciousness.

Fazenda Boa Ventura is a private landholding of some 2,500 ha in the interior of the northeastern state of Ceará. *Moradores* raise subsistence and cash crops under one of two contracts with the landlord: either they pay the landlord one-half of the long-staple cotton they grow for cash (the *meiero* contract) or they pay one-third of their cotton and work two days per week for the landlord at the equivalent of US$0.35 a day, with no meals (the *sujeição* contract). Although it is startling to note (given Brazil's history of dramatic inflation) that the daily wage had the same dollar value in 1967 as it did during the restudy of 1989, the wage was in both eras largely a token payment – workers would flick a finger at the paper currency they were paid and make a customary clicking noise with their tongues, indicating its worthlessness.

Boa Ventura in 1966–67

Boa Ventura as it was in 1966–67 is described in Johnson (1971). For present purposes the following summary identifies the key characteristics for comparison:

1. The *moradores*, whether under the *meiero* or *sujeição* contract, expected to clear a new garden each year from hillside thorn-forest (*mata*) that had lain fallow for more than ten years. These new gardens were very fertile and productive sources of household food, including especially bitter manioc, maize, beans, and a nutritionally diverse array of lesser crops such as squash, sweet potatoes, sesame, and papaya.

2. As a security strategy to counter the frequent droughts for which the region is infamous, they also expected to plant additional gardens in a number of microenvironments, including especially the seasonally flooded margins (*coroa*) of Rio Boa Ventura, the river that bisects the fazenda. The value of coroa and other more humid lands was that they became especially productive in dry years such as 1987, when crops in many hillside gardens withered and died.

3. As a further security strategy, *moradores* actively sought patron-client ties with available elites, especially local storekeepers and landlords. From storekeepers they sought credit. From their landlord they desired loans of food or cash (to tide them over the major period of scarcity just before the new harvest begins), wage work during droughts, help in gaining access to scarce government-supported hospital beds, and intervention with police or other authorities in cases of trouble. They also maintained respectful ties to other landlords in the region and would boast of having invitations to join other fazendas should Boa Ventura prove undesirable.

As noted, however, my research came at a moment of transition. The previous owner, who took class privilege and noblesse oblige for granted, had recently sold Boa Ventura to a new landlord whose lower-class origins disappointed the *moradores*, their own pride being bound up to a degree with the eminence of their fazenda and its owner (cf. Wolf 1959: 209–10). When they discovered that the new landlord also restructured his relationship with them to lower their rent while reducing his obligations, they were openly upset. In him they discovered not a representative of old wealth but a new capitalist whose money was tied up in many ventures and who derived no satisfaction from diverting it to enhance the security of the *moradores*. Although he professed a certain fatherly concern for the *moradores*, he was both less intrusive and less supportive of them than the previous owner had been.

At that time the *moradores* had little knowledge of greater Brazil. Some had travelled south during catastrophic past droughts, but even they were not concerned about what was happening in the government or in other regions of Brazil. For them, all access to good things came from their own labors or through the influence of a powerful patron. Although they voted in regular elections – on ballots that had icons next to candidates' names for the convenience of non-literate voters – in fact they asked the landlord how to vote and rode to the polls in trucks provided by the landlord's political allies or elite patrons. None of this was hidden from view: men told me about it quite freely when I asked, clearly thinking it the natural way to vote.

Boa Ventura in 1988–89

In his field study of 1982 and our collaborative research in 1988–89, Caroso and I found Boa Ventura in many respects unchanged. Its boundaries remained the same, and the overall vista of forested hills checkerboarded with gardens in various stages of production and fallow was entirely familiar. Since 1988 and 1989 were wet years, it was quite lush and beautiful, although previous protracted droughts had caused great suffering. It was still owned by the new-capitalist landlord, and many of the same families occupied the same house sites they had over twenty years before. The most immediately noticeable change was that the number of morador families had declined by one-third, from 45 to 30.

Other important changes soon became apparent that, taken together with the decline in the number of *morador* households, most probably forecast the end of the *morador* way of life on Boa Ventura and perhaps throughout the region.

1. Seu C., the landlord, had substantially reduced the amount of *mata* he was willing to allow the *moradores* to clear for their main hillside gardens. Although one of his explanations for this move was conservation, using the discourse of sustainable development versus deforesta-

tion as a justification for limiting *morador* access to *mata*, a more immediate reason was his desire to increase his cattle herd, which depends upon the *mata* for forage throughout the year. The *moradores* complained bitterly, since it forced them to clear smaller plots in less fertile secondary forest, while fertile land under primary forest was denied them. But Seu C. knows the market value of beef and cattle by-products and is unmoved by the moradores' complaints. Moreover, one of his sons, a lawyer who has significant plans for change once he inherits the fazenda, buys cattle as fast as he can and brings them to Boa Ventura to increase the herd.

2. While reducing their access to prime horticultural plots in the *mata*, the landlord was simultaneously encroaching on the river-margin lands that were their primary back-up in case of drought. His reason here was that, by extending an old irrigation canal that brought water from a distant public reservoir, he could bring the coroa under permanent cultivation in sugar cane. He had already completed one part of the process by converting the existing irrigated areas: where in 1967 a dense orchard of diverse fruit trees flourished, in 1989 only a few remaining coconut trees loomed incongruously over a vast sea of cane. Now he was expanding into areas that had never been irrigated before.

He was most enthusiastic about this project in 1988–89, when he would come to Boa Ventura several times each month for visits of three to five days, supervising canal construction (with *sujeição* labor). He also refurbished an old outbuilding near his mansion house (*sede*), converting it into a processing plant where raw cane could be converted into *rapadura*, the raw brown sugar bars that are a local dietary staple. Several tenants described to me with admiration how clever the landlord was to aim at the local market for *rapadura*, since the price of *rapadura* had remained high even as the market value of raw cane was declining. Indeed, my estimate of the economics showed that the landlord could expect a profit in the neighborhood of 50 percent on his annual investment in *rapadura* manufacture. Even factoring in his capital costs in irrigation canals and processing plant – which were very low-tech and inexpensive – this was a most promising venture. Given the pleasure Seu C. derives from a good business deal, it is understandable that his overseer said of him, "All Seu C. cares about now is cane."

3. The landlord, in allowing their numbers to shrink, indicated that he did not value tenant labor as much as before. Once, when he began to expand his cane fields, he had experimented with hiring cane-cutting crews from the coast. These crews, while expensive, worked much faster than the *moradores* and could be laid off when their work was done. But the *moradores* complained that he owed them a chance to acquire the

necessary skill to work as fast as the coastal crews. Their lower wages certainly made them an attractive labor force if they could bring their productivity anywhere close to that of the skilled outside crews. The landlord agreed, and expressed satisfaction at their progress.

A greater change is in the offing, however. The landlord's sons have openly declared that, when it comes time for their father to turn Boa Ventura over to their control, they will radically convert it from its present management to a modernized, capitalized farm dependent entirely on wage labor. At that time, the *moradores* will be required to leave the fazenda and stop using its land for subsistence purposes. While their father has maintained a semblance of paternalism – for example, he guarantees aging *moradores* that they may stay in their houses even after they are too old to work – the sons feel no such obligation. Indeed, they express a general dislike of the *moradores* and outrage at their dependent attitudes and demands. They openly admire the new economic methods being employed on other modern farms in the region, and want to bring Boa Ventura up to that standard.

A related trend was the rapid growth of independent homesteads in pockets of private land off the fazenda. In part, these represented the offspring of an earlier generation of independent households, who had inherited and divided their parents' land. But in part it also represented the new generation of *moradores*, who were buying small house plots on which to build a house when the funds were available, as a first step in "escaping" (*escapar*) the fazenda: if they are good workers, the landlord allows them to continue to farm his land under the *meiero* contract even after they move into their own house off the fazenda. When the day comes that the *moradores* are asked to leave Boa Ventura, some will have their house plots and may succeed in finding other land to sharecrop. Others – perhaps the majority – will be landless with few options.

The restudy revealed several other dramatic changes. Most astonishing to me was the social security program that allowed even non-literate *moradores* to file for retirement benefits (*aposentadoria*) at age 66, and thereafter go each month to a nearby municipal center and receive their retirement pension in a bank. Everyone among the rural poor and middle class were entirely pleased by this development, which they regarded as virtually life-saving.

Of potentially great importance also was the presence of a public health post in the nearby town of Madalena. Ideally, *moradores* and others could come to the clinic for free medical care and medications. The reality in 1989 was that the health post had no medicines except birth control pills, and consulting hours were severely limited by a lack of personnel. Many tenant families did not appear to believe that they could get medical help in town. On Boa Ventura in 1989, for example, an 11-year-old boy whose ear was encrusted with discharge from a bad infection had received no medical care for weeks until members of our research team took him to town, where he was cured at low cost and completely recovered.

Finally, after electrification from the great Paulo Afonso project reached Boa Ventura in 1983, the landlord brought an old black-and-white television set to be kept in the *sede* and brought onto the veranda each evening so interested people could congregate and watch the popular *telenovelas* (soap operas) on Rede Globo, the leading Brazilian network. The *telenovelas* are preceded by national news programs that cover events from politics to natural catastrophes all over the country. Then a series of *telenovelas* presents dramas of love, power and wealth among largely white and affluent protagonists that draw a picture of modern life with consumer goods and urban occupations. Among the messages being conveyed are middle-class values and aspirations along with information on the workings of the Brazilian polity and the legal rights of the people.

When I asked *moradores* if they noticed much change since my original research, they affirmed strongly that much had improved. When I asked what changes impressed them most, they mentioned health services, social security, bicycles, and electricity. Although electricity affected them little, apart from access to television, the other three represented major changes. The bicycle was rapidly replacing the donkey as the main means of local transportation for tenants, and served as a store of value against inflation and a source of prestige. Public services filled the large gap left by the new owner's refusal to be an old-style patron. The way tenants spoke about Seu C. was sharply different from 1967, and could be summed up in the mildly approving formula, repeated to me often, that "Seu C. does very little for us, but he does not interfere in our lives, either." Although some people would still hold up a fist with tightly clenched fingers to illustrate Seu C.'s stinginess, when I asked one diligent and effective *morador* if he wished his landlord were more of a patron, he replied that he could live without Seu C.'s patronage: "A gente arranja o patrão quando precisa" ("One can get a patron when one needs"). And when another, who was planning to leave the fazenda to live on his own house plot nearby, was told by the landlord's son that he would be in trouble if he left, he replied, "I have nothing to fear: I have the strength of my arms!"

These men, both relatively young, reflect a new attitude of confidence that owes much to the increasing availability of government services. They explicitly commented to me that the landlord is a less important figure than in the past. Several men had been to cities like São Paulo, where they were exposed to a broader range of political knowledge and attitudes. On the one hand, they memorized the sophisticated political poems (*cordéis*) that circulate throughout urban Brazil, such as the following (one among many recited to me by a returned worker):

Já inventaron pacote	They've invented a package
Para embrulhar a nação	To wrap up the nation
Mas nele só tem aperto	But it contains only stinginess
Caristia e inflação	High prices and inflation
Tudo que o governo inventa	Whatever the government invents
O custo de vida aumenta	The cost of living augments
E piora a situação.	And worsens the situation.

On the other hand, this tenant's view of government remained complex, for he also told me that, although urban employers did little to protect their workers, that was because government provides for worker protection, including health care and unemployment insurance. He saw the same trend at work in Ceará.

Why did public services appear in rural northeastern Brazil, especially during the reign of a military dictatorship? Although the first social security benefits programs in Brazil date back to 1923 (Leite 1978), the expansion of social security benefits to the rural poor, including health care, old age pensions, and some aid to the disabled, became significant only following the first, repressive period of the military regime. By the late 1960s, having effectively silenced the left, the regime saw social security programs as a route to greater political legitimacy. With their power base primarily in the established elites, serious land reform was out of the question (Ames 1987: 165). Nor was the regime interested in building a political base among the rural poor. In the northeast, which received a disproportionate amount of government investment in health and education resources, government largesse generally took the form of grants to state and local elites, ensuring their support: "In that clientelistic realm, state and local elites were *patrons* to program beneficiaries but *clients* of the central administration" (Ames 1987: 176).

There was, however, another motivation for the military regime in expanding rural social security: as part of an overall increase in "the tutelary dominance of the bureaucratic (read 'technocratic') patrimonial state ... shaped by the ongoing logic of 'patrimonial statecraft'" (Malloy 1979: 132). In Malloy's view, there was very little rural pressure for these reforms (1979: 140). Perhaps ironically, we could say that the emergence of rural social security, so important to the *moradores* of Boa Ventura, owed little to any perceived danger of rural political activism, and equally little to the class-based political interests of the landlords. It was exogenous to the region, arising in a bureaucratic patrimonial state's goal of "expansion, rationalization, and technification" (Malloy 1979: 132; cf. Moberg 1994).

For our purposes, this represents a shift of rural workers' dependence from the landlord to the institutions that deliver rural health care and provide pension benefits. Since the services are paid for by a 2 percent tax on wholesale transactions in agricultural commerce, and much higher taxes on urban employers and employees, "the situation might fairly be characterized as one in which the urban poor are assuming the greater share of the sacrifice in subsidizing the rural system" (Malloy 1979: 139).

This is not to say that the *moradores'* needs are now being adequately met. Many health problems, including some serious and painful conditions, still go untreated because, although care is free (when available), incidental expenses (travel and lodging while waiting for one's turn) can easily exceed household budgets of poorer families. Yet the landlord's family remains unmoved and unwilling to help. On one occasion, for example, I was with his wife and younger son on the veranda of the mansion when an emaciated and feeble man of perhaps fifty with a walking stick approached to ask for help. Before he had gone far in his plea, mother and son simply got up from their chairs, walked into the house, and closed the door on him in mid-sentence.

This was consistent with the message I received repeatedly from the landlord's family, that Brazil's rural poor are lazy and greedy. This is not the whole picture, because Seu C., at least, says many affectionate things about the workers he feels are most loyal to him. But it is a constant theme in his conversation, primarily because of the growing concern over land reform and peasant invasions (*invasões*). During 1989 Carlos Caroso and I visited the site of an invasion in another part of the northeastern interior. A group of 270 families had taken over 1,260 hectares surrounding the central reservoir of a large (15,000 ha) fazenda. While the overseer emphasized the landlord's generosity (he had paternalistically employed many local poor in wage labor during a recent drought), the leader of the invasion stressed the landlord's injustice and was confident of the tenants' right to the land. The group had received legal and technical advice from a local Catholic priest. Later that year, however, the landlord brought in a strong-arm crew to demolish structures and physically remove squatter families from the fazenda.

Seu C.'s family had recently formed a family trust in an effort to shield their land from similar takeover. But one group of families was already laying the groundwork for a takeover on a strip of land between

Boa Ventura and an adjacent fazenda. Although common understanding was that this land belonged to Boa Ventura, it was never officially included in any deeds going back perhaps 70 years. A local radio station had been running weekly programs describing tenants' rights under the new constitution, until it had been forced off the air by an organization of local landlords. But the tenants had been emboldened by knowledge that a legal infrastructure now existed to help them claim title to land they had been farming for most of their lives.

On the defensive to some degree, although still wealthy and growing more so, Seu C.'s family had hardened its position toward the poor and become angry in talking about them. The following episode from my fieldnotes (July 13, 1989) is illustrative:

When Seu C. came in for the evening and joined me on the veranda, he came up to me and explained that there are people in Brazil who refuse to work, just hold out their hands and ask for money. They are dragging the country down. An old woman, blind in one eye from a head injury, begs around their house [in Fortaleza], earning 4 or 5 cruzados (US$1.50–2.00) a day. Finally, Carlinhos (Seu C.'s son who is graduating this week from law school) went out and yelled at her to get off his street. She no longer begs there.

At various times different members of the family have repeated to me that the poor do not want to work, they just want to be given to. Seu C. even said this to me sitting in the shade, while supervising his *sujeição* workers as they put in their seven-hour day at 5 cents an hour building the irrigation canal that would open more of their subsistence land to sugar cane.

Finally, two further brief episodes will help illustrate the attitudes of the landlord and his family. The first concerns a late evening on the veranda when Seu C. and seven *moradores* were glued to a Brazil–Argentina soccer match on television. At several points, Seu C. hunched forward, intently focused on the exciting game, virtually blocking out the tenants who were all sitting farther from the screen, yet he either never noticed or did not care that they could not see the game. The second occurred when Seu C. and his wife, Dona M., were preparing to leave after a visit to the fazenda: Dona M. upset the *moradores* by asking our research team to give to her all our dining ware and utensils, hammocks, mosquito nets, and other useful items. When we explained to Dona M. that it was our practice (and had been in previous visits) to distribute these as gifts to *morador* families, she was gracious about it. But the *moradores* complained that she knew all along that this was our policy. They saw her request as evidence that, for all her wealth, she enviously coveted our utensils and other possessions for herself and her family and wanted to deprive *moradores* of these gifts.

Generalizing the comparison

Turning now briefly to the other comparative issue – whether the processes identified in our longitudinal study of Boa Ventura apply in other cases of rural transformation – we can cite several examples in support.

1. In a nearby Brazilian case, Hutchinson's (1957) research on a sugar plantation between 1950 and 1956 documented a change in ownership from a traditional family corporation (*engenho*) to a large commercial firm (*usina*):

> The new corporation has brought about many changes in administration ... It has become, from the wider, community point of view, a strictly business enterprise with no family ties and no face-to-face personal relations. (Hutchinson 1957: 180)

Replacing the old, paternalistic ways with modern business methods, the new management alienated its suppliers and its workers:

> What was formerly a peaceful, "all in the family," almost preservelike area has become an area of tensions and of poor business, and social relations ... For the first time in the history of Vila Recôncavo the workers' discontent has taken the form of a strike accompanied by violence. (pp. 183–84)

A comparison between Vila Recôncavo and Boa Ventura would show similar processes at work between time 1 and time 2, in that the changing economic motivation of the owners was the impetus for a change in client consciousness.

In retrospect, Vila Recôncavo was a single instance of the growing rural discontent that accompanied the increased commercialization of the rural economy in northeast Brazil during the 1950s, when two related processes – the conversion of land from subsistence crops to sugar cane production and the reduction in the bargaining power and wages of rural labor – increased the insecurity of moradores throughout the region and fueled a growth in class consciousness (Furtado 1965: 127–43). A major influence radicalizing peasants at this time was the real danger of being made landless by business-minded landlords who, like Seu C.'s sons on Boa Ventura, no longer valued subsistence-oriented tenant farming as an economically viable business strategy (Forman 1975: 183–96). As noted earlier, the peasant leagues that arose in response to this situation precipitated the military coup of 1964, resulting a decade later in the vast expansion of rural social security programs that so dramatically altered the lives of the tenants of Boa Ventura.

2. Handelman (1975) relates the explosion of agrarian protest in rural highland Peru in the 1960s and 1970s to the breakdown of

paternalism as traditional landed oligarchies weakened. As McClintock (1981) has shown, Peruvian haciendas before the 1960s were marked by an extremely powerful landowner class that evoked client consciousness in the dependent peasantry:

> The landowner's wealth and power on the hacienda facilitated clientelist attitudes and behavior among the peasants. Peasants believed that the total pie of benefits could not grow, and hence that each of them was competing against the others for the favors of the patron. All incentives were thus individual ones. The patron was feared, for he could use his power abusively; but he also had to be cultivated, for only he could bestow significant favors on the peasant ... Both peasants and patrons said that the peasants interacted more with the patron than with each other. (McClintock 1981: 77–78)

In the 1970s, however, government pressure led the way in a transformation of haciendas into self-managed cooperatives. Moberg (1994) has described how in Peru and elsewhere a bureaucratic state has sought to weaken the political power of rural elites by encouraging the breakdown of the old paternalistic order. As would be expected from my analysis of the Boa Ventura case, the peasants in Peru did not take the lead in abandoning their client consciousness, but they quickly responded to new opportunities to join in the cooperatives once they had been formed, and to adopt a new set of political attitudes more favorable to collaboration with other peasants to achieve common political goals (McClintock 1981: 105–21). No doubt because a cooperative economic structure was imposed by government plan, peasants on Peruvian cooperatives slowly adopted more participatory attitudes than those seen in the Brazilian case, where cooperatives were absent.

3. Peasant political participation can also turn violent, of course. Throughout the history of agrarian states, even when rural patronage systems were stable, there have been – although perhaps less frequently and regularly than is sometimes assumed – revolts and rebellions, usually centered on various sorts of "outlaws" (Lampião in northeastern Brazil, Robin Hood and Rob Roy more famously elsewhere: Hobsbawm 1981: 59 and *passim*). Some rebellions, like Wat Tyler's in fourteenth-century England (Lindsay 1964), were no doubt strengthened by a growing commercialization of the rural economy that threatened the access of the rural poor to land, but most appear to have been momentary outbreaks of simmering discontent that ultimately failed to achieve lasting social transformation.

An instance relevant to the present argument, however, was the Huk rebellion in the Philippines (Kerkvliet 1977). In the early part of this century, central Luzon was populated by peasant rice farmers, the vast majority of whom cultivated small parcels of land as sharecroppers. Landlords entered into unwritten but widely respected contracts with tenants, that were understood to include such benefits of patronage as loans and aid in case of poor health and natural disasters. In return, the patron benefited from free labor, and his tenants constituted a political following that enhanced his social and political power (Kerkvliet 1977: 6–7).

Tenants had reciprocal relationships with landlords that carried both benefits and obligations. A tenant generally did not object to doing what a landlord asked because he was confident that the landlord would do, in turn, what the tenant expected of him ... [the] old hacendados had *"utang na loob"* – they complied with their moral obligations to reciprocate to the peasants. And they were not *"walang hiya"* – unscrupulous or disrespectful – towards their tenants. (Kerkvliet 1977: 8)

In the 1920s and 1930s, however, landlords in central Luzon changed: they became more concerned with running their lands as efficient businesses, and so did away with the old paternalistic understandings. "The reasons went beyond the behavior of individual landowners. The cause was 'progress.' In particular, rapid population growth, capitalism, and the expansion of the central government dramatically changed central Luzon" (Kerkvliet 1977: 17). Population growth reduced the bargaining power of rural labor, increasing commercialization motivated landlords to emphasize cash cropping over subsistence-oriented sharecropping, and government efforts to survey rural areas and rationalize legal landownership strengthened landlords' power at the expense of peasants' traditional land rights.

The peasants' initial reaction to this change was to insist on the landlords' paternalistic responsibilities. Only when owners refused did peasants turn to rural political organizations for both peaceful and violent actions. Although the government made sympathetic gestures in response to rural activism, little effective change took place and, unlike many of the tenants of Boa Ventura, peasants – as they became more politically astute through their political activities – came to see the government as primarily an arm of the landed class, reaffirming private property and the rights of capital in a free market system.

The whole situation was made more complex by the Japanese occupation and the role of peasants in resisting it, but the rebellion that finally broke out in central Luzon after World War II still drew much of its energy from opposition to the increasingly oppressive and violent alliance of government and landlords bent on maintaining an exploitive economic system without social security protections for the rural poor (Kerkvliet 1977: 161–62). In this light it seems especially likely that, in comparison, the Brazilian government's rural social security support is helping ease the transition to capitalist farming in the northeast without widespread political opposition from peasants.

Discussion

A distinctive type of comparative research involves restudy of the same community over a period of time (Foster et al. 1979). Long-term field research offers a unique opportunity to observe social and cultural changes as they unfold. That the research is done in the same community ensures a higher degree of "experimental control" than is usually possible in anthropology.

On fazenda Boa Ventura, during the period between my original fieldwork in 1966, Caroso Soares's 1981 study, and our collaborative restudy in 1988 and 1989, we can chart in a single instance the breakdown of a paternalistic political ideology that began when Seu C. bought the fazenda from an old-style patron and will be completed when he passes control over to his sons, who are eager to model themselves after the impersonal business practices of modern enterprises in the region. The previous tradition of noblesse oblige and protectiveness toward one's dependents is fading, being replaced by an angry disdain for a rural working class that is increasingly alert to legal options for land redistribution and willing to act accordingly.

The tenants have also changed their views. Younger tenants are eager to become independent, either by buying a small plot of land for building a house and hiring out their labor ("the strength of our arms"), or by squatting or invading fazenda lands under the agrarian reform law. Whereas two decades ago they complained about Seu C.'s indifference as compared to the previous owner, now they seem satisfied that he "doesn't interfere." They confidently claim that they can arrange patronage when they need it.

Although this change is part of a developmental trajectory that includes growing market penetration into rural areas and the developing technocratic state, certain specific changes have been especially salient to the owner and tenants of Boa Ventura. On the one hand, the landlord has increasingly seen his future prosperity to lie in the production of cattle and sugar cane, both of which require a shift of resources away from tenant subsistence production. Although he still benefits from the very low cost of *sujeição* labor, he values it less now, and values the shares of subsistence crops even less. His sons plan to expel all the tenants when he passes control over to them.

On the other hand, tenants' security depends much more on government programs than in the past. The change in landlord attitudes toward rural labor, being repeated in countless ways across northeastern Brazil, could have generated great anxiety and anger in the rural working class, but to some degree that anger appears to have been contained by the expansion of government protection, especially in the form of health care, retirement benefits, and land reform legislation. The tenants are grateful for the social programs that benefit them, and see land reform as a possible direction for them to gain land for themselves. So, although they have clearly begun to abandon their client consciousness, it is not clear that what is replacing it could be called proletarian consciousness (or any kind of class consciousness). True, the land invasions require group action and are political in the sense that activists from outside the community help organize them. But the interest of the tenants in such movements is quite individualistic: they do not seek to form communes or cooperatives, but to parcel out the land into individual homesteads and farms, to replace the fazenda with a neighborhood of free smallholders.

It would seem, therefore, that the solvent power of the market that Wolf referred to is working not only to dissolve ties of patronage and dependence, but to prevent the formation of rural working-class solidarity. Even if, as Malloy suggests, the government services were not provided out of a fear of rural political upheaval, they still have had the effect of calming a rural population undergoing profound social and economic change, giving them the sense that their worst fears – of catastrophic illness and old age penury – will be dealt with now by the state just as once they were dealt with by patrons. Very probably, as appears to have happened to the urban working class in Brazil, many will come to accept "the authoritarian-corporative values embedded in the state ideologies" that now underpin their health and social-security benefits (Cohen 1989: 116).

Conclusion

My original hypothesis has been partially confirmed by evidence from Boa Ventura at two points in time. The prevailing political consciousness of the tenants is undergoing change in the predicted direction, to the degree that the emphasis on paternalistic ties of dependence is lessening. Furthermore, it is clear that this change in consciousness is in response to changes from above, in the behavior and outlook of local elites and in changing policies of the national government. It could even be said that the growing willingness of tenants throughout the region to invade fazendas with the goal of obtaining land for themselves under land reform laws is a sign of emerging class consciousness and readiness for class-based political action.

But my original hypothesis overestimated the likelihood of rural class consciousness arising from the breakdown of paternalism, because in 1967 I did not foresee the social programs of the military regime taking the initiative out of the hands of the rural poor. For the moment, at least, that legislation has paved the way for some rural poor to become independent smallholders, able to get along without a strongly protective patron. Meanwhile the majority of tenant farmers appear headed toward a future as landless rural wage workers, whose political consciousness can be expected to take shape in accordance with the place allotted to them in the evolving political economy.

10 Comparisons in the context of a game theoretic argument

Barbara Geddes

The two roles of comparison in research

For social scientists, comparisons play different roles at different stages of the research process. At the outset, perhaps before the research question is ever formulated carefully, cases and outcomes capture our interest because they differ from other cases or from what theory has led us to expect. Such outcomes call for explanation because they are anomalous when compared with other known or apparently understood instances. At this stage, the comparison may be entirely implicit, and the analyst may focus on the anomalous case, but without the implicit comparison there would be no basis for considering the case under study interesting or puzzling.

At this stage, research may simply involve an unstructured and largely indiscriminate search for information about the puzzling case. As this search proceeds, abstract concepts that illuminate the non-obvious similarities among disparate concrete processes, typologies that order outcomes in ways expected to contribute to causal understanding, and speculations about causes of observed differences flit through the researcher's mind. Concepts and typologies are useful or not useful rather than true or false, and their utility often depends on the specific question the researcher has in mind; there are no tests for assessing concepts and typologies.

Hypotheses, however, can be falsified and thus shown to be useless. Because we have objective criteria and public procedures for assessing the value of hypotheses, testing them has become the central core of the knowledge building process. When causal speculations have been honed to the point where the analyst feels comfortable dignifying them with the label hypotheses, comparisons – sometimes different ones from those that motivated the original search for information – move explicitly and self-consciously to the forefront of the research task. Hypothesis testing requires making comparisons, usually across observations in which outcomes differ.[1] Hypothesis testing is not by any means the only research

196

task, but it is an important one, and ignoring it leads, on the one hand, to ideologically based debates as fruitless as they are acrimonious, and, on the other, to the laborious creation of elaborate deductive sandcastles eventually washed away by inconvenient facts.

The article reprinted below, "A game-theoretic model of reform in Latin American democracies," emerged from just such a sequence of different kinds of comparisons and illustrates the transition from implicit to self-conscious use of comparisons during the course of research. My initial interest in Brazil was motivated by a concern with economic development and the observation at the time (about 1980) that Brazil had grown very rapidly for more than ten years previously and, in fact, had enjoyed an average growth rate substantially higher and less erratic than many other South American countries, at least since the 1930s. It appeared at that time that the Brazilian government's interventions in the economy had generally had greater success in generating rapid growth than had those of other similarly circumstanced countries, and I wanted to understand why. In succeeding years, I explored many aspects of recruitment, training, decision-making, and political influence in the Brazilian economic policy-making bureaucracy.

One strand of this tangled skein focused on civil service reform, an innovation designed to increase reliance on merit as the basis for recruitment and promotion within the bureaucracy. Reforms in the training and recruitment of public employees were expected to increase the competence, honesty, and public service orientation of the individuals making important economic decisions, which would seem to be an unambiguously good thing. Nevertheless, such reforms, when proposed, faced obstacles at every turn, and rarely came to anything in practice. The history of the struggle over civil service reform posed the question of why a reform that seemed harmful to no one, except possibly those public employees who, in Albert Hirschman's (1958: 154) words, had found a "refuge from which to make a last-ditch stand for their right to a quiet, incompetent existence," should fail to occur.

The history of the struggle over civil service reform in Brazil began in the early 1930s with reform initiatives proposed by President Getúlio Vargas. The efforts of Vargas and his political allies failed to make real changes in bureaucratic procedures and performance, however, until after the president's seizure of dictatorial powers in 1937. Before 1937, Congress and the Finance Ministry opposed all significant reforms. Congress was closed in 1937, and the rest of the government was radically centralized. Among many other changes, the Vargas government began holding examinations to choose new entrants into the public service and established a powerful agency, the Departamento

Administrativo de Serviço Público (DASP), to oversee recruitment, promotion, the purchase of government supplies, contracts for services used by the government, and the budget in the rest of the bureaucracy. Other parts of the traditional bureaucracy resented and, where possible, obstructed the DASP and the reforms it implemented, but while Vargas remained in control they lacked the power to prevent change. With the return to democracy in 1945, however, the DASP lost power, much of its leadership cadre resigned in frustration, civil service coverage declined, and traditional patronage-based recruitment retook much of the ground it had lost during the dictatorship.[2]

Many elected politicians and most employees opposed civil service reform because it threatened to remove a traditional political resource from their stock. Jobs in the bureaucracy had been routinely used to pay for the services of local organizers and party workers, the people whose hard work was needed in order to deliver blocs of votes at election time. Party workers employed in the bureaucracy in their turn supplied the thousands of favors and exceptions promised by politicians to their constituents in the course of campaigns. Civil service reform thus threatened to throw a wrench into smooth-running political machines, and, as a result, threatened to undermine the traditional advantage of incumbent politicians (since office holders have much more access to patronage than those excluded from office).

Initially, I saw this situation as a collective action problem among politicians. As long as others used patronage to build support, no individual could afford to eschew its use, no matter how clearly he or she saw the advantages in terms of overall economic development or the provisions of public services of a more competent and honest bureaucracy. This formulation was not entirely satisfactory, however, because it failed to capture the often-observed preference of outsider parties for reform; it treated politicians as though reform would be equally costly to all. In trying to make the game theoretic interpretation more accurately reflect the real Brazilian struggle over reform, I hit upon the form of the game shown in the paper. This game, which assigns different pay-offs to different actors depending on whether they belong to the largest party (and its coalition allies), closely approximates the real situation in Brazil during the democratic period from 1946 to 1964 – no surprise, since I used the game to simplify and illuminate the logic of the struggle over reform during that period of Brazilian history.

In other words, the game is a hypothesis about *why* civil service reforms failed to progress in democratic Brazil. The game theoretic form of this hypothesis requires that the argument be logically consistent, that assumptions about the identity and preferences of relevant actors be explicit, and that plausible arguments about the choices open to actors and the information available to them be made.[3] These requirements inoculate game theoretic hypotheses against some of the conceptual sloppiness that often debilitates hypotheses, but leave entirely open the possibility of empirical disconfirmation. A game theoretic argument, like any other, needs to be tested, and tests are done in the same way as for any other, by comparing implications of the argument to events in the world.

Once this particular game was written down, an implication of the logic, about which I had had no prior intuition, became obvious. In Brazil, one party had remained the largest throughout the democratic period and, as the game theoretic interpretation would predict, no general reform had occurred. The pay-off matrix for this game, however, made clear that if two parties of approximately equal size dominated the legislature and saw their joint domination as safe for the foreseeable future, the game between them would become a prisoner's dilemma, and reform might under certain conditions occur.[4] Since no such distribution of party strength had occurred in Brazil, it was impossible to test this implication of the game theoretic model using Brazilian evidence. And, since the model aspired to the status of a general argument, its implications had to be tested. Fitting the Brazilian case did not constitute a test since the model had been developed to describe the Brazilian case.

The potential universe of cases on which to test the model was all democratic countries in which democracy antedated the professionalization of public service. I limited the cases examined to Latin America to keep the information gathering task manageable, but, in fact, there are few cases of democratization prior to professionalization outside the western hemisphere. In most west European and settler-colony democracies, administrative professionalization occurred prior to democratization.[5]

Though feasibility considerations often limit the cases one can examine, it is always important to think carefully and explicitly about the consequences of the choice of a set of cases within which to undertake comparisons. In this instance, the limitation of the comparison set to Latin America in effect holds constant Iberian culture and colonial heritage, factors that have been suggested as causes of administrative deficiencies in the region. These factors, common to all the countries, provide no leverage for understanding why reform occurred earlier in some Latin American countries than others. At the same time, however, this research design prevents reaching any conclusion about whether the Iberian heritage has, all else being equal, slowed the whole region's bureaucratic development. The research design also somewhat limits variance in economic development. Although the per capita income of Uruguay was several times that of Colombia between 1930 and 1960, all the countries are classified by the World Bank as middle income. In other words, the probability of civil service reform might be affected by gross differences in level of development even though no relationship between level of development and reform exists within this set of middle-income countries; this research design cannot shed light on this potential relationship.

Because the model predicted reform via solutions to prisoners' dilemmas and the literature on prisoners' dilemmas suggests that iteration is necessary in order for actors to achieve solutions to them, I further limited the universe to countries that had experienced fifteen or more years of continuous democracy since 1930.[6] I thought that democratic politicians might need a fairly long period of stability, unmenaced by threats of military intervention, in order to focus their attention on solving this particular prisoner's dilemma – which was not likely to be the most important problem they faced. Fifteen years allowed a generous amount of time for iteration, and I thought that if solutions did not emerge in that time, I would, sadly, have to dismiss the argument. The countries besides Brazil left in the universe at this point were Chile, Colombia, Costa Rica, Uruguay, and Venezuela. I had to exclude Costa Rica because its constitution prohibits the immediate reelection of legislators, which rules out indefinite iteration among legislators.

At the time of making these decisions about which cases to look at, I had no knowledge whatsoever about civil service reform in other Latin American countries – or the United States, for that matter. Like many others, I had always considered the subject boring and had managed to avoid learning anything about it in graduate school. In other words, I did not select these cases because I knew the argument fitted.

I felt great affection for, and pride in, the clever little game I had brought into the world with so much labor, and I was extremely reluctant to discover that it was worthless. This reluctance prevented me for several months from going to the library to examine the history of civil service reform in the four relevant countries, but eventually a deadline loomed, and I had to risk it. Much to my surprise, it turned out that where civil service reform had occurred under democratic auspices, it was initiated in every instance by a legislature or constituent assembly in which the two largest parties were approximately the same size. These initiations are described in the case study section of the paper.

A second implication of the game theoretic model was that if a period of party dominance succeeded a period of relative parity between the largest parties, no legislative extensions of civil service coverage should be expected. This implication also turned out to be consistent with the histories of the five countries. Not only did extensions fail to pass, but civil service coverage was often reduced informally during periods when one party or another dominated the legislature, even if the party had previously campaigned against bureaucratic corruption and incompetence.

In short, two important implications of the game theoretic argument proved consistent with events in the world. These two predictions of the model were tested in a small set of cases that contained two sorts of comparison: a comparison across cases between those that experienced reform and those that did not, and a comparison across time between periods (of approximate party parity) when reforms occurred and periods (of greater inequality) when they did not. Note that, although the number of cases was quite small, both kinds of comparison included variation in the outcome.

To conclude, although this study was in some respects atypical for political science, it used comparisons in the usual ways. It began as an interest in a large sprawling question with grand normative implications. I began to tackle the question through an exploration of an anomalous case, a case that aroused my curiosity because it differed from others that seemed to form a natural, though mostly implicit and unexamined, comparison set.

In the course of carrying out research, one must eventually simplify the discordant hodgepodge of information one discovers.[7] In this study, the first simplification involved a ruthless narrowing of the subject of interest to one of its more manageable component parts, civil service reform. The second simplification reinterpreted the struggle over civil service reform in Brazil in game theoretic terms. The advantage of this second simplification, besides the imposition of clarity and logical consistency, was that it directed my attention to features of the situation that I had not understood while concentrating on the Brazilian case, because they had not arisen in Brazil. Game theory, and formal models more generally, have several advantages over most other forms of causal speculation: they sometimes, as in this case, lead to previously unforeseen substantive conclusions; they tend to be highly fruitful in the generation of testable implications, going beyond what the researcher has already discovered while examining the instance that gave rise to the model; and they define theoretically and with great clarity the universe of cases within which predictions should be expected to occur.

Once the analyst has articulated a causal speculation, whether game theoretic or not, the next stage is to persuade others that it is correct.

Good research approaches this task by drawing out the implications of the causal argument, identifying the universe within which concrete evidence of these implications should be observable, thinking through the consequences of how cases are selected from within this universe, and presenting evidence that confirms or disconfirms expectations. It is at this hypothesis testing stage that comparisons are used most self-consciously by social scientists. A necessary though not sufficient foundation for the claim that a causal relationship exists is the demonstration that variation in entities identified as causes occur in tandem with differences in entities identified as effects. Such differences are only apparent through comparisons across cases, observations, or time periods. The analyst's choice of these comparisons – their theoretical appropriateness, their representativeness of the relevant universe, and their independence from the exploration that gave rise to the causal speculation in the first place – determines how persuasive the argument will be.

A game theoretic model of reform in Latin American democracies[8]

Bureaucratic inefficiency, patronage-induced overstaffing, and outright corruption retard economic development and reduce public wellbeing in developing countries. They prevent governments from effectively carrying out the economic plans to which they devote so much official attention, and they deprive citizens of government services to which they are legally entitled.

The costs associated with bureaucratic deficiencies are widely recognized. Nevertheless, the initiation of reforms has proved difficult. This article explains why reforms which are widely regarded as necessary and desirable often face such severe obstacles to their initiation. It finds the explanation in the interests of the politicians who must make the decisions which would promote or impede reform. The heart of the argument is that these individuals frequently face a choice between actions which serve their individual political interests and actions which would improve the long-run welfare of their societies, and that when this happens, individual interests generally prevail. Reforms only occur in political circumstances which render the individual interests of the politicians who must initiate them consistent with the collective interest in reform.

Struggles over administrative reform have developed in virtually all countries in which political competition preceded the establishment of a professionalized state apparatus. The initiation of reforms entailed as bitter a struggle in Britain and the United States during the nineteenth century as in Latin America during the twentieth. Numerous case studies of the initiation of reforms exist, but few general explanations.

This essay suggests a general explanation. It uses simple game theoretic models to explore how different electoral and party systems affect the incentives of legislators to initiate reforms. It focuses on one type of reform, the introduction of merit-based hiring for civil servants. This aspect of reform was selected for emphasis because the many administrative reform packages which have been proposed during recent decades nearly always include it; rules for merit-based hiring, unlike other kinds of reform, vary only moderately from country to country; and the effects of laws requiring recruitment by exam are relatively easy to assess. Meritocratic recruitment is not always the most important aspect of administrative reform, but it is always at least moderately important, and it is the easiest element of reform to "measure" and compare across nations.

This study analyzes the legislative struggle over reform in South American democracies,[9] some of which have initiated reforms and some of which have not. The choice of this set of cases holds roughly constant several variables which are often mentioned as possible causes of honesty and competence in government: culture, colonial institutional structure, and level of economic development. At the same time, it preserves sufficient variance in contemporary political institutions and reform outcomes to allow the testing of hypotheses.

The need for reform

Demand for reform in Latin America resulted from widespread recognition that the traditional use of government resources for partisan purposes had led to excesses. In Uruguay during the Fifties and Sixties, for example, so large a fraction of the budgets of many government agencies went as wages to pay patronage appointees that there were no funds left for operating expenses. In 1960, Montevideo newspapers reported that because the Ministry of Public Health had created 1,449 new jobs in public hospitals, no money was left to buy medicines and essential hospital equipment (Taylor 1960: 222). The Ministry of Public Works hired 313 new employees during one seven-month period to repair equipment. Since no funds remained to buy spare parts, by the end of the period none of the department's many self-propelled road scrapers remained operable, and all work on the roads had ceased. The "entire budget was being used to pay personnel and none was left for fuel, equipment, and materials" (Taylor 1960: 103, 178–79).

Overstaffing is only one of the forms which government inefficiency can take. In 1983 a group of Peruvian researchers set out to acquire a license to operate a small workshop in Lima. Documenting every step and moving as expeditiously as procedure allowed, they found that it took 289 days to obtain the 11 separate licenses and certificates legally required. Along the way, they were solicited for bribes ten times (de Soto 1986: 173–75).

As governments in the region began trying to promote economic development and as state intervention in economies increased, the need for administrative reform to increase the effectiveness of developmental strategies became increasingly obvious and urgent. Technical experts claimed that intervention in the economy would not produce desired effects unless the individuals making and carrying out policies were better trained (see, for example, Emmerich 1960, 1972 [1958]; IBRD 1961); presidents regularly proposed administrative reforms as elements of their development strategies (see, for example, Morcillo 1975; Brewer-Carías 1975a); political party spokesmen espoused support for reform (Urzúa and García 1971; Brewer-Carías 1975b; Groves 1974); the press campaigned energetically against corruption and incompetence in the bureaucracy, and called for reform (López 1972; Urzúa and García 1971; Taylor 1960; González 1980); and ordinary people expressed a desire for more competent and honest government in their answers to survey questions.[10]

Impediments to reform

In spite of widespread support, however, reforms have occurred only slowly and sporadically. Two groups have opposed reform: those who have found in bureaucratic jobs a ". . . refuge from which to make a last-ditch stand for their right to a quiet, incompetent existence" (Hirschman 1958: 154), and elected politicians and party activists. The opposition of employees who gained their jobs through patronage reflects the expected costs to them of reform. But, perhaps less obviously, administrative reform is also costly to the politicians who must enact it. Traditionally, jobs in the bureaucracy and the multitude of contracts, subsidies, exceptions, and other scarce values distributed by bureaucrats have served as important electoral resources. Politicians and officials have been able to trade help in acquiring these resources for support (Singer 1965; Biles 1972, 1978; Valenzuela 1977).

Administrative reform threatens to eliminate these political resources. Reforms which introduce merit as the main criterion for hiring and promotion reduce the ability of politicians and party leaders to reward supporters with jobs. Efficiency criteria applied to bureaucratic procurement procedures reduce political discretion in the awarding of contracts. The use of economic and technical criteria rather than partisan favoritism to decide who gets subsidized credit, access to foreign exchange, tax exemptions, and so on, further reduces the resources politicians can exchange for support.

The cost of administrative reform to politicians and party activists is thus clear. Under certain circumstances, however, administrative reform may also provide them with benefits. If the national economy improves as a result of increasing the competence of officials and the effectiveness of their decisions, incumbent politicians and their party can claim credit for it in the next election. Moreover, politicians and their party may gain support from voters who favor reform. Politicians may even gain psychological rewards from having helped provide the country with more honest and competent administration. A final possibility is that, as the electorate grows, politicians and party leaders will prefer to switch from offering private goods in exchange for support to offering public goods, because, in a mass electorate, public goods cost politicians less per voter reached (Cox 1986).

To explain why reforms have occurred at some times and places but not others, then, one must answer the question: under what circumstances will the benefits of reform outweigh the costs to the politicians who must at least acquiesce in passing them?

The interests of legislators and party leaders

Whether politicians will initiate administrative reform depends on the incentives they confront. Only if the individual aspirations for power, status, wealth, or even political change on the part of political activists and politicians can be furthered by the provision of reforms will they be provided. A formalization of the incentive structures faced by South American politicians making a choice about whether to use their limited resources to consolidate political support in customary ways or to bring about more efficient administration will yield predictions of when such reforms should occur.

Two groups of political actors play a role in the struggle over reform: elected politicians and party leaders, who often hold no elected office. Simplifying somewhat, one can hypothesize that these individuals want, above all, to further their political careers. Given this first-order preference, their strategic second-order preferences will vary, depending on the specific possibilities available to them.

The interests of elected officials in Latin America resemble the interests of politicians elsewhere. They want to be reelected,[11] and they prefer some policies over others. Without doing them too much of an injustice, we can assume that, for most politicians most of the time, the desire to be elected takes precedence over policy preferences (cf. Ames 1987). For some, the desire for office and its perquisites truly overwhelms their commitment to particular policies. Others may only want to be elected in order to enact preferred policies, but if they fail to be elected, they lose their chance of influencing policy outcomes. Thus, even for the public spirited, the preference for election will be strong since election grants the opportunity to achieve other preferences (cf. Mayhew 1975). This is not to deny that, for some politicians, ideological commitments outweigh the desire to be elected. The electoral process, however, tends to weed out such individuals; they are elected less frequently than those who consider winning of paramount importance. This selection process also contributes to the predominance of electoral motives among those who have already achieved office. As an initial simplification, then, suppose politicians compete with each other in a constant-sum electoral game, and that, for those who compete in it, the desire to win this electoral game overrides other goals.

Party leaders further their careers by increasing the electoral success of their parties and by achieving greater influence within their parties. Many of their goals will thus coincide with those of politicians in their parties since both politicians and party leaders benefit from policies which give their party electoral advantages. In certain other respects, however, their interests diverge. Party leaders benefit from policies which advance the interests of the party as a collectivity over the long run, whereas, in some situations, individual candidates may be injured by such policies. Party leaders, for example, favor rules which enforce party discipline, but in some circumstances individual legislators may be able to improve their electoral chances by breaking ranks. Situations may thus arise in which party leaders have interests which are not shared by the average legislator. Party leaders must then deploy the incentives at their disposal to influence legislators' votes.

The importance of party leaders in the struggle over reform depends on how much they influence candidates' electoral chances. Virtually all Latin American countries elect legislators using systems of proportional representation. The factors that contribute to the probability that candidates will win elections depend on how candidate lists are selected and whether lists are closed (that is, placement on lists is determined by party leaders) or open (that is, determined by voters). In open-list systems, the vote for candidates depends on the popularity of their positions on issues, voters' party loyalty, candidates' personal charisma, and constituency services, patronage, and favors, much as it does in winner-take-all systems such as the United States. In closed-list systems, the candidate's probability of winning depends primarily on his position on the party list. Factors such as charisma, issue position, and constituency service affect the candidate's probability of winning by influencing party leaders' decisions about placement on the list more than by influencing the vote directly.

In systems in which party leaders' control over the list determines who is elected, they exercise great power over the votes of politicians who have to be concerned about future reelection. In systems such as Brazil's, in which party leaders have virtually no control over who runs for office, or Colombia's during the National Front, in which party leaders lost control of the lists, they exercise little. Where party leaders determine election chances, the calculations of legislators considering a vote for reform will focus on the vote's expected effect on the judgments of party leaders.

Meritocratic hiring rules and other reforms which introduce impersonal criteria for the allocation of government resources reduce politicians' and party leaders' discretion over the distribution of the jobs and favors which fuel political machines and thus influence the vote. No politician in competition with others engaged in trading jobs and favors for votes can afford unilaterally to eschew reliance on patronage. Some, however, might be willing to give up this resource if others did. Similarly, no party leader could afford unilaterally for his party to cease distributing patronage, but some might be willing if they could be assured that others also would do so.

The conditions under which legislators can be expected to favor reforms which deprive everyone of some valued electoral resources can be deduced from a simple game theoretic model, as shown in Figure 10.1. In this simplified world, each politician has some baseline probability of winning the next election, v_i, determined by voters' party loyalty, issue preferences, and so on. This baseline probability can be increased by the skillful use of political favors and decreased by his opponents' distribution of favors.

The pay-offs in these matrices reflect the amounts of patronage to which a national party machine has access as a result of its participation in government. Because of the centralization of decision making and resources in Latin America, the patronage resources available to legislators depend more on their party's national position than on local resources.

The matrix in Figure 10.1 shows the incentives faced by candidates from different parties as they decide whether to use patronage to secure

Candidate II

		Merit	Patronage
Candidate I	Merit	v_1, v_2	$v_1 - x_2, v_2 + x_2$
	Patronage	$v_1 + x_1, v_2 - x_1$	$v_1 + x_1 - x_2, v_2 + x_2 - x_1$

Where

Politicians' utilities are assumed linear with the probability of winning the next election; v_i = the probability that Candidate I will be elected if no jobs are distributed for political purposes. V_i rises and falls exogenously with normal political tides. $\Sigma v_i = 1$

x_i = the amount by which Candidate I can increase his chances of election (at his opponent's expense), by rewarding supporters with government jobs. (It is assumed here that, on average, each individual who works to maintain the candidate's political machine, get out the vote, etc., in the expectation of receiving a job will increase the candidate's probability of being elected by some positive, though possibly quite small, amount.)

Figure 10.1. The effect of patronage on the probability of election.

votes during an electoral campaign. The top left cell of the matrix shows the candidates' probabilities of winning when neither distributes favors; these are just the baseline probabilities v_1 and v_2. In the lower left cell, Politician I uses patronage, gaining an electoral advantage of x_1 from it; his opponent, who does not use patronage, then suffers a decline in his probability of winning of $-x_1$. The upper right cell shows the reverse situation. The lower right cell illustrates the pre-reform milieu in which both candidates rely on patronage.

If this pattern of incentives were the whole story, there would never be any reason for legislators to approve administrative reform. Each individual is better off if he or she relies on patronage, no matter what others do, whether the game is repeated or not. If, however, legislators place a positive value on reform, no matter how small, for any reason whatsoever, then the outcome of the game depends on the magnitude of the difference between x_1 and x_2 in relation to the expected political value of the reform. That is, if legislators value reform at all – if, for example, they think supporting reform would sway the votes of a small number of middle-class idealists or improve their standing by a tiny increment with party leaders – they might in some circumstances vote for reform.

Where popular demand for reform exists, giving legislators a reason to vote for it even though that reason rarely outweighs reasons to vote against, the incentives facing legislators as they decide how to vote are

		Legislator from minority party	
		Reform	Patronage
Legislator from majority party	Reform	v_1, v_2	v_1+e, v_2-e
	Patronage	$v_1+x_1, -x_2-e, v_2+x_2-x_1+e$	$v_1+x_1-x_2, v_2+x_2-x_1$

Where
v_i and x_i are defined as in Figure 10.1
e = the amount of credit a legislator can claim for voting for reform.

Figure 10.2. The effect of voting for reform on the probability of reelection.

schematized in Figure 10.2. The lower right cell is the same as in Figure 10.1. Members of both parties vote against reform, so neither can claim credit and neither is hurt by the other claiming credit. The reform fails since neither large party voted for it, and members of both parties continue to rely on patronage during election campaigns. The upper left cell shows the situation when both parties vote for reform. Since both voted for it, the electoral advantage of voting for it cancels out. The reform passes and neither party can rely on patronage during future campaigns. The upper right cell shows the pay-offs that would result if the majority party voted in favor of reform and the minority party voted against. The reform passes so neither party can use patronage in future campaigns, and the majority party reaps a small electoral advantage, e, at the expense of the minority party from voting for reform. The lower left cell shows what happens when the majority party votes against reform and the minority votes in favor. The reform fails to pass so both parties continue to distribute patronage. The minority party gains a small amount of credit at the majority's expense for its vote for reform.

Whether legislators will vote for reform when they face the incentives schematized in Figure 10.2 depends on the relative magnitudes of x_1 and x_2. If $(x_1-x_2)>e$, that is, if x_1 is any significant amount larger than x_2, the majority party will vote against reform and it will fail. If, however, x_1 and x_2 are approximately equal, i.e., if the two parties have approximately equal access to patronage resources, the majority party will vote for reform, and it will pass.[12] The minority party, as long as e has any positive value at all, will always prefer reform.

To reiterate in non-technical language, in an election, all candidates can be expected to rely on patronage, as shown in Figure 10.1.

Members of a party disadvantaged by the distribution of patronage resources, however, would be better off if the merit system were imposed on everyone. Thus, they always have an incentive to support reform in the legislature. Giving up the use of patronage would make them better off as long as everyone else also gave it up. As many observers have noted, the reform issue generally appeals to the "outs" in politics.

Where patronage is equally distributed and politicians can gain even a small amount from a vote for reform, members of both parties have reason to vote for it. In this situation, patronage conveys no relative advantage, but voting for reform may improve electoral chances. Consequently, political interest dictates the passage of reform. The matrix demonstrates the logic underlying these conclusions for political systems dominated by two large parties or coalitions, but the same argument would hold if three or more parties played central roles in electoral competition. Then patronage would need to be distributed approximately equally among all the top parties before it would be rational for legislators in the larger parties to vote for it.

Members of a party with greater access to patronage have no incentive to vote for reform in the legislature and no reason to eschew patronage during the electoral campaign either. They can improve their chances of being elected by relying on patronage, no matter what members of the other party do, and no matter how long the situation continues. Members of a party with more access to patronage, then, could be expected to opt for reform *only* if they thought other gains from voting for reform would outweigh the certain costs that the loss of patronage would entail. One can imagine a situation in which public outrage over bureaucratic incompetence and graft had become so vehement that politicians might fear that they would lose more votes by voting against reform than by reducing their ability to distribute patronage. If public outrage very often reached such proportions, however, legislators would be eager rather than reluctant reformers.

Descriptions of the reform movement in the United States suggest that public outrage over the assassination of President Garfield by a disappointed office seeker played a catalytic role in bringing about reform (Van Riper 1958: 88–94). Even in this case, however, the legislature only voted to pass the reform after the election of 1882. This election, more than a year after Garfield's death, gave Democrats a majority in the House and thus marked the end of the Republicans' post-Civil War dominance over patronage. A few months prior to the 1882 election, the House had "derisively and angrily refused to give a paltry sum and to aid a single experiment of reform" (Hall 1884: 462).

Immediately after the election, faced with the prospect of sharing the spoils in the immediate future, the same Congressmen who had ignored public opinion five months earlier passed the Pendleton Act by an overwhelming majority (Van Riper 1958: 94). Most of the time, legislators and party leaders can afford to ignore the public's desire for reform because reform is only one of many issues which affect voters' choices, and it is rarely, perhaps never, the most important issue to most voters.

To summarize the argument so far, the pay-off matrices above imply a prediction that spoils will be outlawed in democracies when two conditions are met: (i) the benefits of patronage are approximately evenly distributed among the larger parties; and (ii) legislators have some small incentive to vote for reform.

Such reforms may turn out to be fragile if access to patronage again becomes one-sided, a subject to which I will return below. For now, let us look in more detail at how the game theoretic prediction fares when confronted with evidence from the Latin American democracies.

The effect of the distribution of patronage on reform

This section tests the predictions derived from the game theoretic model above on the universe of Latin American countries which have experienced fifteen or more years of consecutive competitive democracy since 1930: Brazil, Chile, Colombia, Uruguay, and Venezuela. Costa Rica was excluded because its legislators cannot be immediately reelected, so the simplifying assumptions about the interests of legislators used here could not be expected to apply to them. The 1930 cut-off date was chosen because interest in state-fostered development, and hence in administrative reform, began in most countries during the Depression. Prior to that time, administrative reform was not typically seen as an issue having much importance for public welfare.

Of the five countries examined, three, Colombia, Venezuela, and Uruguay, passed initial civil service reforms during more-or-less democratic periods.[13] Brazil's initial reform occurred during the Vargas dictatorship in the late 1930s. Most attempts to extend the reform during the democratic period failed. No comprehensive civil service reform passed in Chile during its long period of democracy. This section will examine the circumstances under which reforms occurred in Colombia, Uruguay, and Venezuela to see if they are consistent with the predictions of the model noted above. Then it will discuss Brazil and Chile as contrasting cases.

In the real world, there is no way to measure amounts of patronage or how much influence on the vote it has. In the case studies that follow, I deal with these measurement problems by relying on two plausible assumptions. First, all else equal, the distribution of jobs and favors increases the probability of being elected (otherwise politicians would not expend so much of their energy providing such services); the more a politician distributes, the better his chances. And second, the amount of patronage to which a candidate has access for distribution depends on his party's control of elective and administrative offices at the national level. Such control depends on the party's present and past electoral success. Electoral victories allow the more successful party to appoint its adherents to bureaucratic posts. These appointees become the source of the favors that influence later elections. (Generally, a waning party which has lost many of the seats it formerly held in the legislature will still be able to call upon loyalists in the bureaucracy for a number of years.)

These assumptions permit an approximate rank ordering of each party's access to patronage, a level of measurement sufficient for the simple model used here. They imply that if two parties control roughly equal numbers of seats in the legislature over a period of years, each party will have access to about the same amount of patronage. If, in contrast, one party dominates the legislature, we can assume that it also dominates patronage opportunities.

Colombia

Competition between the Liberal and Conservative parties for control of government and the spoils associated with control has structured all of Colombia's modern history. Until 1958, transfers of power from one party to the other were accompanied by largescale turnovers of personnel and partisan violence (Solaún 1980). Public welfare suffered from the inefficiency of a bureaucracy composed of patronage appointments as well as from periodic outbreaks of violence. As early as the 1920s, critics identified the parties' excessive reliance on patronage as one of the pathologies of Colombian life. Reforms have been undertaken, however, only during two time periods, both of which correspond to periods of approximate equality between the two parties.

Colombia's first experiments with merit-oriented administrative reforms occurred during the presidency of Enrique Olaya Herrera, 1930–34. The Olaya administration marked the first electoral victory of the Liberal Party in the twentieth century. Olaya won by a slim margin, and the reformist Liberals' hold on government during his first two years was tenuous. Several administrative reforms were passed at this time, the most important of which aimed at improving the performance of the Ministry of Public Works and other agencies responsible for the construction and maintenance of railroads and highways (Hartwig 1983: 105–7).

By 1934, the Liberals had consolidated their electoral dominance, and Alfonso López won the presidency easily. He continued many of the new economic policies of Olaya, but permitted the reassertion of partisan considerations in hiring. The Olaya administration's merit-based reforms quietly disappeared during the Liberal hegemony from 1934 to 1946 (Hartwig 1983: 106–11).

Colombia's next attempt to establish merit as the basis for recruitment to the civil service occurred in 1958. At that time, each of the major parties controlled exactly half of the legislature and half of the available administrative appointments. This was due to a pact, the National Front, between the Liberal and Conservative parties that established parity between the two traditional rivals in the national legislature, in departmental (i.e., state) legislatures, in municipal councils, and in administrative appointments. This pact, designed to end a decade of repression and partisan violence in which more than 200,000 people had been killed, was scheduled to remain in effect for sixteen years. Each party would receive 50 percent of the seats in legislatures and councils. The presidency was to alternate between the two parties. A career civil service was proposed as a means of removing key jobs from partisan control, and other administrative jobs were to be distributed equally between supporters of the two parties. In short, the pact established an equal sharing of power and patronage regardless of electoral outcome for sixteen years (Hartlyn 1988; Berry *et al.* 1980; Dix 1980).

The pact called for the creation of a merit-based career civil service, but presidential and legislative action were required to initiate it (Morcillo 1975; Groves 1974). Individual legislators facing this decision about whether to forgo a portion of customary patronage, would have to consider the electoral costs and benefits associated with patronage, as shown in Figure 10.2 above. By law, each party could claim an equal share of patronage. Nevertheless, no individual legislator could afford to eschew the use of patronage unilaterally.

Two factors contributed to making a vote for reform more attractive than it might otherwise have been. The first was the interest of all politicians in reestablishing a democratic system, which depended on ending partisan violence. Administrative reform was expected to help end the violence by providing a fair means of distributing jobs and also by contributing to better quality economic policy. Leaders in both parties had committed themselves to agreements, including complicated parity arrangements as well as civil service reform, as a way of reducing the violence and reestablishing a competitive political system. Thus party elites had managed to forge an enforceable cooperative solution to the prisoner's dilemma of unrestrained party competition. The career interests of high level party leaders in reestablishing the competitive electoral system explain their support for the pact. Legislators' second reason for voting for reform was the expectation that it would affect future placement on electoral lists. Party leaders in Colombia at that time could influence legislators' decisions with special effectiveness because of party cohesion and a closed-list proportional representation system (cf. Duff 1971). Although the proliferation of factions within Colombia's two major parties during the pact subsequently reduced the influence of party leaders over legislators, in 1958 both parties were still relatively cohesive (Archer 1990).

Evidence from the Colombian case is thus completely consistent with the model. Reform occurred when access to patronage was distributed equally. Party discipline enforced by the closed-list system provided legislators with an additional incentive to vote for reform.

Uruguay

In Uruguay, the career civil service was first mandated by the 1934 Constitution. This constitution legalized a pact between two factions of the traditional dominant parties, the *terrista* faction of the Colorado Party and the *herrerista* faction of the National, or Blanco, Party.

Uruguay has historically had a two-party system within which multiple factions have independent legal status and run their own lists of candidates in elections, thus creating a de facto multiparty system. Prior to the reform, Gabriel Terra, head of the *terrista* faction, had been elected president on the Colorado ticket. In the face of severe economic distress caused by the Depression, and an apparently insurmountable policy immobilism caused by Uruguay's collegial executive and powerful but factionalized legislature, Terra staged a coup d'état in 1933. Luis Alberto Herrera, caudillo of the most important Blanco Party faction at the time, collaborated with Terra, and the two faction leaders entered into a pact to share government offices, excluding other factions of both parties (Taylor 1960: 23–29).

The sitting legislature was dismissed. Terra and Herrera chose a Deliberative Assembly of ninety-nine members, made up of approximately equal numbers of Colorado supporters of Terra and Blanco supporters of Herrera, to act as a provisional legislature. They in turn elected a Constituent Assembly made up of Terra and Herrera supporters. The resulting Constitution institutionalized the pact by mandating minority representation in the president's Council of Ministers and the equal division of Senate seats between the most voted lists of the two most voted parties. The division of the Senate assured these two factions equal control of appointments of all important administrative positions, the boards of directors of state enterprises, Supreme Court justices, and members of the Accounts Tribunal (Taylor 1960: 171). At the same time, it excluded other factions from access to spoils. In effect, it transformed what had been a de facto multiparty system into a two-party system with approximately equal access to patronage for both parties.

Traditionally, the Colorado Party had attracted more electoral support and controlled more patronage than had the Blancos. More popular parties usually have access to more patronage, but the pact resulted in an equal division of patronage in spite of electoral inequality. In this setting, the Constituent Assembly was able to agree to establish a career civil service, which would remove some appointments from the discretion of party activists. As in Colombia, the closed-list system provided faction leaders with incentives they could deploy to affect the votes of members of the Constituent Assembly.

This brief period of relative equality between two factions was unique in Uruguayan history. The two parties achieved approximate equality in electoral strength in 1962 and 1971, but the largest factions within each party remained unequal (Fabregat 1963: 31; Venturini 1984: 25, 50; Rial 1985: 12–13). No legislation passed to enforce the principle of meritocratic hiring in practice. Legislative and constitutional additions to the civil service law after the Thirties generally focused on providing job security, vacations, grievance procedures, and so on. In other words, later additions to the civil service laws were designed to benefit well-organized civil servants and thus contribute to electoral gains for legislators, not to require further sacrifice of electoral interests.

Venezuela

At the beginning of the democratic period in Venezuela, administrative reform seemed to be supported by everyone. Excessive corruption had helped discredit the dictator, Marcos Pérez Jiménez, and administrative reform was widely seen as needed, both to reduce corruption and to improve the state's ability to use oil revenues to foster development and increase social welfare. President Rómulo Betancourt expressed strong support for reform, foreign experts were hired to help formulate a reform and train Venezuelans to implement it, and a reform agency attached to the presidency was created (Brewer-Carías 1975a, 1975b; Stewart 1978).

The agency completed its draft plan for civil service reform in 1960, and the president submitted it to Congress. The president had a coalition majority in Congress. Since party discipline in Venezuela is strong, in part because of party leaders' control of electoral lists, prospects for reform should have been good. Nevertheless, the civil service reform bill was never reported out of committee (Groves 1967).

It continued, moreover, to languish in Congress throughout the Betancourt presidency and through that of his successor, Raúl Leoni. Venezuelan observers note that, despite flamboyant public statements supporting reform, neither president really pushed the bill (Brewer-Carías 1975a: 454–57). Throughout this period, the party Acción Democrática (AD) controlled the presidency and a strong plurality in Congress. AD party leaders had much more to lose from giving up patronage than had the other parties.

In 1968, Rafael Caldera of the Social Christian Party (Copei) was elected president with 28.9 percent of the vote, as compared with the AD-led coalition vote of 28.1 percent. In the legislature, the vote was split between the two largest parties, with 25.8 percent for AD and 24.2 percent for Copei (Ruddle and Gillette 1972). The civil service reform was brought forward for consideration in Congress again, revised to make it congruent with recent constitutional and institutional changes, and passed in 1970 with support from both AD and Copei (Brewer-Carías 1975a: 475–79; Stewart 1978: 39–40). Thus, Venezuela's first merit-based civil service law also passed during a period of temporary equality between parties.

Brazil

Getúlio Vargas established a career civil service in Brazil during the dictatorship from 1937 to 1945. The reform had made a fair amount of headway in imposing merit as the criterion for hiring and promotion by the time Vargas was overthrown in 1945. But, after the return to democracy, earlier reforms were to a considerable extent undermined (Siegel 1966: 148–75).

From the establishment of democracy until the military coup in 1964, the distribution of electoral strength and patronage in Brazil was quite unequal. The country had a multiparty system with open-list proportional representation in the lower house and a majoritarian system in the Senate. The three most important parties were the Partido Social Democrático (PSD), a traditional, conservative party despite its name, the Partido Trabalhista Brasileiro (PTB), the Labor Party, and the União Democrática Nacional (UDN), a middle-class reformist party. The PSD and PTB had developed from the traditional and labor wings of the political machine created by Vargas during the dictatorship (Souza 1976; Oliveira 1973). They were entrenched in the government bureaucracy prior to Vargas' overthrow, and their patronage resources remained impressive throughout the democratic period. In spite of apparently important ideological differences, the PSD and PTB formed frequent electoral alliances. The UDN, in contrast, developed in opposition to the Vargas political machine (Benevides 1981). Over the years, it achieved some access to patronage as a result of entering coalitions and winning some elections, but it never equalled the other parties.

During the 1950s and 1960s, as economic development became the most important goal of the Brazilian government, concern about administrative reform reached new levels. Presidents Getúlio Vargas (during his second administration), Juscelino Kubitschek, and Jânio Quadros all proposed reforms (Graham 1968: 143–53). Public demand for reform, as expressed in the press and in answers to survey questions, was widespread. For example, a 1964 survey asked: "Which one of these do you think our country needs most: honest government without corruption; a government that gets things done; a fair distribution of wealth; national unity; or individual freedom?" Even though the income distribution in Brazil was one of the most skewed in the world, 62 percent of those who answered chose "an honest government without corruption." The second most frequent choice was "a government that gets things done."[14] When asked whether "the only really important problem in Brazil is the problem of lack of character and honesty," only 15 percent of those who had an opinion disagreed. When asked what was the most important reason for their party preference, 44 percent mentioned honesty first, more than twice as many as mentioned party program or past record.[15]

Even in the face of such expressions of public opinion, however, legislators making the decision whether or not to vote for reform had to take into account the costs and benefits associated with patronage. Members of the UDN would have been better off if they had been able to pass a reform. Under these circumstances, it is not surprising that the UDN espoused "the struggle against the forces that have been dominant for many years, administrative corruption . . ." in platforms, campaigns, and speeches (Benevides 1981, 99). Individual members of the party could still improve their chances of being elected, however, by relying on promises of patronage during the campaign.

Members of the UDN behaved as would be expected, given the costs and benefits they faced. Most members relied on patronage and deals in electoral campaigns, but advocated the passage of reform bills in Congress (Geddes 1990). This stance, though rational, left them vulnerable to charges of hypocrisy from both idealists within the party and opponents outside.

PSD and PTB legislators, in contrast, had no reason to vote for reform and every reason to continue relying on patronage during electoral campaigns. During the democratic period, the career civil service remained on the books, but control over new hiring returned, for the most part, to the realm of patronage. Congress reduced the status and powers of the Departamento Administrativo de Serviço Público (DASP), the agency in charge of enforcing civil service laws (Siegel 1966: 148–72). During much of the democratic period, examinations were not held, and appointments were made in the temporary and extranumerary (that is, outside the merit system) categories of employment. The dividing line between merit-based career and non-career civil servants was blurred by the passage of laws conferring career civil service status and perquisites on "temporary" employees who had not taken the examination but who had spent five years or more in public employment (Graham 1968: 140–58).

Reform laws were proposed at various times, but only two kinds of civil service laws made it through Congress: those which granted benefits to civil servants and thus involved no electoral cost to legislators; and those which extended meritocratic norms into agencies controlled by one particular party and thus involved gains rather than costs for the majority of legislators. In the realm of granting benefits, Congress increased the wages of civil servants and passed several laws granting job security and higher status to unclassified employees.

The one exception to the overall decline in the merit-based civil service during the democratic period occurred when Congress extended the merit system to cover the social security institutes. Thousands of jobs in these institutes had been used during the second Vargas and Kubitschek presidencies to reward the presidents' Labor Party (PTB) coalition partner (Amaral 1966: 17–19; Siegel 1963: 6). Hiring in the institutes had, in effect, been turned over to Labor Party activists. By voting to include the institutes in the merit system, Congressmen from other parties could decrease the resources available to the Labor Party without incurring any cost themselves. Given the unusual circumstance of the existence of a group of agencies dominated by one particular party, the vote for reform did not depend on parity in the legislature.

Chile

During its long history of democracy, Chile never passed a comprehensive civil service reform. It had no civil service commission and no uniform system of recruitment and promotion (Valenzuela 1984: 256;

López 1972). It did have some requirements for entry, such as completion of tenth grade, but even these were violated in practice. Each agency controlled its own recruitment system. As a result, some agencies were highly professionalized and others extremely politicized (Ascher 1975: 57–86; Urzúa and García 1971: 175–78).

The Chilean party system was more fragmented than those of the other countries discussed. Traditionally, the Radical Party had greatest access to patronage. Radical Party dominance began to decline in the early Fifties, but no conjuncture occurred which gave approximately equal patronage to the largest parties in Congress (Valenzuela 1985: 44–47).

Two characteristics of the Chilean democratic system further decreased the likelihood of passing a reform: the open-list system of proportional representation initiated in 1958 and the fragmented party system. It might appear at first that in a fragmented party system such as Chile's, in which the "dominant" party often receives only 20 to 30 percent of the vote in legislative elections, several smaller parties could band together to pass reforms that would deprive the largest party of its disproportionate access to patronage. In this way, a group of smaller parties with less access to patronage could improve their ability to compete against the party with the closest ties to the bureaucracy.

In an open-list system, however, incumbents' interest in maintaining their advantage over competitors in their own parties outweighs their interest in depriving members of other parties of access to patronage resources. In open-list systems, the candidate's place on the party list is determined by the vote he receives. In other words, a candidate runs not only against candidates from other parties but also against other candidates from his own party.

Patronage thus becomes an even more valuable resource to those candidates who have access to it. Candidates can distinguish themselves from the candidates of other parties on the basis of programmatic appeals, offers of public goods, and ideology, but attention to casework and the distribution of private goods are among the few ways of distinguishing themselves from other candidates in the same party. Incumbents have a great advantage over other candidates in terms of their ability to distribute favors. Consequently, incumbents of all parties in an open-list proportional representation system can be expected to be especially reluctant to give up patronage.

Had Chilean party leaders had an interest in reducing reliance on patronage, they might have succeeded in overcoming incumbents' reluctance to vote for reform. Despite the open-list system, Chilean party leaders, in contrast to Brazilian, had substantial influence over the political careers of legislators. They influenced them through control over: who achieved a place on the list; whose name appeared at the top of the ballot (and thus who received a disproportionate share of the votes of the unsophisticated); and who received cabinet appointments, often a stepping stone to executive office. Given the unequal distribution of patronage among parties and the importance of patronage to the organizational survival of parties, however, party leaders had no interest in reform.

The fragmented party system necessitated government by coalition. Agreements on the distribution of spoils among coalition partners held these coalitions together (Valenzuela 1978; López 1972: 89). Even if the president's party had been willing to make an agreement with the opposition to eschew patronage, it could not have done so because of the almost certain disintegration of its governing coalition which would have followed. Such an agreement with the opposition would, in effect, constitute defection in the ongoing cooperative game between the president and his coalition partners, and he could expect to be punished for defection by loss of support.

Given the fragmented party system, unequal access to patronage, open-list proportional representation, and the need for coalitions in order to govern, the game theoretic approach would predict no civil service reform in Chile, and none occurred. With regard to the occurrence or non-occurrence of an initial reform, then, game theoretic predictions seem to be consistent with events in all the countries examined.

The return to an unequal distribution of patronage

Up to this point, this study has dealt with the situations in which the first step toward a merit-based civil service was taken. I turn now to consideration of whether these initial steps have been, or will be, followed by others. Given the notorious inefficiency of post-reform bureaucracies in Venezuela, Colombia, and Uruguay, one must conclude either that civil service reform does not work in Latin America or that initial reforms were subsequently undermined.

Evidence suggests that professionalization does occur and does increase competence and public service orientations in the parts of the bureaucracy in which it occurs (Wahrlich 1964; Lafer 1970; Vieira 1967; Hartwig 1983; Schmidt 1974), but that initial reforms affect only a small part of the bureaucracy. Where conjunctures favoring the passage of reforms have lasted only a short time, additional increments of reform have not followed initial reforms. Further, subsequent legislation and executive decrees have sometimes vitiated earlier reforms.

In Venezuela, when Acción Democrática returned to its then customary dominant role with the election of Carlos Andrés Pérez in 1973, non-partisan administration suffered a setback. Pérez won the presidency with a strong plurality (48.4 percent, compared with 36.7 percent for Copei). He was the first elected Venezuelan president to have an absolute majority in both houses of Congress (Karl 1982: 182–84). He asked for, and eventually got, special powers to enact by executive decree a package of proposals aimed at controlling and using effectively the windfall of oil money threatening to engulf the nation. Included among these projects were several administrative reforms. Pérez expressed strong support for administrative reform, including professionalization of personnel. His actions, however, tended to belie his words.

Decree 211, issued by Pérez, allowed the administration to increase the number of non-classified (that is, temporary and low status employees who need not pass exams to enter the service) public employees as well as the number of positions *de confianza* (high status appointments in which loyalty is considered an appropriate criterion for recruitment). Employees *de confianza* in 1982 included all division chiefs, those employed in fiscal sections, buying, supplies, and document reproduction, and all secretaries in these areas. Copei claimed that 80,000 people had lost their jobs for political reasons during the administration turnover when Pérez came to power (Karl 1982: 267). Pérez, in other words, took the opportunity provided by having a majority in the legislature to build the political machine which would form the foundation of his second successful campaign for the presidency.

Some administrative reforms have occurred, however, since the Pérez administration. An anti-corruption law, for example, was passed in 1982 when AD and Copei each received 39.7 percent of the vote in legislative elections.[16] The problem of professionalizing personnel, however, remains unsolved (Brewer-Carías 1985).[17] Partisan considerations still affect most hiring decisions, and turnover in the bureaucracy when a new administration comes into power is so high that administrative output falls noticeably (Cova and Hannot 1986). Corruption continues to be a serious problem.

The situation in Uruguay resembled that in Venezuela, but in a more extreme form. After the end of the pact between Terra and Herrera, Uruguay never again experienced equality among the largest party factions. The 1934 Constitution mandated that hiring and promotion be based on merit, but did not establish an agency to conduct examinations. Instead, each bureaucratic entity set its own standards. Some evidence about the strictness of these standards can be inferred from education statistics. In the mid-1950s, 46 percent of public employees had not finished primary school, and 70 percent had completed ten or fewer years of schooling (Taylor 1960: 215–19). Entrance examinations in many agencies guaranteed little more than literacy. There was one important barrier to entry, however: applicants were not permitted to take the test unless it was signed by the neighborhood *sublema* (that is, party faction) boss (Cf. Biles 1972, 1978).

Most legislation regarding the civil service and additional provisions added to subsequent constitutions dealt with job security and grievance procedures. These issues involve no cost to legislators as long as the number of jobs keeps expanding, and brings them electoral benefits in the form of support from government employees (estimated at 27.6 percent of the working population of Uruguay in 1956 (Taylor 1960: 100)).

As a result of this series of laws and constitutional provisions, by the 1960s it had become virtually impossible to dismiss government employees. The 1952 Constitution provides that the Senate must approve the dismissal of a classified employee. Even the dismissal of temporary employees led to serious political repercussions (Taylor 1960: 215). As noted at the beginning of this essay, such a large proportion of agency budgets was spent on wages that, at times, agencies could not afford to buy equipment needed in order to carry out their functions and supply government services.

To summarize, in Uruguay's factionalized political system, legislators supported those elements of career civil service which could be converted into electoral advantage, especially job creation and job security. They did not provide for the imposition of merit as the criterion for hiring and promotion, which would have reduced the ability of factions to service their clients.

The pattern of implementation of the 1958 reform in Colombia resembles that in Uruguay. Once parity between the two major parties was established, competition among the factions within each party for shares of the party's half intensified. Struggles for patronage among factions of the same party became increasingly vitriolic over time. As in Uruguay, the party pact has led to a sharp increase in the number of government jobs.

All Colombian presidents during the early democratic period made some effort at administrative reform, and quite a few reforms gained legislative approval. Merit-based hiring has been an exception, however. By 1966, when Carlos Lleras Restrepo came to power, only 5 percent of public employees were included in the merit-based career civil service.

Lleras mounted an aggressive campaign against corruption and patronage and for administrative reform. Congress, however, successfully blocked his proposed personnel reforms. Unable to extend the merit system to cover more jobs, near the end of his term Lleras issued a decree allowing public employees to enroll themselves in the career service without taking the exam, thus undermining the meritocratic element of civil service.

As the party pact neared its end, conflict between the parties increased, and interest in administrative reform waned, even in the executive branch. With the failure to extend the merit system, civil service in Colombia, as in Uruguay, had become synonymous with inflexibility and the inability to fire incompetents (Hartlyn 1988). Misael Pastrana, the last president during the pact, showed little interest in reform, being more interested in consolidating his party's position before the first election unfettered by parity agreements. His successor, Alfonso López Michelsen, suspended the career civil service during a state of siege.

The general assessment by observers of the current Colombian scene is that professionalization of some key sectors of the Colombian bureaucracy has occurred, but personnel reform in general has failed (Hartwig 1983; Vidal 1982). In spite of considerable presidential support, campaigns against corruption in the press, and supportive public opinion, legislators in the factionalized party system have not found it in their own interest to extend the merit system. Since the end of the National Front, party parity has not occurred. Because of the ease of forming faction lists, party leaders failed to exert much influence over legislators' votes (Archer 1990).

In brief, then, in all the countries examined, reforms initiated during periods of party equality or during a dictatorship suffered reverses when the distribution of power among the competitive parties became unequal. Even in the United States, when the election of 1896 resulted in renewed Republican dominance, the merit system was seriously threatened. President McKinley removed the exam requirement for 10,000 jobs. Further, during the McKinley administration Congress passed legislation excluding thousands of new appointments from the system (Van Riper 1958: 171–75). If McKinley's assassination had not brought Theodore Roosevelt unexpectedly to the presidency, administration in the United States might look less different from Latin America than it does today.

Civil service reforms generally include two kinds of provisions: requirements for merit-based hiring and promotion; and guarantees to employees of job security, fair treatment, union representation, and so on. In unequal or fragmented party systems, legislators have been reluctant to increase the number of jobs included in the merit system since each new inclusion reduces the resources available to politicians and party leaders for use in their struggle with each other. Laws extending perquisites and job guarantees to larger numbers of employees have posed no problem for legislators, however, since they bring electoral benefits from grateful employees.

Implications for the future of reform

In the United States, where both parties enjoyed similar access to patronage from 1882 until 1896, civil service was gradually extended "by executive order, taking advantage of feeble statutory authorization" (Schattschneider 1942: 138). By 1896, the merit system had been extended to cover about half of all appointments, which included "the bulk of the offices which it was then either legal or politically and administratively practical to place under the merit system" (Van Riper 1958: 130). Most of these extensions occurred when the party in control of government had lost an election and expected the incoming party to dismiss its supporters (Skowronek 1979). This pattern of incremental extension was possible because, in a system of two approximately equal parties, occasions recur when it is temporarily in the interest of one party or the other to extend the merit system. Over time, this series of instrumental decisions creates a professional civil service.

The same thing is likely to happen in South America, but will take longer because of differences in party systems. The initial establishment of a merit-based civil service, an agency to administer it, and, usually, a school to train civil servants creates islands of competence within the bureaucracy and concentrates advocates of further reform strategically inside government. Though they lose many battles, they rarely disappear from the scene completely.

Reform continues to be strenuously advocated from within the executive branch of government and, also, in the press. Elected officials, as shown above however, often feel reluctant to extend reform. Even in the two countries with two-party systems, the institutionalization of factions which run separate electoral lists has transferred the struggle for patronage from a struggle between parties into a struggle among factions within each party. This makes it extremely unlikely that equality can be maintained for any length of time, since it must be maintained among factions, not just parties.

Multiparty systems in Latin America have so far not produced lasting periods of relative equality between the two most popular parties or coalitions. One party has usually tended to dominate, and it has not served that party's interest to extend the merit system. If two approximately equal parties were to emerge as the only serious competitors for power in a multiparty system, however, as seems quite possible in Venezuela, the game theoretic model would predict further extensions of reform. And, as noted above, some extensions have occurred in Venezuela.

Conclusion

The very simple game theoretic model proposed at the beginning of this essay implies two predictions about when administrative reform should occur: (i) reforms are more likely to pass the legislative hurdle when patronage is evenly distributed between the strongest parties; (ii) initial reforms are more likely to be followed by further extension of reform where the electoral weight of the two top parties remains relatively even and stable.

The rational actor assumptions on which the model is based also imply several predictions about the effects of certain institutions on the probability of reform. Open-list proportional representation, for example, because it makes patronage a valuable resource to incumbents in their struggle against challengers within their own party, reduces the probability of reform. Electoral rules which result in the proliferation of candidate lists, for example, minimal requirements for party qualification, or easy formation of dissident electoral lists within parties – also reduce the probability of reform because fractionalization reduces the probability of an equal distribution of patronage among the larger parties. Institutional features of the party system which give party leaders more influence over legislators, such as control over placement on the list, can work in either direction. Where party leaders have an interest in reform, their ability to impose party discipline increases the probability of reform, but, where party leaders have no interest in reform, their influence makes reform less likely.

The evidence examined in this paper has proved consistent with these predictions. All the instances of initial civil service reform in democracies occurred during periods of party parity with regard to patronage. Reforms did not occur in democracies with open-list proportional representation. Factionalism seemed to undercut the ability of two-party systems to produce recurrent situations of equality. And, finally, when the parties returned to their normal situation of inequality after a temporary period of parity, reforms were not extended and, in fact, were often cut back.

Moreover, evidence from these cases has proved inconsistent with other explanations of reform. It is, for example, sometimes suggested that administrative reform occurs when countries attain a level of economic development that makes the continuation of government incompetence economically costly. The dates of initial reforms in these cases, however (Uruguay 1934, Brazil 1937, Colombia 1930–34 and 1958, Venezuela 1970, and Chile none prior to 1973), offer little support for a direct link between development and reform. A related but more political argument hypothesizes that reforms occur when the demographic changes which accompany development give reformist parties supported by middle-class and manufacturing interests the chance to defeat traditional machine parties. Latin America offers few examples of victories by unambiguously reformist anti-machine parties. The Christian Democratic Frei administration in Chile comes closest to what North Americans think of as a reform government. It did not introduce civil service; rather, the many administrative changes initiated by the Christian Democrats sought to monopolize offices for their own party. In contrast, the reforms which actually introduced meritocratic hiring – as demonstrated in the case histories above – occurred when traditional machine parties found themselves forced to share power with other traditional machines.

In contrast to the above arguments advanced to explain reform in the United States, Latin American specialists have sometimes suggested that the Iberian colonial heritage shared by Latin American countries predisposes them toward clientelism and against impersonal procedures such as meritocratic recruitment to civil service. There may be some truth in this argument, but it obviously cannot explain the very considerable differences among Latin American cases.

The game theoretic model has thus proved sufficiently useful to deserve further research. Claims about its generality have to be somewhat cautious because of the small number of culturally and historically similar cases examined here. It may be that the domain of this model is limited to the western hemisphere. None the less, its implications are quite far reaching. It suggests that administrative reforms will be difficult to achieve and maintain in democracies, especially democracies with fragmented party systems. Certain characteristics which are often thought of as increasing representativeness, such as multiparty systems that reflect a wide spectrum of interests and openlist proportional representation, may paradoxically cause elected officials to be less responsive to the public interest.

One of the promises of democracy is that it makes government services available to all citizens regardless of wealth or status. The failure to professionalize public administration, however, makes that promise hard to keep. Stories abound in Latin America about the need for bribes or pull in order to get everyday services such as renewal of a driver's license. More seriously, inefficiency and incompetence in government agencies can be so extreme that clients' needs cannot be served at all. For example, Montevideo's *El País* reported in 1960 that the Fund for Pensions for Rural, Domestic, and Aged Workers was up to two years behind in the commencement of payments to nearly 4,000 people (Taylor 1960: 222). During the democratic period, Chileans eligible for pensions routinely sought the help of elected officials to avoid the months or even years of red tape involved for the politically unconnected to initiate payments (Valenzuela 1977: 120–37; Tapia-Videla 1969: 300–13). All but one of Brazil's many social security institutes had gone bankrupt, in part because of excessive employment of untrained Labor Party supporters, by 1964 (Malloy 1979). In these instances – and many others could be cited – the failure of public service directly affects the quality of life of the ordinary people whom democracy is supposed to benefit.

It is ironic that the reforms which would improve efficiency and fairness in the provision of government services should be impeded by the same representative institutions whose manifest purpose is to reflect constituents' interests.

Notes

1 See Geddes (1990) for an elaboration of the logic that supports this statement. As has been pointed out by Douglas Dion (1998), arguments that some antecedent factor is necessary but not sufficient can be tested on sets of observations in which all share the same outcome. Even when testing this form of argument, however, comparisons across observations are required.

2 This history is discussed in much more detail in Geddes (1994: ch. 3).

3 See Geddes (1995) and Tsebelis (1990) for much fuller discussions of the circumstances in which game theoretic arguments are useful.

4 In principle, the same result could occur if three or more parties of about equal size dominated a legislature, but this has not occurred in practice. The caveat about expected future dominance is necessary to the logic of the argument because reform disadvantages incumbents relative to parties excluded from power. Two large approximately equal parties can agree to give up this advantage without changing their relative standing as long as no challenging outsider parties are waiting in the wings. If the political system contains smaller parties with an obvious potential for overtaking the lead currently held by the largest parties, however, incumbents will have to consider the effect of the loss of their patronage advantage on the probability

of being defeated by one or more of these smaller parties. The game between a larger party and one or more smaller parties is never a prisoner's dilemma, and the larger party always has reason to vote against reform.

5 As numerous African countries take steps toward democratization, more countries may now be entering the potential universe. And since I have not tested the model outside Latin America, it may turn out that some feature of Latin American circumstance that I failed to see or give sufficient weight limits the domain of the argument to Latin American countries.

6 The 1930 cut-off point was chosen because in most Latin American countries demands for administrative reform first began to be made in the Thirties. Prior to the articulation of the need for better bureaucratic performance, there is little reason to expect democratic politicians to initiate such reforms.

7 I believe that the drive to transform chaotic perceptions into causal arguments inheres in human nature, but, like other inherent traits such as timidity or the ability to carry a tune, it is not uniformly distributed.

8 Originally published in the *American Political Science Review* 85, 2 (June 1991). Reprinted here with permission from the editors.

9 Although bureaucratic incompetence and corruption also plague authoritarian regimes, I shall examine only democracies, because the incentives that determine whether political leaders will initiate reform depend on institutional features of the political system. Consequently, one would need a different model to explain reform in an authoritarian institutional setting.

10 See nn. 14 and 15.

11 Presidents sometimes appear to be an exception to the assertion that politicians care most about reelection, since, in many Latin American countries, they cannot be immediately reelected. They can, however, serve again after one or two terms have elapsed. Many do so (e.g., Fernando Belaúnde and Carlos Andrés Pérez), and more hope to but are prevented from doing so either by military intervention (e.g., Eduardo Frei and Juscelino Kubitschek) or by ambitious competitors within their own parties (e.g., Carlos Lleras Restrepo).

12 Speaking of majority parties in the Latin American context involves a degree of simplification. In fact, legislative majorities are often coalitions. This should not, however, affect the logic of the argument.

13 The categorization of Uruguay as a democracy at the time of the reform is somewhat dubious. The elected president had staged a coup and replaced the elected legislature. Still, two factions continued to function as the most important political competitors. Since party competition continued during this period of modified democracy, Uruguay was retained in the small universe of democracies (Taylor 1952).

14 This question comes from a survey conducted by the United States Information Agency in March 1964 (World Survey II: Attitudes toward Domestic and Foreign Affairs [N = 466]), made available by the Inter-University Consortium for Political and Social Research (ICPSR 7048), University of Michigan.

15 These questions come from a survey conducted by Júlio Barbosa *et al.* (Political Behavior and Attitudes in a Brazilian City, 1965–1966 [N = 645]),

made available by the Inter-University Consortium for Political and Social Research (ICPSR 7613), University of Michigan.
16 Ley Orgánica de Salvaguarda del Patrimonio Público (*Gaceta Oficial*, no. 3077, *extraordinario*, December 23, 1982). My thanks to Michael Coppedge for bringing this law to my attention.
17 "Burocracia: Ciudadano [Bureaucracy: Citizen]," in *El Diario de Caracas*, August 2, 1987.

11 The role of microhistories in comparative studies

John R. Bowen

All the essays included in this volume involve the use of comparisons, and yet, in my view, their central arguments turn on something other than an inductive "comparative method." What the arguments *do* depend on, crucially, is the historical analysis of motives, ideas, and events. They indicate, I believe, a general movement in comparative studies toward theoretically informed, microhistorical accounts of complex social processes.

Not that comparisons are unimportant in these analyses: they play two critical roles. First, the authors use comparisons as ways to generate ideas about the processes and mechanisms underlying particular social phenomena. They then try out these ideas by closely inspecting micro-historical sequences of events. Secondly, the authors give added plausibility to their arguments by tracing such sequences in several different social contexts. Comparisons thus play a role both in generating ideas and theories, and in making the claim that the mechanisms enjoy some degree of generality. The critical test of the theory, however, is in the historical account, the fit between observed sequences of events, on the one hand, and social or cultural models of how events ought to unfold, on the other.

Recall what was entailed in the classical forms of "comparative method," as delineated, in different ways, by John Stuart Mill and E. B. Tylor. The comparative method followed a logic of induction; it assumed comparability of units across cases; and it aimed to establish synchronic associations among variables. The social scientist began with a small or large number of cases, identified variables, and established relationships among those variables. In its "small-n" forms, which resemble some of the analyses included here, claims were based, not on statistical significance, but on the presence or absence of one or two key variables. Allen Johnson mentions two instances of small-n, "controlled" comparisons that have themselves becomes classics in social anthropology: Fred Eggan's studies of social structure in the

North American southwest, and S. F. Nadel's analysis of the social origins of witchcraft and sorcery beliefs in Africa. Nadel's account, in particular, relied on the assumption that the relevant causal variables are those that differ between the societies studied, an assumption commonly made in this type of inductive argument (see Lieberson 1991).[1]

The authors included in this volume have developed their research projects in very different ways. They began their projects when, after a long period of field or archival research, they noticed anomalies, paradoxes, or simply interesting differences between two or more cases. These initial contrasts suggested mechanisms of potentially greater generality, leading some of the authors to develop models that incorporated those mechanisms. (In some cases, such as Levi's, the general model had been developed in earlier projects and was modified to take account of the new cases.) Those authors proceeded to test their models in two sorts of ways: by seeing whether other cases fitted the model as well as did the initial cases, or by seeing whether a sequence of events unfolded in the way implied by the model.

I argue that in every analysis included here, the most telling evidence for the author's general claims is to be found in the inspection of event sequences, and that these sequences are detected at a microsocial level, that is, are made up of individuals, actions, and specific chains of events (which, although integrally connected to structures, institutions, and forces, are not subsumable under them). I will try to support my claim by pointing to what I think is the key moment of demonstration in each of the papers. I begin by exploring the reasons why the authors reject macrosociological comparative answers to their questions; I then consider the ways they develop models about microsocial processes; finally, I examine how they try out models against cases.

The limits of inductive comparisons

When David Laitin tries to explain why political violence has been much higher in Spanish Basque Country than in Catalonia, he begins by considering a number of older social and cultural explanations for Basque violence. His reason for devoting so much space to this review is not to refute all the accounts which compete with his own, but rather to indicate a logical weakness in these accounts, namely, that every variable proffered as explaining Basque violence could have been used to explain Catalan violence as well, had the latter occurred. On a standard inductive comparative account, then, all these variables fail to distinguish between the two cases. One could imagine other possible variables, and perhaps find one or two that are present in the one case, but not in the other. But what would lead someone to suppose that such a difference explained outcomes, rather than merely occurred? Laitin argues that the analyst needs a model that offers a psychosociologically convincing story about how violence might rise to high levels or not do so. This story then can be tried out against cases where, within a single country or state, one region or community exhibits violence and the other does not.

Margaret Levi also notes that the contrasts she wishes to explain, such as differences in enlistment rates between francophone and anglophone regions of Canada, are not explained by any standard sociological variables. The most important differences between the two regions are highly specific to Canadian history: memories and interpretations of the initial social compact, levels of trust in the state, and judgments about what members of the other community are likely to do in the future. These variables are the outcomes of the particular history of interactions between the two communities as political and cultural blocs in Canada. They are not usefully generalized to other countries and thus cannot serve as the building blocks for an inductive, cross-country comparison. (Generalizability is important to Levi, however, and she finds it in a model of "contingent consent," developed out of this and other cases.)

Fredrik Barth points out an additional problem with inductive, cross-cultural comparative method: it presumes that a representative type, an average, or a main tendency can be identified for each society or "culture." But, he continues, variation may be as great within societies as across them, and may be due to the same mechanisms. (A similar logical problem exists regarding comparing of means between any two distributions – most explosively, in US contexts, means and distributions of IQ scores.) By focusing only on between-society variation, one may misunderstand the sources of variation.

Greg Urban's essay provides a theoretical argument for why sequences of events in one place would provide more convincing evidence for a hypothesis than would comparisons of traits or events across very different societies. As did Barth, Urban notes that before we can compare things we have to classify them as tokens of particular types: what will count as a weapon? what will count as crying? what will count as "nationalism" or "electoral reform"? Urban argues that, as practiced in cross-cultural studies, coding loses sight of the meanings attached to objects in particular times and places, and of changes in objects (their "mercuriality") as they are transmitted through time and space. Urban's anthropological comments on cross-cultural coding resemble Sartori's (1970) political science critique of the conceptual "stretching" used to incorporate ideas or processes from different countries within the same analytical framework. In the same vein, Barth points out that comparisons are in fact made of *descriptions* of social processes or institutions, not the processes or institutions themselves, and that these descriptions are always preshaped by theoretical approaches.

Contrasts and models

The process of developing models usually involves noting a contrast – often a puzzling one – and then asking what ideas about human motives and actions would plausibly account for it. Miriam Golden had spent considerable time in Italy gathering information for a book about Italian trade unions. She had difficulty understanding why union leaders would call for strikes in some situations and not in others, when workforce reductions were equally likely. She realized that she was assuming that these leaders would base their decisions about a strike on the likelihood of the reductions, and that this assumption was probably what prevented her from making sense of their actions. Consequently, she tried out a different set of assumptions. In her revised view, union leaders, taking the long view, sought above all to keep the unions in business by looking after the survival of their shopfloor organizations. They gave less priority to maintaining overall workforce levels. Because strikes are costly, she reasoned, union leaders would call for a strike only when union activists were targeted. In those countries where institutions were in place that prevented such targeting, one would expect to see lower rates of striking over workforce reductions than in countries where such institutions were absent.

The model here is a simple and reasonable set of ideas about how union leaders in all modern industrialized countries would be likely to behave. It accorded well with available literature on the general vulnerability of unions in all countries.

Other models developed by the authors consist of similarly elemental ideas about how actors might weigh competing possible actions. Many citizens of large, modern states wish to comply with the law, and to make their contribution to social welfare, through enlisting in the army or paying taxes, but will be much less likely to do so if they believe that other citizens are not doing their fair share (Levi). Politicians will respond to voter enthusiasm for civil service reform, but not if they believe that benefits at the polls will be outweighed by a potential loss of support from those people benefiting from patronage jobs (Geddes). In some cases the models concern cognitive and emotional processes, as when Greg Urban argues that because certain forms of speaking are cross-culturally associated with certain emotions (such as "creaky voice" with displays of sadness and mourning), if they are given other meanings, then those other meanings will always be in addition to, never instead of, their basic meanings. Barth and Urban emphasize that fieldwork generated a set of axes of variation, much as reading descriptive studies led Laitin and Levi to develop their models of processes.

In every case, the process of developing models about mechanisms has depended on prior acquisition of extensive area knowledge. Anthropologists typically carry out long periods of fieldwork, but so did some of the political scientists included here. For Barbara Geddes (in Brazil), Roger Petersen (in Lithuania), and Miriam Golden (in Italy), the study of an initial country led them to uncover the patterns that then provoked the development of a more general model. David Laitin's work has involved ethnographic and historical study in Africa and Europe. Margaret Levi's studies have been based on archival work. Indeed, precisely because the models advocated by these political scientists include highly contextualized accounts of motives, variation, and history, their development required the kind of in-depth knowledge associated with area studies.[2]

Cases and narratives

I now put forward my more contentious claim, that it is the historical analysis of motives and events, and not cross-country comparisons, that offers the most telling evidence for each contributor's argument.

Let me begin with the chapters by Laitin and Petersen, which are very similar in method. Laitin's evidence comes from two pairs of regions within a country (or former country): the Basque and Catalan regions of Spain, and, in the former Soviet Union, Georgia and Ukraine. Basque Country and Georgia are the members of the pairs with high levels of political violence, but Laitin shows that many plausible comparative stories could have accounted for higher levels in Catalonia or the Ukraine, had they arisen. How, then, do we explain the different levels of nationalist-oriented violence for these pairs?[3]

Drawing on Petersen's work, Laitin argues that certain features of local social groups, combined with the relative difficulty of getting people to commit to a nationalist program (which he identifies here with language choice), will favor the escalation of violence in some communities vis-à-vis others. Once the tipping point is reached, a culture of violence becomes self-sustaining. In Laitin's narrative of violence in Basque Country, some of the events are "random," but their social and cultural consequences are illuminated by the model. The account employs the idea of a psychosocial mechanisms, which serves to account for why cycles of violence *can* develop under certain circumstances, but, given the random nature of events, cannot predict that they *will* do so.[4]

Laitin gives the model further plausibility by testing it against a second contrast, that of relatively peaceful Ukraine and relatively violent Georgia. The key variables turn out to be the same: the density of social networks, the level of Communist Party membership, the difficulty of learning the regional language. Laitin cautions us not only that one could construct a plausible story, using the same mechanisms, to "explain" Ukrainian violence and Georgian peace, but also that the future may deliver precisely such a reversal of polarity.[5]

The "test" of the model that Laitin offers is that he can tell the stories of violence and the stories of peaceful bargaining by referring to the same factors. Laitin tells two stories of contrasting trajectories within roughly uniform macrosocial environments, and he tells those stories using approximately the same mechanisms. The robustness or generality of the model lies in the sequence of mechanisms employed in the narratives of escalating or non-escalating violence. It does not lie in the strength of associations between explanatory variables and outcome variables across a number of cases – after all, tomorrow could bring an outbreak of violence in Ukraine, and either a massive coding headache or the collapse of an inductive claim.[6]

Petersen's overall research strategy has been to develop an ethnohistorical data base in Lithuania, and then work outward to other parts of the Balkans and to other regions of eastern Europe. His major finding from the Lithuanian data is that, when members of villages were interviewed about events of anti-Soviet resistance in the mid-1940s, they reported a sequence of mechanisms that corresponded to the sequence in the model he and Laitin have proposed. Some mechanisms, such as the reliance of certain families on norms of honor, come into play at an early stage of resistance; others, such as threats against non-resisters, become effective only at later stages.

Petersen does make comparisons across villages – for example, in testing the hypothesis that the larger the percentage of community residents who are of draft age the more likely a higher level of resistance activities in the village. However, his argument (Petersen forthcoming: 148–75) rests crucially on the detailed tracing of the sequence of events in his main study village, Svainikai. In that village, the western social (*talka*) group had a particularly high level of face-to-face contact, and indeed it was that group that initiated anti-Soviet resistance in the 1940s. Resistance was able to grow in that village because of the presence of key actors with multiple group memberships, who were able to bring new villagers into resistance activities.

Having explained that particular sequence, Petersen then looks to several other villages to show what happened when these key social characteristics were absent. The village referred to as "#21" did not continue along this path, and one plausible reason, as Petersen modestly puts his case, is that they lacked the overlapping social groups that pushed along resistance in Svainikai.

Laitin and Petersen's analyses are not inductive comparisons along Mill's lines, but narratives of social processes that are illuminated by a model and then given added plausibility by the use of contrasting cases. Their accounts direct us to look for divergent pathways as ways of discerning (and then trying out) models of social processes.

My own chapter does not develop an overall model, but does resemble the studies just discussed in its examination of contrasting trajectories followed in neighboring regions. Here the general social phenomenon is not "nationalism" or "resistance", but "religious reformism." I identify three kinds of differences between pairs of Islamic reform movements. First, I delineate processes of self-differentiation within a region or city. Townspeople in the highland Sumatran town of Takèngën engage in their own comparative activity (recall Urban's point) when they define their reformed ways of worship over and against those of their unenlightened neighbors. Their brand of reformism contrasts with that practiced in the neighboring lowland society, and this difference is better explained as adaptations to different microenvironments (although some degree of self-differentiation enters in). Finally, I offer a "most different case" comparison, between Indonesia and Morocco. Certain general cultural differences, for example concerning ideologies and practices of gender, create contrasts between all Indonesian and all Moroccan religious reformisms. I focus on those mechanisms that plausibly underlie historical processes of differentiation, but do not, given this approach, find it necessary to assume that one has the same object, "reformism," in all societies.

The essays by Levi, Geddes, and Golden employ comparisons across countries and through time, and could be read as growing out of Mill's inductive tradition. I do not read them in this way, however, nor do I believe the authors intend them to be so understood.

Levi refers to her approach as an "analytic narrative." In her efforts to account for differences in enlistment across countries, Levi identifies intriguing contrasts, most interestingly within one of her countries,

Canada, where far fewer francophones than anglophones enlisted. She thus starts from the same point as does Laitin, by pointing to a highly contextualized contrast within a country. In Canada, the two linguistic communities are highly interdependent; indeed, through their interactions and perceptions of one another they nearly define the state of political play in Canada at any time. Her account emphasizes the different policy implications of these interactions: francophone concern for fairness led fewer Quebecois than anglophones to volunteer; this hesitancy led the majority anglophone community to support conscription (to compel the francophones to carry their share of the war burden); laws on conscription then had additional consequences for inter-community relations. Levi's study is a good example of how comparativists can explicitly build "path dependency" into their models.[7]

Geddes explicitly addresses the question of explanation in her comparative study of civil service reform in Latin America. She derives her hypothesis from the case of Brazil and tests it against several other countries – but I would argue that she clinches the case when she explores historical shifts in each country. Geddes controls for macrosocial context by limiting her study to five middle-income countries in Latin America in which democracy had been fairly well established but had predated efforts at civil service reform. This strict delimitation of region holds constant Iberian culture, colonial influence, and economic development, and ensures that politicians had time to consider alternative electoral and patronage strategies.

As in Levi's case, Geddes' model includes mixed motives and a specification of the conditions under which politicians take one or another course of action. Politicians would like to reform their bureaucracies, because patronage systems prevent them from making the social and economic improvements that, for reasons of self-interest and concern for public welfare, they would like to see accomplished. But they hesitate to undertake reform, because patronage is a way of building up electoral support. If public pressure for reform is low, a majority party will have little reason to weaken their political base by initiating civil service reform. But if two parties are about equal, and if there is some public demand for such reform, each might seek to become the majority party by gaining electoral support as the party of reform.

These predictions are born out by the cases, but each case also introduces a number of country-specific institutions and histories. In Colombia, party leaders agree to stop intolerably high levels of political violence. In Uruguay, leaders of factions within parties out-maneuver their intra-party rivals by setting up a new patronage system. Additional assumptions are required to make the cases turn out as expected. In Chile, for example, the small parties do not band together to pass reform measures, as predicted by the model. Geddes explains this apparent deviation by noting that Chile's open-list rule allows candidates from the same party to compete against one another, making patronage especially important and reform unattractive. Not only do the situations differ substantially from one country to the next, but, as Geddes acknowledges, the variables do not admit of independent measurement – how much patronage? how much demand for reform?

Given these complexities of explanation, Geddes' argument is best supported, I find, when she examines sequences of events within each country. It is more convincing to claim that the demand for reform, or the relative power of a party or faction, rose or fell within one country than to try to compare levels of demand or power across countries. Her finding, that in each country reforms are reversed when the balance of power among parties becomes unequal, does not require comparability of variables across countries, only comparability of *processes*, and makes her overall argument compelling.

Golden also limits her sample to countries with similar ideas and histories: in her case, to four industrialized countries with labor unions capable of calling for strikes. She recounts how in Italy, Japan, and Britain, union successes were followed by disastrous union defeats. She derives a model in which unions primarily work to safeguard activists, and applies it to the four countries. Were the only comparisons offered those between countries, then the reader would be likely to raise numerous questions about how to interpret differences in strike frequency between, say, the United States and Japan. Many relevant factors other than union strength or labor laws differ substantively between these two countries, among them the degree of power held by a centralized state in Japan compared with the relatively diffused power in the United States. But Golden's crucial data is the set of parallel histories of strikes over workforce reductions in each country, each of which confirms her model. In Japan, for example, unions sharply reduced the number of such strikes after about 1960, because firms guaranteed job security to unionized employees and stopped targeting activists. Golden also can draw on her model to explain cross-industry contrasts: in Britain strikes are called against mining authorities, but not against automobile manufacturers, for predictable reasons.

Allen Johnson's study is the most explicitly historical. Initially he identifies it as a "controlled comparison" (citing Nadel and Eggan), but he then points to the systemic nature of the social changes examined. In the region of Brazil under study, changes occurred in demography, technology, market conditions, class consciousness, public health, and so forth. Although he had formulated a general hypothesis in 1967 – that paternalism and proletarian consciousness will appear in complementary distribution, one strong and the other weak – the restudy is not a test of that general hypothesis but an account of a very particular set of transformations. The welfare state, in the form of health facilities, land reform, and retirement benefits, reached Boa Ventura at about the same time as the new landlord began to practice less paternalism and more capitalism. As a result, in this region, but not everywhere, "client consciousness" has not become "proletarian consciousness" but rather "smallholder consciousness."

Conclusions

This is not a monological venture. Recalling that this project has itself involved a "most different case" strategy in choosing contributors, one would be highly surprised to find a single path of analysis. By and large, the political scientists highlight the possibility of telling a deductive story; the anthropologists, of exploring fields of variation. Some combination of disciplinary and career histories make this contrast inevitable.

This initial difference makes the areas of agreement all the more interesting. Taken together, the essays point both to the ubiquity of comparisons in social science, and to the critical role played therein by microhistorical accounts. Comparisons – or, as I would prefer to call them, contextualized contrasts – help generate initial ideas about the mechanisms underlying a type of social process. These ideas are limited to a certain region – Amazonia, post-Franco Spain, modern states with military drafts. They may be ideas about how ritual forms are transmitted, or how a culture of violence is created, or what leads union leaders to change their propensity to call a strike. They have microhistorical content: about changes in ideas, motives, or actions. Proving these ideas – trying, testing, demonstrating them – requires offering a narrative account, one that takes maximal account of multiple causes and massive contingencies. Often the proof involves several such accounts, using two or more cases that are matched according to various criteria of similarity and difference. Proving the argument is, therefore, not inducing a general association from the presence or absence of variables, but offering to readers a plausible narrative of credible social complexity.

Notes

1 In a recent reanalysis of macrohistorical studies, William Sewell (1996) makes a parallel argument to that presented here, claiming that several authors in historical sociology misleadingly represent what are in fact good analytical histories as if they were inductive proofs of causal relationships.

2 We continue to disagree about what counts as evidence for motives, and this disagreement probably reflects both different types of fieldwork and different theoretical commitments. Golden, for example, claims that union leaders were uninformative sources on their own motives, and that better evidence lay in patterns of action. Her point is probably most relevant when the fieldwork consists of surveys or brief discussions, and less so when it includes long-term ethnographic work. The political scientists included here are probably also more sympathetic to the idea of "revealed preference" than are the anthropologists.

3 David Collier (1991) discusses the importance of how pairs are selected for comparative analysis. I would call Laitin's approach one of "contextualized contrasts", in that the focus is on difference between two cases that share a deep historical and regional context. Skocpol and Somers' (1980) "contrast of contexts" is related to this contrastive approach, but ultimately they return to an inductive model.

4 See the lengthy discussion of this point in our introduction to this volume.

5 One might note that the concepts of honor, nation, and language that play a central role in Laitin's account probably delimit the scope of its applicability to certain areas of the world. For example, in Indonesian history, the Indonesian language has served as an emblem of nationalism, but, perhaps because speaking many languages is taken for granted, language commitment has not played a major role in recruitment to nationalist movements. Perhaps functional equivalents could be identified for this and other areas.

6 Laitin's study probably fits into what Andrew Abbott (1992) calls the "interactionist" model of narrative account, where patterns and contingency are both expected.

7 For a fuller account see Levi (1997: 134–64), in which she develops parallel historical accounts of enlistment, conscription, and conscientious objection in several countries.

References

Abbot, Andrew 1992. "What Do Cases Do? Some Notes on Activity in Sociological Analysis," in Charles C. Ragin and Howard S. Becker (eds.), *What Is A Case? Exploring the Foundations of Social Inquiry*, Cambridge: Cambridge University Press, 53–82.

Abraham, Katherine G. and Medoff, James L. 1984. "Length of Service and Layoffs in Union and Nonunion Work Groups," *Industrial and Labor Relations Review*, vol. 38, no. 1 (Oct.), 87–97.

Almond, Gabriel 1990. *A Divided Discipline*, Newbury Park: Sage.

Alt, J. and Shepsle, Kenneth (eds.) 1990. *Perspectives on Positive Political Economy*, Berkeley and Los Angeles: University of California Press.

Amaral, Carlos Verissimo do 1966. *Politica e Administracao de Pessoal: Estudos de Dois Casos* [Politics and Personal Administration: Two Case Studies], Cadernos de Administracao Publica 60, Rio de Janeiro: Fundacao Getulio Vargas.

Ames, Barry 1987. *Political Survival: Politicians and Public Policy in Latin America*, Berkeley: University of California Press.

Anderson, Benedict 1983. *Imagined Communities*, London: Verso.

Archer, Ronald 1990. "Clientelism and Political Parties in Colombia: A Party System in Transition?" Presented at the annual meeting of the Midwest Political Science Association, Chicago.

Ascher, William 1975. "Planters, Politics, and Technocracy in Argentina and Chile," Ph.D. dissertation, Yale University.

Barnes, Robert 1980. "Marriage, Exchange and the Meaning of Corporations in Eastern Indonesia," in J. K. Comaroff (ed.), *The Meaning of Marriage Payments*, London: Academic Press.

1987. "Anthropological Comparisons," in L. Holy (ed.), *Comparative Anthropology*, Oxford: Basil Blackwell.

Barth, Fredrik 1953. *Principles of Social Organization in Southern Kurdistan*, Oslo: Universitetets Ethnografiske Museum Bulletin no. 7.

1959. *Political Leadership Among Swat Pathans*, London: The Athlone Press.

1971. "Tribes and Intertribal Relations in the Fly Headwaters," *Oceania* XLI (3).

1975. *Ritual and Knowledge Among the Baktaman of New Guinea*, New Haven: Yale University Press.

1987. *Cosmologies in the Making: A Generative Approach to Cultural Variation in Inner New Guinea*, Cambridge: Cambridge University Press.

241

1989. "The analysis of culture in complex societies," *Ethos* 54 (III–IV): 120–42.

1992. "Towards greater naturalism in conceptualizing societies," in A. Kuper (ed.), *Conceptualizing Society*, London: Routledge.

1993. *Balinese Worlds*, Chicago: University of Chicago Press.

Benevides, Maria Victoria Mesquita 1981. *A UDN e o Udenismo* [The UDN and UDNism], Rio de Janeiro: Paz e Terra.

Bendix, Reinard 1978. *Kings or People*, Berkeley: University of California Press.

Biles, Robert 1972. "Patronage Politics: Electoral Behavior in Uruguay," Ph.D. dissertation, Johns Hopkins University.

1978. "Political Participation in Urban Uruguay: Mixing Public and Private Ends," in *Political Participation in Latin America*, I, *Citizen and State*, John Booth and Mitchell Seligson (eds.), New York: Holmes & Meier.

Boas, Franz 1887a. "The Occurrence of Similar Inventions in Areas Widely Apart," *Science*, 9: 485–86.

1887b. "Museums of ethnology and their Classification," *Science*, 9: 587–89.

1887c. "Museums of ethnology and their Classification," *Science*, 9: 614.

Booth, Allison L. 1987. "Extra-statutory Redundancy Payments in Britain," *British Journal of Industrial Relations*, 25, 3 (Nov.), 401–18.

Bourdieu, Pierre 1972. *Esquisse d'une Theorie de las Pratique*, Geneva: Droz.

Bowen, John R. 1992. "On Scriptural Essentialism and Ritual Variation: Muslim Sacrifice in Sumatra and Morocco," *American Ethnologist*, 19: 656–71.

1993a. *Muslims Through Discourse: Religion and Ritual in Gayo Society*, Princeton: Princeton University Press.

1993b. "A Modernist Muslim Poetic: Irony and Social Critique in Islamic Verse," *Journal of Asian Studies*, 45: 629–46.

Brewer-Carías, Allan-Randolph 1975a. *Cambio Politico y Reforma del Estado en Venezuela* [Political Change and State Reform in Venezuela]. Madrid: Tecnos.

1975b. "La Reforma Administrativa en Venezuela (1969–1973): Estrategias, Tacticas y Criterios" [Administrative Reform in Venezuela: Strategies, tactics, and criteria]," in *Reforma Administrativa: Experiencias Latino-americanas* [Administrative Reform: Latin American Experiences]. Mexico City: Instituto Nacional de Administration Publica.

1985. *El estado incomprendido: Reflexiones sobre el sistema politico y su reforma* [The Misunderstood State: Reflections on the Political System and its Reform], Caracas: Vadell Hermanos.

Briggs, Charles L. 1992. "'Since I am a woman, I will chastise my relatives': Gender, Reported Speech, and the (Re)production of Social Relations in Warao Ritual Wailing," *American Ethnologist*, 19 (2): 337–61.

1993. "Personal Sentiments and Polyphonic Voices in Warao Women's Ritual Wailing: Music and Poetics in a Critical and Collective Discourse," *American Anthropologist*, 95 (4): 929–57.

Buettner-Janusch, John 1957. "Boas and Mason: Particularism Versus Generalization," *American Anthropologist*, 59, 318–25.

Bunce, Valerie, and Chong, Dennis 1990. "The Party's Over: Mass Protest and the End of Communist Rule in Eastern Europe," unpublished manuscript.

Burton, Michael L. and White, Douglas R. 1987. Cross-cultural Surveys Today," *Annual Review of Anthropology*, 16: 143–60.

Calmfors, Lars and Driffill, John 1988. "Bargaining Structure, Corporatism and Macroeconomic Performance," *Economic Policy*, 3, 1 (April): 13–61.

Carr, Raymond and Fusi, Juan Pablo 1979. *Spain: Dictatorship to Democracy*, London: George Allen and Unwin.

1985. *Catalunya terre lliure: documents del moviment de defensa de la terra 1985–1988*, Sant Boi: Lluita.

Chernela, Janet n.d. "Ethnopoetics of Wept Greetings among Eastern Tukanoan Speakers of the Brazilian Northwest Amazon."

Christelow, Allan 1992. "The Muslim Judge and Municipal Politics in Colonial Algeria and Senegal," in Juan R. I. Cole (ed.), *Comparing Muslim Societies*, Ann Arbor: University of Michigan, 113–62.

Clark, Robert 1984. *The Basque Insurgents: ETA, 1952–1980*, Madison: University of Wisconsin Press.

Clifford, James and Marcus, George (eds.) 1987. *Writing Culture*, Berkeley and Los Angeles: University of California Press.

Cohen, Youssef 1989. *The Manipulation of Consent: The State and Working-Class Consciousness in Brazil*, Pittsburgh: Pittsburgh University Press.

Collier, David 1991. "The Comparative Method: Two Decades of Change," in D. Rustow and T. H. Eriksen (eds.), *Comparative Political Dynamics: Global Research Perspectives*, New York: HarperCollins, 7–31.

Combs-Schilling, M. E. 1989. *Sacred Performances: Islam, Sexuality, and Sacrifice*, New York: Columbia University Press.

Cotler, Julio 1968. "Le Mecanica de la Dominacion Interna y del Cambio Social en la Sociedad Rural," in Jose Matos Mar et al., (eds.), *Peru Problema*, Lima: Francisco Moncoa.

1978. *Clases, Estado y Nacion en el Peru*, Lima: Instituto de Estudios Peraunos.

Cova, Antonio and Hannot, Thamara 1986. "La Administracion publica: Otra forma de ver a una villana incomprendida" [Public administration: Another view of a misunderstood villain], in Moises Naim and Roman Pinango (eds.), *El Caso Venezuela: Una ilusion de armonia* [The Venezuelan case: An illusion of harmony], Caracas: Ediciones IESA.

Cox, Gary 1986. "The Development of a party-oriented Electorate in England, 1932–1918," *British Journal of Political Science*, 16: 187–216.

Davies, James C. 1969. "The J-Curve of Rising and Declining Satisfactions as a Cause of Some Great Revolutions and a Contained Rebellion," in H. Graham and T. Gurr (eds.), *Violence in America*, New York: Signet, 671–709.

Derrida, Jacques 1986. "Structure, sign and play in the discourse of the humans sciences," in Hazard Adams and Leroy Searle (eds.), *Critical Theory Since 1965*, Tallahassee: University Presses of Florida, 83–94.

de Soto, Hernando 1986. *El otro Sendero: La Revolucion Informal* [The Other Path: The Informal Revolution], Lima: Editorial El Barranco; published in English as *The Other Path: The Invisible Revolution in the Third World*, New York: Harper & Row, 1989.

Deutsch, Karl 1954. *Nationalism and Social Communication*, Cambridge, MA: MIT Press.

Díez Medrano, Juan 1995. *Divided Nations: Development, Class and Nationalism in the Basque Country and Catalonia*, Ithaca: Cornell University Press (page numbers in text refer to a prepublication draft of 1992).

DiGiacomo, Susan M. 1985. "The Politics of Identity: Nationalism in Catalonia," Ph.D. thesis, University of Massachusetts.

Dion, Douglas 1998. "Evidence and Inference in the Comparative Case Study," *Comparative Politics*, 30, 2 (January): 127–45.

Dix, Robert H. 1980. "Consociational Democracy: The Case of Colombia," *Comparative Politics*, 12: 303–21.

Duff, Ernest. 1971. "The Role of Congress in the Colombian Political System." in Weston Agor (ed.), *Latin America Legislatures*, New York: Praeger.

Dunlop, John T. 1944. *Wage Discrimination under Trade Unions*, New York: Macmillan.

Durkheim, Emile 1965 [1915]. *The Elementary forms of the Religious Life*, trans. Joseph Ward Swain, New York: Free Press.

Eckstein, Harry 1975. 'Case Study and Theory in Political Science," in F. I. Greenstein and N. Polsby (eds.), *Handbook of Political Science*, VII, *Strategies of Inquiry*, Reading: Addison-Wesley.

Eggan, Fred 1950. *The Social Organization of the Western Pueblo*, Chicago: University of Chicago Press.

    1954. "Social Anthropology and the Method of Controlled Comparison," *American Anthropologist*, 56: 743–63.

    1966. *The American Indian*, Chicago: Aldine.

Elster, Jon. 1983. *Explaining Technical Change: A Case Study in the Philosophy of Science*, New York: Cambridge University Press.

    1989. *The Cement of Society: A Study of Social Order*, Cambridge: Cambridge University Press.

    1989. *Nuts and Bolts for the Social Sciences*, Cambridge: Cambridge University Press.

    1993. *Political Psychology*, Cambridge: Cambridge University Press.

Elorriaga, Gabriel 1983. *La Batalla de las Autonomias*, Madrid: Azara.

    1988. *Esprai*, no. 2, organ of Terra Lliure.

Emmerich, Herbert 1960. "Administrative Roadblocks to Coordinated Development," prepared for the Expert Working Group on Social Aspects of Economic Development in Latin America. Mexico City.

    1972 [1958]. "Informe sobre un Estudio Preliminar acerca de posibilidades de mejoras en la Administración Pública de Venezuela" [Report on a preliminary study of possible improvements in Venezuelan public administration], in *Informe sobre la reforma de la Administración Pública Nacional* [Report on the reform of national public administration], I, Caracas: Comisión de Reforma de la Administracion Public.

Farber, Henry S. 1986. "The Analysis of Union Behavior," in Orley Ashenfelter and Richard Layard (eds.), *Handbook of Labor Economics*, II, Amsterdam: North Holland.

Fabregat, Julio T. 1963. *Elecciones Uruguayas* [Uruguayan Elections]. VI, Montevideo: Corte Electoral.

Fanon, Frantz 1968. *The Wretched of the Earth*, New York: Grove Press.

FBIS (Foreign Broadcast Information Service), Washington, DC [dates noted as year, month, day, so 911001 = October 1, 1991).

Feder, Luis 1971. *The Rape of the Peasantry*, Garden City: Anchor Books.

Ferejohn, John 1991. "Rationality and Interpretation: Parliamentary Elections in Early Stuart England," in Kristen Monroe (ed.), *The Economic Approach to Politics*.

Fischer, Michael M. J. and Abedi, Mehdi 1990. *Debating Muslims: Cultural Dialogues in Postmodernity and Tradition*, Madison: University of Wisconsin Press.

Fitzpatrick, David 1989. "'A peculiar tramping people': the Irish in Britain, 1801–1870," in W. E. Vaughan (ed.), *A New History of Ireland: Ireland Under the Union* I, *1801–1870*, ch. 28, vol. V, Oxford: Clarendon Press.

Flora, Peter, Kraus, Franz and Pfenning, Winifred 1987. *State, Economy, and Society in Western Europe, 1815–1975*, II, *The Growth of Industrial Societies and Capitalist Economies*, London: Macmillan.

Floud, Roderick, Gregory, Annabel and Wachter, Kenneth 1990. *Height, Health, and History: Nutritional Status in the United Kingdom, 1750–1980*, Cambridge: Cambridge University Press.

Forman, Shepard 1975. *The Brazilian Peasantry*, New York: Colombia University Press.

Foster, George, Scudder, Thayer, Colson, Elizabeth and Kemper, Robert V. (eds.) 1979. *Long Term Field Research in Social Anthropology*, New York: Academic Press.

Foucault, Michel 1973 [1966]. *The Order of Things: An Archaeology of the Human Sciences*. New York: Vintage Books.

Fox, James J. (ed.) 1980. *The Flow of Life*, Cambridge, MA: Harvard University Press.

Freedman, Paul 1988. "Cowardice, Heroism and the Legendary Origins of Catalonia," *Past and Present*, 21, November: 3-28, 1988.

Freeman, Richard B. and James L. Medoff 1984. *What Do Unions Do?*, New York: Basic Books, 1984.

Fujita, Wakao 1974. "Labor Disputes," in Kazuo Okochi, Bernard Karsh and Solomon B. Levine (eds.), *Workers and Employers in Japan: The Japanese Employment Relations System*, Tokyo: Princeton University Press and University of Tokyo Press.

Furtado, Celso 1965. *Diagnosis of the Brazilian Crisis*, Berkeley: University of California Press.

Galjart, Benno 1964. "Class and 'Following' in Rural Brazil," *American Latine* 7(3): 3–24.

Geddes, Barbara. 1990. "How the Cases You Choose Affect the Answers You Get: Selection Bias in Comparative Politics," *Political Analysis*, 2: 131–50.

   1994. *The Politician's Dilemma: Building State Capacity in Latin America*, Series on Social Choice and Political Economy, Berkeley: University of California Press.

   1995. "The Uses and Limitations of Rational Choice," in Peter Smith (ed.), *Latin America in Comparative Perspective: New Approaches to Analysis and Methods*, Boulder: Westview.

Geertz, Clifford 1968. *Islam Observed*, Chicago, IL: University of Chicago Press.

1973. *The Interpretation of Culture*, New York: Basic Books.

1984. "Anti anti-relativism," *American Anthropologist*, 86 (2): 263–78.

Gellner, Ernest 1983. *Nations and Nationalism*, Ithaca: Cornell University Press.

Gennard, John 1982. "Great Britain," in Edward Yemin (ed.), *Workforce Reductions in Undertakings: Policies and Measures for the Protection of Redundant Workers in Seven Industrialized Market Economy Countries*, Geneva: International Labour Office.

Godelier, Maurice and Strathern, Marilyn (eds.) 1990. *Big Men and Great Men: Personification of Power in Melanesia*, Cambridge: Cambridge University Press.

Golden, Miriam A. 1988. *Labor Divided: Austerity and Working Class Politics in Contemporary Italy*, Ithaca: Cornell University Press.

1989. "Le sconfitte eroiche della classe operaia," *Politica ed Economia*, 19, 1 (Jan.): 33–34.

Goldstone, Jack A. 1994. "Is Revolution Individually Rational? Groups and Individuals in Revolutionary Collective Action," *Rationality and Society*, 6: 139–66.

González G., Fernan 1980. "Clientelismo y administracion publica" [Clientelism and public administration], *Enfoques colombianos: Clientelismo*, 14: 67–106.

Goody, Jack 1990. *The Oriental, the Ancient, and the Primitive*, Cambridge: Cambridge University Press.

Gould, Roger 1993. "Collective Action and Network Structure," *American Sociological Review*, 58: 182–96.

Graham, Laura 1984. "Semanticity and melody: parameters of contrast in Shavante vocal experience," *Latin American Music Review*, 5: 161–85.

1986. "Three Modes of Shavante Vocal Expression: Wailing, Collective Singing, and Political Oratory," in J. Sherzer and G. Urban (eds.), *Native South American discourse*, Berlin: Mouton de Gruyter, 83–118.

Graham, Lawrence 1968. *Civil Service Reform in Brazil: Principles vs. Practice*, Latin American Monographs no. 13, Institute of Latin American Studies, Austin: University of Texas Press.

Granovetter, Mark 1978. "Threshold Models of Collective Behavior," *American Journal of Sociology*, 83: 1420–43.

Green, Donald and Shapiro, Ian 1994. *The Pathologies of Rational Choice*, New Haven: Yale University Press.

Greif, Avner 1994. "Cultural Beliefs and the Organization of Society: A Historical and Theoretical Reflection on Collectivist and Individualist Societies," *Journal of Political Economy*, 102, 5 (October): 912–50.

Groves, Roderick 1967. "Administrative Reform and the Politics of Reform: The case of Venezuela," *Public Administration Review*, 27: 436–51.

1974. "The Colombian National Front and Administrative Reform," *Administration and Society*, 6: 316–36.

Gunther, Richard et al. 1986. *Spain after Franco*, Berkeley: University of California Press.

Gurr, Ted 1970. *Why Men Rebel*, Princeton: Princeton University Press.

Haas, Ernst 1993. "Nationalism: An Instrumental Social Construction," *Millennium*, 22, 3: 505–46.

Hall, E. F. 1884. "Civil Service Reform," *New Englander*, 43: 453–63.

Hammoudi, Abdellah 1993. *The Victim and Its Masks*, Chicago, IL: University of Chicago Press.

Hanami, Tadashi 1984. "Conflict Resolution in Industrial Relations," in Tadashi Hanami and Rober Blanpain (eds.), *Industrial Conflict Resolution in Market Economies: A Study of Australia, the Federal Republic of Germany, Italy, Japan and the USA*, Deventer: Kluwer.

Handelman, Howard 1975. *Struggle in the Andes: Peasant Political Mobilization in Peru*, Austin: University of Texas Press.

Hanham, H. J. 1973. "Religion and Nationality in Mid-Victorian England," in M. D. R. Foot (ed.), *War and Society*, London: Paul Elek, 159–82.

Hansen, Edward C. 1977. *Rural Catalonia under the Franco Regime*, Cambridge: Cambridge University Press.

Hartley, Jean, Kelly, John and Nicholson, Nigel 1983. *Steel Strike: A Case Study in Industrial Relations*, London: Batsford Academic and Educational.

Hartlyn, Jonathan 1988. *The Politics of Coalition Rule in Colombia*, Cambridge: Cambridge University Press.

Hartwig, Richard E. 1983. *Roads to Reason: Transportation, Administration, and Rationality in Colombia*. Pittsburgh: University of Pittsburgh Press.

Hayes, Carlton J. H. 1931. *Historical Evolution of Modern Nationalism*, New York: R. R. Smith.

Hays, Terence E. 1993. " 'The New Guinea Highlands': Region, Culture Area, or Fuzzy Set?" *Current Anthropology*, 34: 141–64.

Hewitt, B. G. 1990. "Aspects of Language Planning in Georgia (Georgian and Abkhaz)," in Michael Kirkwood (ed.), *Language Planning in the Soviet Union*, New York: St Martin's Press.

Hibbs, Douglas A. Jr. 1978. "On the Political Economy of Long-Run Trends in Strike Activity," *British Journal of Political Science*, 8, 2 (April): 153–77.

Hibbs, Douglas A. Jr. and Locking, Hakan 1995. "Wage Dispersion and Productive Efficiency: Evidence for Sweden," FIEF Working Paper no. 128, Stockholm: Trade Union Institute for Economic Research.

Hirschman, Albert O. 1958. *The Strategy of Economic Development*, New Haven: Yale University Press.

Hobsbawm, E. J. 1981. *Bandits*, New York: Pantheon Books.

1990. *Nations and Nationalism Since 1780*, Cambridge: Cambridge University Press.

Holy, Ladislav 1987. "Introduction," in L. Holy (ed.), *Comparative Anthropology*, Oxford: Basil Blackwell.

1991. *Religion and Custom in a Muslim Society: The Berti of Sudan*, Cambridge: Cambridge University Press.

Huntington, Samuel P. 1968. *Political Order in Changing Societies*, New Haven: Yale University Press.

Hutchinson, Bertram 1966. "The Patron-Dependent Relationship in Brazil: A Preliminary Examination," *Sociologia Ruralis*, 1: 3–30.

Hutchinson, Harry 1957. *Village and Plantation Life in Northeastern Brazil*, Seattle: University of Washington Press.

IBRD (International Bank for Reconstruction and Development 1961. *The*

Economic Development of Venezuela, Baltimore: Johns Hopkins University Press.

Ingold, T. 1993. "The art of translation in a continuous world," in G. Palsson (ed.), *Beyond Boundaries: Understanding, Translation, and Anthropological Discourse*, Oxford: Berg Publishers.

Institute for Comparative Study of Political Systems n.d. *Methods for Electing National Executives and National Legislatures in South America*, Washington, DC: Operations and Policy Research.

Johnson, Allen 1961. *Sharecroppers of the Sertão*, Stanford: Stanford University Press.

1975. "Landlords, Patrons, and 'Proletarian Consciousness' in Rural Latin America," in June Nash and Juan Carradi (eds.), *Ideology and Social Change in Latin America*, New York: CUNY.

1991. Regional Comparative Field Research. *Behavior Science Research*, 25: 3–22.

1997. The Psychology of Dependence Between Landlord and Sharecropper in Northeastern Brazil, Political Psychology, special issue, John Duckitt (ed.), *Culture and Cross Cultural Dimensions of Political Psychology*, 18: 411–38.

1998. "Repression: A Re-examination of the Concept as Applied to Folktales," *Ethos*, 26 (3): 295–313.

Johnson, Allen and Earle, Timothy 1987. *The Evolution of Human Societies*, Stanford: Stanford University Press.

Johnson, James 1996. "How Not to Criticize Rational Choice Theory: Pathologies of 'Common Sense'," *Philosophy of the Social Sciences*, 26 (1): 77–91.

Johnston, Hank 1991. *Tales of Nationalism: Catalonia 1939–1979*, New Brunswick: Rutgers University Press.

Karklins, Rasma and Petersen, Roger 1993. "Decision Calculus of Protesters and Regimes: Eastern Europe, 1989," *Journal of Politics*, 55: 588–614.

Karl, Terry 1982. "The Political Economy of Petro-dollars: Oil and Democracy in Venezuela," Ph.D. dissertation, Stanford University.

Keddie, Nikki R. (ed.) 1971. *Scholars, Saints, and Sufis*, Berkeley, CA: University of California Press.

Keman, Hans (ed.) 1993. *Comparative Politics: New Directions in Theory and Method*, Amsterdam: VU University Press.

Kerkvliet, Benedice J. 1977. *The Huk Rebellion: A Study of Peasant Revolt in the Philippines*, Berkeley: University of California Press.

King, Gary, Keohane, Robert O. and Verba, Sidney 1994. *Designing Social Inquiry: Scientific Inference in Qualitative Research*, Princeton: Princeton University Press.

Kirkwood, Michael (ed.) 1990. *Language Planning in the Soviet Union*, New York: St. Martin's Press.

Kiser, Edgar 1996. "The Revival of Narrative in Historical Sociology: What Rational Choice Theory Can Contribute," *Politics and Society*, 24: 249–71.

Kiser, Edgar and Hecter, Michael 1991. "The Role of General Theory in Comparative-Historical Sociology," *American Journal of Sociology*, 97: 1–30.

Knauft, Bruce 1993. *South New Guinea Cultures: History, Comparison, Dialectic*, Cambridge: Cambridge University Press.

Kohn, Hans 1944. *The Idea of Nationalism: A study in its Origins and Background*, New York: Macmillan.

Koike, Kazuo 1983. "Internal Labor Markets: Workers in Large Firms," in Taishiro Shirai (ed.), *Contemporary Industrial Relations in Japan*, Madison: University of Wisconsin Press.

1987. "Japanese Redundancy: The Impact of Key Labor Market Institutions on the Economic Flexibility of the Japanese Economy," in Peter T. Chinloy and Ernest W. Stromsdorfer (eds.), *Labor Market Adjustments in the Pacific Rim*, Boston: Kluwer-Nijhoff.

1988. *Understanding Industrial Relations in Modern Japan*, Houndmills, Basingstoke: Macmillan.

Korpi, Walter and Shalev, Michael 1980. "Strikes, Power, and Politics in the Western Nations, 1900–1976," in *Political Power and Social Theory*, Maurice Zeitlin (ed.), 1, Greenwich: JAI Press.

Kreps, David M. 1990. "Corporate Culture and Economic Theory," in James Alt and Kenneth Shepsle (eds.), *Perspectives in Positive Political Economy*, 90–143, New York: Cambridge University Press.

Kuran, Timur 1991. "Now out of Never: The Element of Surprise in the East European Revolution of 1989," *World Politics*, 44, 1 (October) 7–48.

1995. *Private Truths, Public Lies: The Social Consequences of Preference Falsification*, Cambridge: Harvard University Press.

Lafer, Celso 1970. *The Planning Process and the Political System: A Study of Kubitschek's Target Plan, 1956–1961*. Latin American Studies Program Dissertation Series, no. 16, Ithaca: Cornell University Press.

Laitin, David 1986. *Hegemony and Culture: Politics and Religious Change Among the Yoruba*, Chicago: The University of Chicago Press.

1988. "Language Games," *Comparative Politics*, 20: 289–302.

1989. "Linguistic Revival: Politics and Culture in Catalonia," *Comparative Studies in Society and History*, 31, 2 (April): 297–317.

1991. "The National Uprisings in the Soviet Union," *World Politics*, 44, 1 (October): 139–77.

Laitin, David and Rodrigues, Guadaluppe 1992. "Language, Ideology and the Press in Catalonia," *American Anthropologist*, 94, 1 (March): 9–30.

Laitin, David, Petersen, Roger and Slocum, John W. 1992. "Language and the State: Russian and the Soviet Union in Comparative Perspective," in A. Motyl (ed.), *Thinking Theoretically About Soviet Nationalities*, New York: Columbia University Press.

Layard, Richard, Nickell, Stephen and Jackman, Richard 1991. *Unemployment: Macroeconomic Performance and the Labour Market*, Oxford: Oxford University Press.

Lee, Raymond M. 1987. "Introduction," in Raymond M. Lee (ed.), *Redundancy, Layoffs and Plant Closures: Their Character, Causes and Consequences*, London: Croom Helm.

Leite, Celso Barroso 1978. *A Protecao Social no Brasil*, São Paulo: Edicoes Ltd.

Léry, Jean de 1972 [1578]. *Viagem a terra do Brasil*, São Paulo: Martins/ EDUSP.

Levi, Margaret 1988. *Of Rule and Revenue*, Berkeley and Los Angeles: University of California Press.

1991. "Are There Limits to Rationality?" *Archives Europeans de Sociologie*, 32: 130–41.

1997. *Consent, Dissent, and Patriotism*, Cambridge: Cambridge University Press.

Lévi-Strauss, Claude 1969. *The Raw and the Cooked* (Mythologiques I), trans. J. and D. Weightman, New York: Harper & Row.

Liber, George O. 1992. *Soviet Nationality Policy, Urban Growth, and Identity Change in the Ukrainian SSR 1923–1934*, Cambridge: Cambridge University Press.

Lieberson, Stanley 1991. "Small N's and Big Conclusions: An Examination of the Reasoning in Comparative Studies Based on a Small Number of Cases," *Social Forces*, 70 (2): 307–20.

Lijphart, Arend 1971. "Comparative Politics and Comparative Method," *American Political Science Review*, 65: 682–93.

Lima, Antonio Carlos de Souza 1991. "On indigenism and nationality in Brazil," in G. Urban and J. Sherzer (eds.), *Nation-States and Indians in Latin America*, 236–58, Austin: University of Texas Press.

Lindsay, Jack 1964. *Nine Days' Hero: Wat Tyler*, London: Dennis Dobson.

Linz, Juan. "Early State-Building and Late Peripheral Nationalisms against the State" in *Building States and Nations*, S. N. Eisenstat and Stein Rokkan (eds.), Beverly Hills: Sage, 1973.

Lippi de Oliveira, Lucia 1973. "O Partido Social Democratico" [The Social Democratic Party], Master's thesis, Instituto Universitario de Pesquisas do Rio de Janeiro.

Lipset, Seymour Martin 1981. *Political Man: The Social Basis of Politics*, Baltimore: Johns Hopkins University Press.

1985. *Consensus and Conflict*, New Brunswick: Transaction Books.

Little, David 1991. *Ukraine: The Legacy of Intolerance*, Washington, DC: USIP Press.

1993. "On the Scope and Limits of Generalizations in the Social Sciences," *Synthese*, 97: 183–207.

Lohmann, Susanne. 1992. "Rationality, Revolution, and Revolt: The Dynamics of Informational Cascades," Graduate School of Business Research Paper 1213, Stanford University.

López Pintor, Rafael 1972. "Development Administration in Chile: Structural, Normative, and Behavioral Constraints to Performance." Ph.D. dissertation, University of North Carolina.

Mace, Ruth and Pagel, Mark 1994. "The Comparative Method in Anthropology," *Current Anthropology*, 35 (December): 549–64.

McClintock, Cynthia 1981. *Peasant Cooperatives and Political Change in Peru*, Princeton: Princeton University Press.

Malloy, James 1979. *The Politics of Social Security in Brazil*, Pittsburgh: University of Pittsburgh Press.

Mandelbaum, David G. 1988. *Women's Seclusion and Men's Honor*, Tucson and London: University of Arizona Press.

Mardin, Serif 1978. "Youth and Violence in Turkey," *Arch. europ. sociol.*, XIX, 1978, 229–54.

Marwell, Gerald and Oliver, Pamela E. 1993. *The Critical Mass in Collective Action: A Micro-Social Theory*, Cambridge: Cambridge University Press.

Mars, Gerald and Altman, Yochanan, 1993. "The Cultural Bases of Soviet Georgia's Second Economy," *Soviet Studies*, 35, 4: 546–60.

Mason, Otis T. 1886. "Resemblances in arts widely separated," *American Naturalist*, 20: 246–51.

1887. "The occurrence of similar inventions in areas widely apart," *Science*, 9: 534–35.

Mayer, Lawrence, C. 1989. *Redefining Comparative Politics: Promise Versus Performance*, Newbury Park: Sage Publications.

Mayhew, David 1975. *Congress: The Electoral Connection*, New Haven: Yale University Press.

Mead, Margaret 1935. *Sex and Temperament in Three Primitive Societies*, New York: William Morrow.

Meyers, Frederic 1964. *Ownership of Jobs: A Comparative Study*, Institute of Industrial Relations Monograph No. 11, Los Angeles: University of California, Los Angeles.

Miller, Barbara D. 1997. *The Endangered Sex: Neglect of Female Children in Rural North India*, Ithaca: Cornell University Press.

Millward, Neil and Stevens, Mark 1986. *British Workplace Industrial Relations 1980–1984: The DE/ESRC/PSI/ACAS Surveys*, Aldershot: Gower.

Moberg, Mark 1994. "An Agency Model of the State: Contributions and Limitations of Institutional Economics," in James M. Acheson (ed.), *Anthropology and Institutional Economics*, Lanham: University Press of America.

Morcillo, Pedro Pablo 1975. "La Reforma Administrativa en Colombia" [Administrative Reform in Colombia], in *Reforma Administrativa: Experiencias latinoamericanas* [Administrative Reform: Latin American Experiences], Primer Seminario Interamericano de Reforma Administrativa, Mexico City: Instituto Nacional de Administracion Publica.

Morgan, L. H. 1871. *Systems of Consanguinity and Affinity of the Human Family*. Smithsonian Contributions to Knowledge, vol. XVII. Washington, DC: The Smithsonian Institution.

Morris, R. J. 1979. *Class and Class Consciousness in the Industrial Revolution 1780–1850*, London: Macmillan.

Moy, Joyanna and Sorrentino, Constance 1981. "Unemployment, Labor Force Trends, and Layoff Practices in 10 Countries." *Monthly Labor Review*, 104, 12 (Dec.): 3–13.

Munson, Henry 1993. *Religion and Politics in North Africa*, New Haven, CT: Yale University Press.

Nadel, S. F. 1952. "Witchcraft in Four African Societies: An Essay in Comparison," *American Anthropologist*, 54: 18–29.

Nakamura, Mitsuo 1983. *The Crescent Arises over the Banyan Tree*, Jogjakarta: Gajah Mada University Press.

Noer, Deliar 1973. *The Modernist Muslim Movement in Indonesia, 1900–1942*, Kuala Lumpur: Oxford University Press.

North, Douglass C. and Weingast, Barry R. 1989. "Constitutions and Commitment: The Evolution of Institutions Governing Public Choice in

Seventeenth Century England," *Journal of Economic History*, 49, 4: 803–32.

Oaklander, Harold 1982. "United States," in Edward Yemin (ed.), *Workforce Reductions in Undertakings: Policies and Measures for the Protection of Redundant Workers in Seven Industrialized Market Economy Countries*, Geneva: International Labour Office.

Oberschall, Anthony 1994. "Rational Choice in Collective Protests," *Rationality and Society*, 6: 79–100.

Oliver, Pamela, E. and Marwell, Gerald 1988. "The Paradox of Group Size in Collective Action: A Theory of the Critical Mass II," *American Sociological Review*, 53: 1–8.

Olson, Mancur 1982. *The Rise and Decline of Nations: Economic Growth Stagflation, and Social Rigidities*, New Haven: Yale University Press.

Organization for Economic Cooperation and Development 1986. *Labour Market Flexibility. Report by a High-Level Group of Experts to the Secretary-General*, Paris: OECD.

Ortner, Sherry B. 1990. "Patterns of History: Cultural Schemas in the Foundings of Sherpa Religious Institutions," in Emika Ohnuki-Tierney (ed.), *Culture Through Time: Anthropological Approaches*, Stanford: Stanford University Press.

Ostrom, Elinor 1990. *Governing the Commons: The Evolution of Institutions for Collective Action*, New York: Cambridge University Press.

Oswald, Andrew J. and Turnbull, Peter J. 1985. "Pay and Employment Determination in Britain: What Are Labour 'Contracts' Really Like?" *Oxford Review of Economic Policy*, 1, 2 (summer): 80–97.

Otyrba, Gueorgui 1994. "War in Abkhazia," in Roman Szporluk (ed.), *National Identity and Ethnicity in Russia and the New States of Eurasia*, London: M. E. Sharpe, 281–309.

Padoa-Schioppa, Fiorella 1988. "Underemployment Benefit Effects on Employment and Income Distribution: What We Should Learn from the System of the *Cassa Intergrazione Guadagni*," *Labour*, 2, 2 (Autumn): 101–24.

Parkin, David 1980. "Kind Bridewealth and Hard Cash: Eventing a Structure," in J. L. Comaroff (ed.), *The Meaning of Marriage Payments*, New York: Academic Press.

Payne, Stanley 1975. *Basque Nationalism*, Reno: University of Nevada Press.

Perez-Agote, Alfonso 1984. *La Reproduccion del nacionalismo: el caso vasco*, Madrid: CIS.

Petersen, Roger 1989. "Rationality, Ethnicity, and Military Enlistment," *Social Science Information*, 28: 564–98.

1991. "Rebellion and Resistance," Ph.D thesis, University of Chicago.

1993. "A Community-Based Theory of Rebellion," *European Journal of Sociology*, 34: 41–78.

(forthcoming). *Resistance and Rebellion: Lessons from Eastern Europe*, Cambridge: Cambridge University Press.

Pinto, Magalhães 1960. "Relatorio politico do Presidente Magalhães Pinto" [The Political Statement of President Magahlaes Pinto], Archives of the UDN, Fundação Getúlio Vergas.

Pizzorno, Alessandro 1978. "Political Exchange and Collective Identity," in Colin Crouch and Alessandro Pizzorno (eds.), *Comparative Analyses, Vol. 2 of The Resurgence of Class Conflict in Western Europe Since 1968*, New York: Holmes & Meier.

Pontusson, Jonas and Swenson, Peter 1996. "Labor Markets, Production Strategies, and Wage Bargaining Institutions: The Swedish Employer Offensive in Comparative Perspective." *Comparative Political Studies*, vol. 29, no. 2 (Spring): 223–50.

Popkin, Samuel L. 1979. *The Rational Peasant*, Berkeley: University of California Press.

Posen, Barry 1993a. "Nationalism, the Mass Army, and Military Power," *International Security*, 18, 2: 80–124.

1993b. "The Security Dilemma and Ethnic Conflict," *Survival*, 35, 1 (Spring): 27–47.

Powell, John Wesley 1887. "Museums of ethnology and their classification," *Science*, 9: 612–14.

Przeworski, Adam and Teune, Harry 1970. *Logic of Comparative Social Inquiry*, New York: John Wiley and Sons.

Quijano Obregon, Anibal 1967. "Contemporary peasant movements," in Seymour M. Lipset and Aldo Solari (eds.), *Elites in Latin America*, New York: Oxford University Press.

Ragin, Charles C. 1987. *The Comparative Method: Moving Beyond Qualitative and Quantitative Strategies*, Berkeley and Los Angeles: University of California Press.

Ramírez Goicoechea, Eugenia 1991. *De jovenes y sus identidades: socianthropologia de la etnicidad en Euskadi*, Madrid: CIS.

Reinares, Fernando 1990. "Sociogenesis y Evolucion del Terrorismo en Espana," in Salvador Giner (ed.), *Espana: sociedad y politica*, Madrid: Espana Calpe.

RFE (Radio Free Europe) Reports (dates noted as year, month, day, so 911001 = October, 1991).

Rial, Juan 1985. *Elecciones 1984: Un triunfo del centro* [Elections of 1984: Triumph of the Center], Montevideo: Ediciones de la Banda Oriental.

Riker, William 1990. "Political Science and Rational Choice," in James Alt and Kenneth A. Shepsle (eds.), *Perspectives on Positive Political Economy*, Cambridge: Cambridge University Press.

Riviere, Peter 1984. *Individual and Society in Guiana*, Cambridge: Cambridge University Press.

Roff, William R. 1987. "Islamic Movements: One or Many?" in William R. Roff (ed.), *Islam and the Political Economy of Meaning*, 31–52. Berkeley: University of California Press.

Rogowski, Ronald 1995. "The Role of Theory and Anomaly in Social-Scientific Inference," *American Political Science Review*, 89: 467–70.

Romero Maura, J. 1968. "Terrorism in Barcelona and its Impact on Spanish Politics, 1904–1909," *Past and Present*, 41: 130–83.

Rosen, Lawrence 1984. *Bargaining for Reality*. Chicago: University of Chicago Press.

Rosenthal, Jean-Laurent 1992. *The Fruits of Revolution*, Cambridge: Cambridge University Press.

Ross, Arthur M. 1948. *Trade Union Wage Policy*, Berkeley: University of California Press.

Rothstein, Bo 1992. "Labor-Market Institutions and Working-Class Strength," in Sven Steinmo, Kathleen Thelen and Frank Longstreth (eds.), *Structuring Policies: Historical Institutionalism in Comparative Analysis*, Cambridge: Cambridge University Press.

Ruddle, Kenneth and Gillette, Philip (eds.) 1972. *Latin American Political Statistics: Supplement to the Statistical Abstract of Latin America*, Los Angeles: University of California, Los Angeles Latin American Center.

Rustow, Dankwart and Eriksen, Thomas Hylland (eds.) 1991. *Comparative Political Dynamics: Global Research Perspectives*, New York: HarperCollins.

Sahlins, Marshall 1958. *Social Stratification in Polynesia*, Seattle: American Ethnological Society.

Sartori, Giovanni 1970. "Concept Misinformation in Comparative Politics," *American Political Science Review*, 64: 1033–53.

Schattschneider, Emil E. 1942. *Party Government*, New York: Rinehart.

Scharpf, Fritz 1990. "Games Real Actors Could Play," *Rationality and Society*, 2 (October), 471–94.

Schelling, Thomas 1978. *Micromotives and Macrobehavior*, New York: Norton.

  1985. *Micromotives and Macrobehavior*, New York: Gordon & Breach.

Schmidt, Steffen 1974. "Bureaucrats As Modernizing Brokers?" *Comparative Politics*, 6: 425–50.

Scognamiglio, Renato 1990. *Diritto del lavoro*, Naples: Jovene.

Scott, James C. 1976. *The Moral Economy of the Peasant*, New Haven: Yale University Press.

  1985. *Weapons of the Weak: Everyday Forms of Peasant Resistance*, New Haven: Yale University Press.

Sen, Amartya K. 1967. "Isolation, Assurance and the Social Rate of Discount," *Quarterly Journal of Economics*, 81: 112–24.

Sewell, William H. Jr. 1996. "Three Temporalities: Toward an Eventful Sociology," in Terrence J. McDonald (ed.), *The Historic Turn in the Human Sciences*, Ann Arbor: University of Michigan Press, 245–80.

Shabad, Goldie 1992. "Still the exception? Democratization and Ethnic Nationalism in the Basque Country of Spain," paper presented at the Conference of Europeanists, Chicago.

Shabad, Goldie and Llera, Francisco 1994. "Political Violence in a Democratic State: Basque Terrorism in Spain," in *Terrorism in Context*, Martha Crenshaw (ed.), University Park: Pennsylvania State University Press.

Shafir, Gershon 1995. *Immigrants and Nationalists*, Albany: SUNY Press.

Ash-Shiddieqy, T. M. Hasbi n.d. *Tuntutan Qurban* [The demands of sacrifice], Jakarta: Bulan Bintang.

Shigeyoshi, Tokunaga 1984. "Some Recent Developments in Japanese Industrial Relations, with Special Reference to Large Private Enterprises," Discussion paper IIVGH/dp84-208, Berlin: Wissenschaftszentrum fur Sozialforschung.

Shirai, Taishiro 1968. "Income Patterns and Job Security in Japan," in B. C.

Roberts (ed.), *Industrial Relations: Contemporary Issues*, First World Congress of the International Industrial Relations Association, Geneva, 4–8 September, 1967, London: Macmillan.

Siegel, Gilbert 1963. "Administration, Values and the Merit System in Brazil," in Robert Daland (ed.), *Prospectives of Brazilian Public Administration*, I, Comparative Series in Brazilian Public Administration, Los Angeles: University of Southern California and Fundacao Getulio Vargas, Escola Brasileira de Administraca Publica.

1966. "The Vicissitudes of Government Reform in Brazil: A Study of the DASP," Ph.D. dissertation, University of California.

Siegel, James T. 1969. *The Rope of God*, Berkeley: University of California Press.

1979. *Shadow and Sound: The Historical Thought of a Sumatran People*, Chicago: University of Chicago Press.

Singer, Paulo 1965. "A politica das classes dominates" [Politics of the dominant classes], in Octavio Ianni et al. (ed.), *Politica e revolucao social no Brasil* [Politics and social revolution in Brazil], Rio de Janeiro: Civilizacao, Brasileira.

Skocpol, Theda, and Somers, Margaret 1980. "The Uses of Comparative History in Macrosocial Inquiry," *Comparative Studies in Society and History*, 22, 2 (April): 174–97.

Skocpol, Theda (ed.) 1984. *Vision and Method in Historical Sociology*, Cambridge: Cambridge University Press.

Skowronek, Steven 1979. *Building a New American State: The Expansion of National Administrative Capacities, 1877–1920*, Cambridge: Cambridge University Press.

Smith, A. D. 1979. *Nationalism in the Twentieth Century*, New York: New York University Press.

Smith, Leonard V. 1994. *Between Mutiny and Obedience: The Case of the French Fifth Infantry Division During World War I*, Princeton, Princeton University Press.

Snouck, Hurgronje, C. 1903. *Het Gajoland en Zijne Bewoners* [Gayoland and its Inhabitants], Batavia (Jakarta): Landsdrukkerij.

1906. *The Achehnese*, 2 vols. Leiden: E. J. Brill.

Soares, Carlos Caroso 1983. "Sharecroppers of the Sertao: Boa Ventura Revisited," unpublished research report, Department of Anthropology, Los Angeles: University of California.

Solaún, Mauricio 1980. "Colombian Politics: Historical Characteristics and Problems," in R. Albert Berry, Ronald G. Hallman and Mauricio Solaún (eds.), *Politics of Compromise: Coalition Government in Colombia*, New Brunswick: Transaction Books.

Soltis, Joseph, Boyd, Robert and Richerson, Peter J. 1995. "Can Group-functional Behaviors Evolve by Cultural Group Selection?" *Current Anthropology*, 36: 473–94.

Souza, Maria do Carmo Campello de 1976. *Estado e partidos politicos no Brasil* [The State and Political Parties in Brazil], Sao Paulo: Alfa-Omega.

Spencer, Herbert 1876–1896. *Principles of Sociology*, London.

Spinrad, William 1960. "Correlates of Trade Union Participation: A Summary of the Literature," *American Sociological Review*, 25, 2 (April): 237–44.

Spiers, Edward M. 1980. *The Army and Society, 1815–1914*, London: Longman.

Stewart, Bill 1978. *Change and Bureaucracy: Public Administration in Venezuela*, James Sprunt Studies in History and Political Science, vol. 56, Chapel Hill: University of North Carolina Press.

Stinchcombe, Arthur 1991. "On the Conditions of Fruitfulness of Theorizing About Mechanisms in Social Science," *Philosophy of the Social Sciences*, 21: 367–88.

Stocking, George, Jr. 1968. *Race, Culture, and Evolution: Essays in the History of Anthropology*, New York: The Free Press.

    1974. *A Franz Boas Reader: The Shaping of American Anthropology, 1883–1911*, Chicago: The University of Chicago Press.

    1994. "Dogmatism, Pragmatism, Essentialism, Relativism: The Boas/Mason Debate Revisited," *History of Anthropology Newsletter*, 21 (1): 3–12.

Subtelny, Orest 1988. *Ukraine: A History*, Toronto: University of Toronto Press.

Suny, Ronald Grigor 1988. *The Making of the Georgian Nation*, Bloomington: Indiana University Press.

    1995. "Elite Transformation in Late-Soviet and Post-Soviet Transcaucasia, or What Happens When the Ruling Class Can't Rule," in Timothy J. Colton and Robert C. Tucker (eds.), *Studies in Post-Soviet Leadership*, Boulder: Westview Press.

Tapia-Videla, Jorge Ivan 1969. "Bureaucratic Power in a Developing Country: The Case of the Chilean Social Security Administration." Ph.D. dissertation, University of Texas.

Taylor, Philip B. 1952. "The Uruguayan Coup d'Etat of 1933." *Hispanic American Historical Review*, 32: 301–20.

    1960. *Government and Politics of Uruguay*. Studies in Political Science no. 7, New Orleans: Tulane University Press.

Tsebelis, George 1990. *Nested Games: Rational Choice in Comparative Politics*, Berkeley and Los Angeles: University of California Press.

Tylor, E. B. 1889. "On a Method of Investigating the Development of Institutions; Applied to Laws of Marriage and Descent," *Journal of the Royal Anthropological Institute*, 18: 245–69.

Ujihara, Shojiro 1974. "The Labor Market," in Kazuo Okochi, Bernard Karsh and Solomon B. Levine (eds.), *Workers and Employers in Japan: The Japanese Employment Relations System*, Tokyo: Princeton University Press and University of Tokyo Press.

Urban, Greg 1988. "Ritual wailing in Amerindian Brazil," *American Anthropologist*, 90, 2: 385–400.

    1991. *A Discourse-centered Approach to Culture, Native South American Myths and Rituals*, Austin: University of Texas Press.

Urzúa Valenzuela, German and García Barzelatto, Ana Maria 1971. *Diagnostico de la Burocracia Chilena (1818–1969)* [Diagnosis of the Chilean Bureaucracy (1818–1969)]. Santiago, Editoral Juridica de Chile.

Valenzuela, Arturo 1977. *Political Brokers in Chile: Local Government in a Centralized Polity*, Durham: Duke University Press.

    1978. *The Breakdown of Democratic Regimes: Chile*, Baltimore: Johns Hopkins University Press.

1984. "Parties, Politics, and the State in Chile: The Higher Civil Service," in Ezra Suleiman (ed.), *Bureaucrats and Policy Making: A Comparative Overview*, New York: Holmes & Meier.

1985. "Origins and Characteristics of the Chilean Party System: A Proposal for a Parliamentary Form of Government," Working Paper No. 164, Washington: Woodrow Wilson Center.

Vallier, Ivan (ed.) 1971. *Comparative Methods in Sociology*, Berkeley and Los Angeles: University of California Press.

Van Riper, Paul 1958. *History of the United States Civil Service*, Evanston: Row, Peterson and Company.

Ventura, Luciano 1990. "Licenziamenti collecttivi," *Enciclopedia giuridica treccani*, XIX, Rome: Creccano.

Venturini, Ángel R. 1984. *Estadísticas Electorales: Elecciones Nacionales 1926–1982. Elecciones Internas 1982* [Electoral Statistics: National Elections 1926–1982, Primary Elections 1982], Montevideo: Ediciones de la Banda Oriental.

Verba, Sidney 1991. "Comparative Politics: Where Have We Been, Where Are We Going?" in Howard J. Wiarda (ed.), *New Directions in Comparative Politics*, Boulder, CO: Westview Press.

Vidal Perdomo, Jaime 1982. "La reforma administrativa de 1968 en Colombia" [The 1968 administrative reform in Colombia], *International Review of Administrative Science*, 48: 77–84.

Vieira, Astério Dardeau 1967. *A Administração do perroal vista pelos chefes de servico* [Personnel administration as seen by agency heads], Rio de Janeiro: Fundação Getúlio Vargas.

Wahrlich, Beatriz 1964. *Administração de pessoal: Principios e technicas* [Personnel administration: Principles and techniques], Rio de Janeiro: Fundação Getúlio Vargas.

Waldmann, Peter 1985. "Gewaltsamer Separatismus. Am Beispiel der Basken, Franko-Kanadier und Nordiren," *Kolner Zeitschrift fur Soziologie und Sozialpsychologie*, 37.

Weber, Max 1968. *Economy and Society*, 2 vols., Berkeley: University of California Press.

Werbner, Pnina 1988. "'Sealing' the Koran: Offering and Sacrifice Among Pakistani Labour Migrants," *Cultural Dynamics*, 1: 77–97.

Whiting, John W. M. 1954. "The Cross-cultural Method," in Gardner Lindzey (ed.), *Handbook of Social Psychology*, I, 523–31. Cambridge, MA: Addison-Wesley.

Whyte, Martin King 1978. *The Status of Women in Preindustrial Societies*, Princeton: Princeton University Press.

Wiarda, Howard J. (ed.) 1991. *New Directions in Comparative Politics*, Boulder: Westview Press.

Wolf, Eric 1959. *Sons of the Shaking Earth*, Chicago: University of Chicago Press.

1966. *Peasants*, Englewood Cliffs: Prentice-Hall.

1969. *Peasant Wars of the Twentieth Century*, New York: Harper & Row.

Wolf, Eric and Hansen, Edward C. 1972. *The Human Condition in Latin America*, New York: Oxford University Press.

Woodward, Mark 1989. *Islam in Java: Normative Piety and Mysticism in the Sultanate of Yogyakarta*, Tuscon: University of Arizona Press.

Yalman, Nur 1978. *Under the Bo Tree*, Berkeley and Los Angeles: University of California Press.

Zelditch, Morris, Jr. 1971. "Intelligible comparisons," in Ivan Vallier (ed.), *Comparative Methods in Sociology*, Berkeley and Los Angeles: University of California Press, 267–307.

Zulaika, Joseba 1988. *Basque Violence*, Reno: University of Nevada Press.

Author Index

259

Subject Index

Abkhazia, 45, 49, 50, 56
Abkhazis, 52, 55
Aceh, 148
Acehnese ideology, 150
Acehnese people, 141, 144, 145
Acehnese poetry, 145, 146
Acehnese religious forms, 145
Africa, 7, 23, 228n.5, 234
Algeria, 21, 23, 137, Kabyle society, 13
Morocco, 16
Rwanda, 9
Senegal, 137
South Africa, 9
Tunisia, 23
analytical narrative, 2, 4, 155–72, 236
Armenians, 44
Asia, 7, 23 (*see also* Aceh, Gayo, New
Guinea)
Bali, 78, 85
Dutch East Indies, 137
Indonesia, 7, 16, 137, 240n.5
Sumatra (highlands), 137
Australia, 153, 159
Australian War Memorial, 157

behavioralist approach, 9
Belarusans, 45
Belgium, 21
Brazil, 16, 17, 93, 94, 207, 211, 216–18,
219, 226, 227, 234, 239
Boa Ventura, 173–95, 239
Departamento Administrativo de
Serviço Público (DASP), 198
ligas camponesas, 174
P. I. Ibarama, 94, 97–102
Vargas dictatorship, 211
Vila Reconcavo, 190
bureaucratic-authoritarianism, 9

Canada, 153, 159, 163, 165, 168, 232,
237
King, Mackenzie, 167
Ontario, 163

Quebec, 21, 163, 167
capitalism, 23, 177, 178, 192
causation, 64, 108, 231
charisma, 206, 207
Chechens, 45
civil service reform, 197–27
class, 180
class solidarity, 179
clientelism, 226
collective action, 17, 121, 152
collective action problem, 17, 198
comparisons, 3, 19n.1, 159, 180, 239
community-level comparison, 81, 83,
85, 87, 235
comparative approach, 13, 23, 24, 137,
190
comparison and social learning, 90
controlled comparison, 5, 16, 180, 230,
238
correlationist approach, 103, 108
covariation, 11
creating fields of diversity, 82, 89, 239
cross-cultural comparison, 7, 106, 232
crucial case, 19
generality, 15, 25, 70, 75, 103, 137, 146,
158, 169, 226, 230–32, 235
implicit and explicit comparison, 105,
108
induction, 230, 232
large-scale comparison, 6
longitudinal comparison, 16, 173, 180,
181, 192
macrosociological comparison, 231
Mill's analysis of difference, 13
measurement problem, 211, 212
most different case strategy, 3, 4, 146,
236, 239
museum debate, 92
paired comparisons, 57, 58
regional comparison, 6, 16
robustness, 15, 24, 25, 44, 169, 170,
171, 235
role of anomaly, 14, 231, 196, 201